Maya: Secrets of the Pros

Second Edition

Maya®: Secrets of the Pros™

Second Edition

John Kundert-Gibbs
Dariush Derakhshani
et. al.

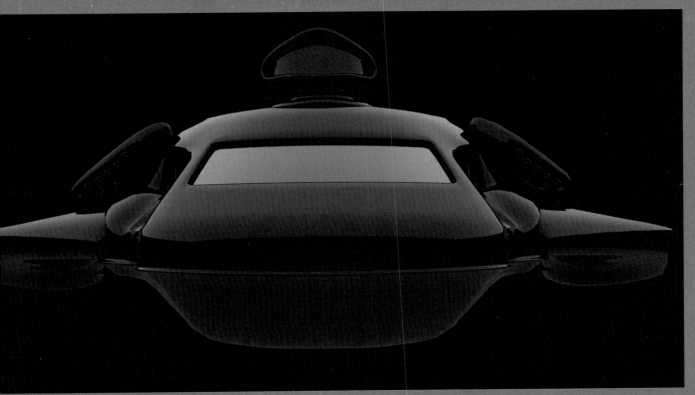

San Francisco • London

SYBEX®

Publisher: Dan Brodnitz
Acquisitions and Developmental Editor: Mariann Barsolo
Production Editor: Elizabeth Campbell
Technical Editor: Keith Reicher
Copyeditor: Pat Coleman
Compositor: Side by Side Studios
CD Coordinator: Dan Mummert
CD Technician: Kevin Ly
Proofreaders: Nancy Riddiough, Jim Brook, Candace English, Katherine Perry
Indexer: Nancy Guenther
Book and Cover Designer: Mark Ong, Side by Side Studios

Software License Agreement: Terms and Conditions

To all our family, friends, and colleagues
And to Kristin, Joshua, and Kenlee
—John Kundert-Gibbs

And to Tirdad, an inspiration for me
—Dariush Derakhshani

Acknowledgments

A work of this scope, involving so many, means that there are a great number of people to thank for their contributions and support.

First, we would like to thank the wonderful crew at Sybex for their untiring efforts to get this book looking so great and out the door on time. We especially thank the book team: Mariann Barsolo, Elizabeth Campbell, Pat Coleman, Keith Reicher, Keith McNeil, Dan Mummert, and Kevin Ly. Thanks also to Mark Ong and Susan Riley at Side by Side Studios.

At Alias, a special thanks to Danielle Lamothe, who always helps us find an answer, and to Duncan Brinsmead for taking the time to give us a hand and a thought.

Our employers, who have generously allowed us the time and freedom to write, also deserve thanks. At Clemson University, special thanks to James Barker, Doris Helms, Bonnie Holaday, Robert Geist, and Mike Westall. At Sight Effects thanks to Alan, Melissa, and Rudy as well as the crew, and to Gary J for all his support.

Finally, our family and friends deserve a great deal of credit for their untiring loyalty and support not only for this book, but of our chosen careers, which often involve late nights and weekends. We especially thank Kristin, Joshua, Kenlee, and Randi. Without the support of our family, friends, and colleagues, this book could never have been.

Letter from the Publisher

Dear Reader,

Thank you for choosing the second edition of *Maya Secrets of the Pros*. This book is part of a new wave of Sybex graphics books, all written by outstanding authors—artists and teachers who really know their stuff and have a clear vision of the audience they're writing for. It's also part of our growing library of truly unique 3D graphics books.

Founded in 1976, Sybex is the oldest independent computer book publisher. More than twenty-five years later, we're committed to producing a full line of consistently exceptional graphics books. With each title, we're working hard to set a new standard for the industry. From the paper we print on, to the writers and photographers we work with, our goal is to bring you the best graphics books possible.

I hope you see all that is reflected in these pages. I'd be very interested to hear your comments and get your feedback on how we're doing. To let us know what you think about this, or any other Sybex book, please visit us at www.sybex.com. Once there, go to the product page, click on Submit a Review, and fill out the questionnaire. Your input is greatly appreciated.

Please also visit www.sybex.com to learn more about the rest of our graphics line.

Best regards,

Dan Brodnitz
Publisher

About the Authors

Maya Secrets of the Pros, Second Edition is the work of co-lead authors John Kundert-Gibbs and Dariush Derakhshani, along with a cadre of Maya professionals.

John Kundert-Gibbs

John Kundert-Gibbs is director of the Digital Production Arts program at Clemson University, which prepares the technical directors of the future. Author of a number of publications on Maya, computer graphics, and dramatic literature, he directs students in producing animated shorts, creates effects for live-action projects, and designs electronic media for theatrical productions. He is co-author of *Maya 5 Savvy* and *Maya: Secrets of the Pros*. He has a Bachelor of Arts degree in physics from Princeton University and a Ph.D. in dramatic literature from The Ohio State University.

Dariush Derakhshani

Dariush Derakhshani is currently a digital effects supervisor and part-time teacher. He has worked in Los Angeles at Sight Effects, a prominent commercial effects house, as well as a CGI animator on a variety of projects in film and television.

His writing credits include *Maya: Secrets of the Pros*, *Maya 5 Savvy*, and the best selling *Introducing Maya 6: 3D for Beginners* as well as several print and online magazines.

He has won the Bronze Plaque from the Columbus Film Festival and has shared honors from the AICP and London International Advertising Awards. He has worked as a CGI animator and compositor on a variety of projects from films to television and was a Supervising Technical Director for the *South Park* television series. Dariush spends his time consulting and teaching at a variety of schools and writing as frequently as he can. His works have appeared in *CGW* and *Post* magazines and on various sites of the digitalmedianet.com. Dariush holds a Bachelor of Arts in architecture and in theater from Lehigh University and a Master of Fine Arts in animation from USC Film School. He is bald and lists to one side.

Tom Capizzi

Tom Capizzi is currently the lighting director on a computer-generated feature film called *The Barnyard* at Omation Studios. Tom has more than 15 years' experience creating digital content and has worked on more than 20 feature films. Some of the most recent films are *Garfield*, *Scooby Doo 1 & 2*, *Daredevil*, *Elf*, and *X-Men 2*. He has also taught digital modeling at Art Center in Pasadena, CA; Center of Creative Studies in Detroit; Gnomon School of Visual Effects in Hollywood; and several other colleges. Tom is a published author and constantly stays up-to-date with cutting-edge digital production techniques.

Jake Carvey

Jake Carvey has been producing and directing computer animation for broadcast, film, and games since 1994. 3D animation was a logical culmination of his passionate interest in diverse disciplines, from stage lighting to dramatic writing. He is obsessed with the development, practice, and teaching of techniques and strategies for consistently delivering high production values within small studio environments. As president of Spin Cycle Animation & FX, he led the animation team responsible for creating and producing well over 100 unique animated promos for Kids' WB!, harvesting truckloads of industry awards along the way. Since 2000, Jake has been working as a freelance director and animator, continuing to deliver projects for Disney, NBC, ABC, PBS, Sony, Target, Wal-Mart, Circuit City, and many others. He works from a two-story loft in downtown Los Angeles, where his average commute is running down a single flight of stairs.

Krishnamurti M. Costa

Krishnamurti M. Costa, aka Antropus, is a 32-year-old, Brazilian, self-taught CG artist. Kris is a character animator on *The Barnyard*, a CG feature written and directed by Steve Oedekerk and distributed by Nickelodeon Movies/Paramount Pictures. He started working in computer graphics about 12 years ago. He won the Anima Mundi Festival (the biggest animation festival in Latin America) as an animator and art director. He is also working on a short-movie called *SenzaAzione*, still in progress, as a personal project. In 2004, he won the 3D main prize on CGTalk / CGNetwork's "MachineFlesh Challenge," competing with more than 1400 others in the 3D category. He is also known for his tutorial series published on his web site and other online CG resources. Please visit www.antropus.com for more information on Kris.

Timothy A. Davis

Timothy A. Davis is currently an Assistant Professor in the Computer Science Department at Clemson University and has played an active role in developing the interdisciplinary master's program in Digital Arts Production, which trains students to produce special effects for entertainment and commercial projects. His teaching and research interests include parallel/distributed rendering, ray tracing, spatio-temporal coherence, and nonphotorealistic rendering. He received his Ph.D. from North Carolina State University in 1998 and has worked in technical positions for the Environmental Protection Agency and NASA Goddard Space Flight Center.

Petre Gheorghian

Petre Gheorghian is a Senior Product Specialist at Alias, providing training and consulting to Maya users globally. His areas of focus include modeling, rendering, and character animation. He is a Certified Maya Instructor and holds graduate degrees in both Fine Art and Engineering. Petre's versatility, both as a technician and an artist, has allowed him to master the complexity in many aspects of Maya. Petre is also the author of the Alias learning tools *Maya Techniques | Modeling a Human Head* and *Maya Techniques | Exploring Maya 5 Features* and co-author of several other learning tools. He was an Alias MasterClass presenter at Siggraph 2003 and Siggraph 2004.

Kenneth Ibrahim

Kenneth Ibrahim began his career in visual effects as an Alias application engineer in Tokyo, Japan, in 1994 just as Maya was entering its alpha phase. After returning to the United States and spending three years at Alias demonstrating and supporting Maya, Ken moved into production proper by joining PDI's C.A.F.E. group and working on a number of TV spots during which he helped integrate Maya into the PDI pipeline. Ken has since worked at a number of companies on films, including *Shrek*, *Final Fantasy*, *Matrix Revolutions*, *X2*, *Peter Pan*, and *I, Robot*. He can be reached at his web site and online shop www.shuri-ken.com.

Robert Kosai

Robert Kosai works for PDI/Dreamworks where he has developed and animated Maya Cloth garments on *Shrek 2* and *Shrek 4D*. Prior to that, his experience includes character animation for Electronic Arts' The Sims franchise. Robert has a B.S. in computer science from the University of Southern California and is a graduate of Sheridan College where he studied classical animation. When not behind a computer, he can be found riding his bicycle around the San Francisco Bay Area.

Stephen K. Mann

Stephen K. Mann is currently the Senior Character TD for Charlex|3D, where he leads the character department for commercials and their current short-film project *Lab Rats*. Previously he worked for several studios, including BlueSky Studios, Klieser-Walczak, Hornet Animation, and Sony Imageworks. Stephen also has been teaching advanced character rigging and animation for the New York School of Visual Arts for the past four years. As well as working on TV commercials, he has worked on feature films, including *X-Men*, *The One*, and the upcoming FOX project *Robots*. Stephen holds a Bachelors in Studio Art from the University of Vermont and an MFA in Animation and Digital Art from the University of Southern California's School of Film and Television.

Keith Reicher

Keith Reicher is a layout animator for PDI/DreamWorks, an affliate of DreamWorks Animation SKG. He has worked on *Shrek 2* and *Madagascar* and is currently working on the upcoming *Shrek* release. Born and raised in New York, he studied at The New York Institute of Technology and holds an MFA in computer graphics from Pratt Institute.

Kevin Vassey

Kevin Vassey is an FX Animator at PDI/Dreamworks where he developed clothing for *Shrek 2* and is currently working on crowds for the upcoming film *Madagascar*. Previously, he worked as a Render TD at Big Idea Productions on their first film *Jonah: A Veggietales Movie*. Prior to that he worked as an animator for Disney i.d.e.a.s in Orlando, FL. Kevin holds a BFA from Clemson University.

Contributors

Some current and former Clemson University students also had a hand in Maya *Secrets of the Pros, Second Edition*:

Brian Cumming is a Software Engineer at Electronic Arts in Vancouver, BC. He holds a BS and an MFA in Digital Production Arts from Clemson University. Brian's research interests involve writing plug-ins for Maya and creating collaborative virtual environments.

Jerry Gardiner received his BFA degree at Clemson University and is currently finishing his MFA in Digital Production Arts at Clemson. A contributor to *Maya 5 Savvy*, he primarily works in modeling and texturing. Jerry created the award-winning short *Artbot* with fellow student Brian Cumming and took on multiple roles, including art director, for the DPA production *Demons Within*.

Rebecca Johnson is a Matchmover and Technical Animator at Rhythm and Hues Studios. She has an MFA in Digital Production Arts from Clemson University and a degree in Visual Arts from Lander University. Rebecca is interested in nonphotorealistic rendering and facial animation.

Contents

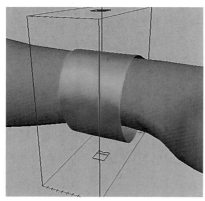

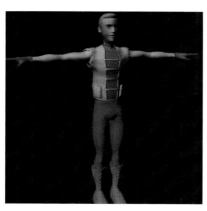

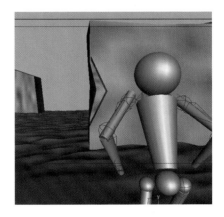

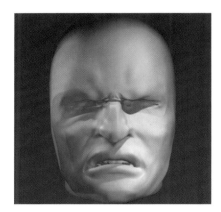

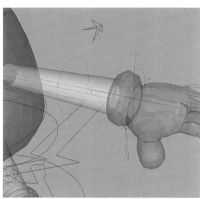

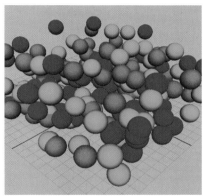

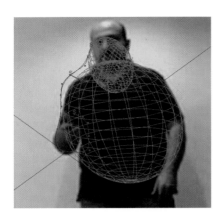

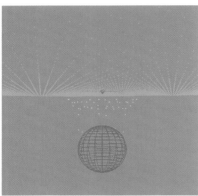

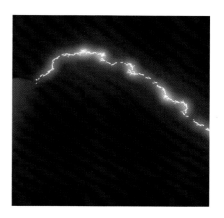

Chapter 9   Advanced Character Modeling Using Polygons and Subdivision Surfaces   229

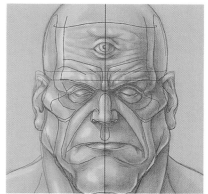

Introduction

After the wild success of *Maya: Secrets of the Pros*, we began thinking about the future of the *Secrets* books. Although it was originally conceived as a single, stand-alone work, it was obvious that a large audience was hungry for information from those who do professional 3D work on a day-to-day basis and that we should feed this appetite! Many "second edition" books are simple rewrites of the previous title; not so with *Maya: Secrets of the Pros, Second Edition*. Here we have nine all new chapters containing a whole new set of professional secrets arising from years of experience getting production quality results from Maya. Thus, *Secrets II* makes a companion volume to *Secrets (I)*, but it also stands on its own. As with the first edition, we have authors from around the globe who work at studios large and small, as well as at universities that train the next generation of effects artists.

Here again, you have at your fingertips a fantastic resource: insights and instruction from professionals in the field. Whether you're a relative "newbie" or a wizened old pro, you will learn new tricks and skills from the chapters and included CD files that will have you working better and smarter in no time. Some of the material contained in these pages was, up to this point, trade secrets of individuals and companies—secrets that allow them to win bids and produce world-class effects for film and television. Now you too can enter this world, gaining understanding about the business, science, and art of 3D effects and animation. We trust you will find the chapters exciting and inspiring, and we look forward to your contributions to the next edition of this book!

About This Book

One thing worth noting is that *Maya: Secrets of the Pros, Second Edition* is not for the neophyte. If you don't know the difference between a manipulator handle and a spline curve, you're probably better off getting another book first (like, say, *Maya 5 Savvy* from Sybex). If, however, you're an advanced hobbyist or especially a professional who makes your living doing 3D graphics, this book is definitely for you—we built it from the start to be for you! In fact (and this is worth pointing out in boldface), **even if you use other 3D packages along with or instead of Maya, this book is still for you**. Although the scene files are all Maya, the work-flow strategies and insights apply to just about any professional 3D package.

We have attempted, whenever possible, to keep this book version-agnostic, if not package-agnostic. In other words, we feel the information in this book is too timeless to go out of style whenever the next version of Maya comes out, so we concentrated on presenting work flow, technique, and creative problem-solving practiced by professionals rather than just the latest bells and whistles Maya provides (though there's plenty of "wow" factor to each of the chapters). So, whether you're working in Maya 6 or Maya 21, the information in this book will challenge and inspire you to create better, more efficient, and more beautiful work.

For the first time, Alias has made the Unlimited version available for the Macintosh with Maya 6. If you're a Mac user reading this book, you already know that most of the Maya key commands are the same in both Windows and the Mac. Just remember to use the Command key for Ctrl, the Option key for Alt, and the Home key (above End) for Insert.

To get a better feeling for the buffet of tasty 3D dishes in store for you, try flipping through the book's pages (as if you didn't do that already). Just in case you want a little more of an appetizer for each chapter, here's what's in store, chapter by chapter.

Chapter 1 unfolds secrets of Maya Cloth. Robert Kosai and Kevin Vassey take you on a tour of Cloth, from underlying concepts, to creating simple garments, to a more advanced use of Cloth: simulating a bracelet. This chapter will get you up and running with Maya Cloth so that you can create garment effects, whatever your project.

In Chapter 2, John Kundert-Gibbs et al. discuss two disparate nonphotorealistic rendering techniques. The first uses hand-drawn (pen-and-paper) textures to create a "comic book" rendering style. The second involves using Maya's MEL scripting language to create rendered images similar in style to that of Impressionist painters such as Monet. Together, these techniques let you use Maya to create a variety of animation looks.

Chapter 3 blurs the line between the real and virtual worlds. Here, Keith Reicher shows how to create camera motion that looks and "feels" like real-world camera motion, including camera shake, lag, and "human" error in handling the controls of a camera. Not only does the chapter go over cinematic terminology and its application to virtual cameras, Keith also shows how to use Maya Live (included with Maya Unlimited) to extract the motion of a real camera to use in your virtual scenes.

In Chapter 4, Dariush Derakhshani and Jake Carvey take you into the world of HDRI (High Dynamic Range Imagery), global illumination, and image-based lighting, the hot lighting techniques taking Hollywood by storm. As the authors point out, however, it's one thing to know the words, quite another to understand how to use these techniques to achieve the look you want in the most efficient manner possible. The authors cut through the layers of buzzwords in this chapter, laying out proper techniques, and, just as important, when to throw these techniques at your lighting situation.

Chapter 5 examines one of the fundamental elements of 3D work: the production pipeline. In this chapter Stephen K. Mann goes over the reasons for creating an effective pipeline and then discusses how to create an efficient one, separating the technical issues from the artistic. Once a good pipeline is in the works for your studio (or for your home projects), you can concentrate on being creative, not solving logistical problems.

Chapter 6 discusses Maya's new Hair system (available with Maya Unlimited), a powerful tool for creating natural effects such as long hair and for controlling other objects such as skeleton chains. In a series of tutorials, Petre Gheorghian and Dariush Derakhshani walk you through the powerful tools awaiting you in Maya's Hair, getting you familiar with the basics of the system and showing you how to use it to create various effects such as adding secondary motion to a character's walk cycle. In the end, you'll have a solid base from which to build hair and other effects for your animation projects.

Chapter 7 uncovers the potential that dynamics hold for creating great effects. In this chapter, Dariush Derakhshani shows you several ways to work in dynamics using particles, dynamic curves, soft bodies, and expressions to create and animate flexible objects such as car antennae and even water puddles in a rain. Dynamics can create a variety of wonderful, complex effects, and this chapter provides you with a roadmap for exploring them.

In Chapter 8, Kenneth Ibrahim and John Kundert-Gibbs show off the capabilities of an underused MEL function: noise. After a quick introduction to the math behind the noise function, the authors get right to the fun stuff: building cool effects using noise. Some effects are simple to create, while looking great; others, like the arcing electricity effect that ends the chapter, while complex to build, are so compelling that they are useable in big-budget effects films.

Chapter 9 shows off advanced modeling techniques. In it, Tom Capizzi and Krishnamurti M. Costa take you through the process of creating a compelling human face using subdivision surfaces and polygons. When finished, you should feel comfortable tackling just about any organic modeling task!

About the CD

The CD that accompanies this book is packed with useful material that will help you master Maya for yourself. Included are scene files, animations, and even source code relating to the chapters in the book.

Some CD highlights are:

- A model complete with animation and simulated cloth
- A "hand-drawn" textured character
- Scenes with realistic camera movement
- HDRI images and lit scenes
- Scenes featuring Maya Hair
- Scenes with soft body dynamics
- Scenes and MEL scripts for generating effects using Maya's noise (MEL) function
- A complete head modeled using subdivision surfaces and polygons

As you can see from this list, rather than having to create entire scenes from scratch for each chapter, the accompanying scenes and animations get you started and help guide you to appropriate solutions quickly and efficiently. Additionally, after you go through a chapter once, you can grab a sample scene file or bit of code and play with it, finding your own unique and wonderful solutions to the challenges presented in each chapter.

Staying Connected

To stay up-to-date on *Maya: Secrets of the Pros*, please go to the book's page at www.sybex.com. If you have any questions or feedback, please contact John Kundert-Gibbs at jkundert@cs.clemson.edu or Dariush Derakhshani at dariushhome@koosh3d.com.

Sharing Our Experiences

As you can see, the subjects covered in this book unveil a large swath of intermediate to advanced techniques using Maya. Often authors of these chapters reveal little-known secrets or point out ways to make a task much quicker than you might have imagined. Whether you're an effects animator, a modeler, a surfacing artist, a pipeline technical director, or someone who loves all the phases of 3D production, something is waiting for you in the pages of this book. And whether you proceed from beginning to end, or just pick and choose your chapters, you will find something in *Maya: Secrets of the Pros, Second Edition* to satisfy your appetite for knowledge for months if not years to come.

What has become clear to all of us who worked on this book is that, no matter how long you have worked with Maya or in 3D graphics, there is always more to learn, and the joy of learning is half the fun of working in this profession. We have all been inspired and amazed by one another's work and have been witness to one of the greatest aspects of working in the graphics community: the openness, generosity, and willingness to share. As you sample the chapters in this book, recall that someone is delivering years of hard-won experience with every page you read and every exercise you work through. All you have to do is bring along a thirst for knowledge and a passion for 3D work.

Working on these pages has been a reinvigorating experience. All of us have felt again the joy of discovery and the equally wonderful joy of helping others who appreciate our unique talents. We trust you will feel our heartfelt love of what we do. And don't forget to share *your* passion with others!

We have had great pleasure preparing this new edition and invite you to join us in celebrating more secrets of the pros!

—John Kundert-Gibbs and Dariush Derakhshani
    January, 2005

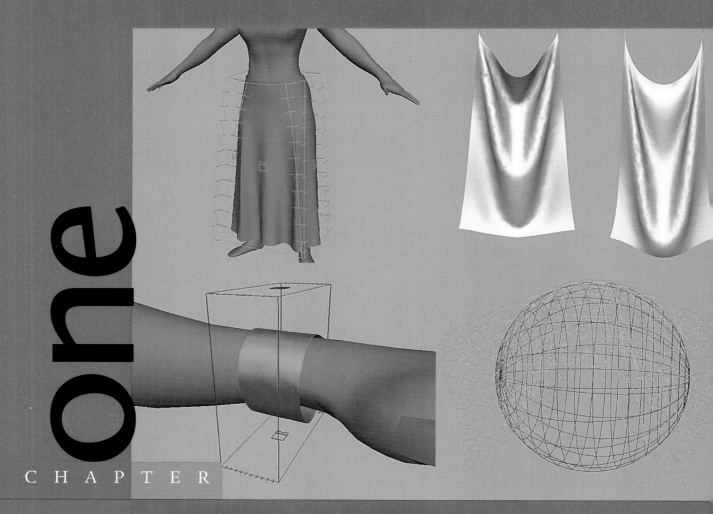

one

Working with Maya Cloth

Robert Kosai and Kevin Vassey

Maya Cloth *is a powerful deformation tool that can generate complex motion which is difficult to achieve using traditional methods. Packaged as part of Maya Unlimited, Cloth has been used with success on several live action effects films such as* The Matrix *and* The Lord of the Rings *trilogies as well as all CG productions such as* Shrek 2.

Cloth derives its motion using simulation based on a mass-spring system. By setting up a garment for use with Maya's Cloth Solver, you allow it to perform the tedious tasks of deforming the garment to match the character's motion and posing while giving your animation a lot of nice secondary action and an increased sense of fluidity and realism.

This chapter gives the experienced Maya Cloth user some ins and outs to help you improve your work flow and master some of the intricacies of this powerful tool. A step-by-step tutorial guides the new user of Maya Cloth through the process of fashioning a skirt and animating it. Once you grasp the major concepts, you can handle the second tutorial that demonstrates how to deform a bracelet as an example of an alternate application for Cloth.

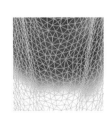

Work Flow with Cloth

When you are working with Maya Cloth, as you would with real cloth, you must have a plan before you start to "sew." As part of the planning phase, you need a clear idea about

Figure 1.1: Various valid panel shapes

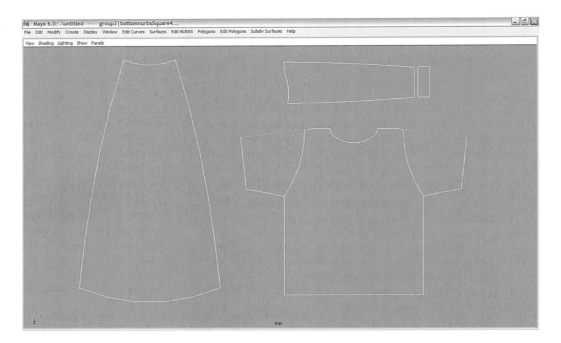

the garment you will be creating. Many studios have artists whose job is to visualize and then produce concept drawings of characters and their costumes. Emulating the look and feel evoked from these concept drawings is the goal of the cloth animator. If you are working on your own design, collect reference photos of items similar to your garment. Keep the references pinned on the wall or under a coffee mug but always within arm's reach, as they are a constant reminder of what you're striving toward and are handy to have when discussing your work with others.

The next step is to design the panel layout of your intended garment. A good place to begin is looking at your own clothing. Find where the seams are. Imagine the fabric

unstitched and laid flat. How many separate pieces of fabric were used? Like a tailor, you will want to measure to achieve a proper fit. Maya panels are created from shaping curves into the desired look (see Figure 1.1).

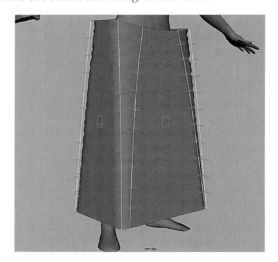

There is no restriction on the number of curves used to create panels, but keep in mind the following two rules.

- The curves must form a closed loop.
- The curves must be coplanar, meaning all curves must lie flat on the same plane.

After you create the panels, you can stitch them together into a single garment. Initially, the shape will match the planar contour of the panel curves, as shown here.

To make the sewn panels look natural, let the simulation run and allow it to settle into a stable configuration (see Figure 1.2). In order to get the best "fit" out of your cloth simulation, you will adjust numerous attributes and create constraints that influence the motion characteristics.

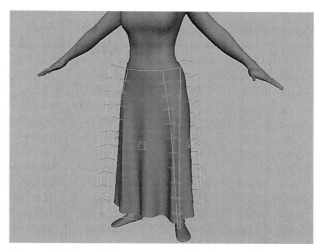

Tutorial: Making a Skirt

This tutorial provides the steps to create a skirt that is tailored around a female model's waist and is about ankle length. Like most artistic endeavors, achieving the desired aesthetic can take many possible paths. This example is one approach, and it is designed to cover many concepts. Your goal is to produce a garment that simulates quickly and maintains stability through a variety of animations. If you are working in

Figure 1.2: The cloth garment settled after simulation

a collaborative environment, the ability to make quick revisions is essential as well.

Creating the Panels

The garment in Figure 1.2 is created from 4 panels stitched together and simulated to a relaxed state. The first decision to make is the number of panels. Why not 2, 6, or 16? Building a garment with fewer panels does require less work to set up and is easier to manage if changes are needed down the road, but the garment's requirements ultimately drive panel construction. Sometimes extra panels are necessary to put more fabric in a specific location, to control tessellation resolution or to assign unique cloth properties to a particular portion of a garment. In this case, we chose a 4-panel design because it tends to have few issues with stretching around the waist and tends to drape nicely; certainly good results can be achieved with other panel designs.

You will begin with 4 identical rectangular panel shapes, determining the width of each by measuring the circumference of the model's waist. Extra fabric is created at the bottom to help generate folds. Once the general shape of the garment is blocked in, you can adjust individual panels to achieve a better fit.

Creating a Guide Curve

The guide curve is the reference for where the cloth garment is to fit in relation to the model. To create a guide curve, follow these steps:

1. Open clothModel.mb.
2. Create a curve using the EP Curve tool to draw around the waist of the model.
   a. Select Inuyasha_skin and choose **Modify → Make Live**.
   b. Choose **Create → EP Curve Tool**, and draw around the waist, finishing the curve just short of the first point. Close the curve by choosing **Edit Curves → Open/Close Curves**.
   c. Scale the curve vertices away from the body slightly. Cloth is more stable if it has a small cushion from the surface against which it collides.

3. Choose **Edit Curves** → **Rebuild Curve** ❐.
4. Set **Rebuild Type** to Uniform, set **Parameter Range** as 0 to 1, and set the number of spans to 25. This will clean up the curve for use with some scripts later.
5. Rename the curve to skirtAttachCurve.
6. Measure the curve's length. This will take the guesswork out of how much fabric is needed. A properly fit garment will have fewer stability issues during simulation. Choose **Create** → **Measure Tools** → **Arc Length Tool**. LMB click the curve and drag. You should see the length, from the beginning of the curve, displayed (see Figure 1.3).

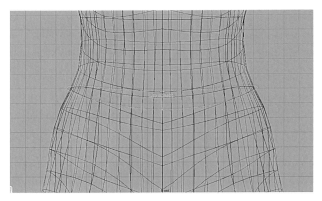

Figure 1.3: *The skirt attach curve is offset away from the waist. The ArcLength tool displays the length of the curve.*

Creating the Panel Curves

You now have a few guidelines to help determine the shape of your panels. Start each panel with a top width that is ¼ the length of the reference curve. The height of each panel will lie between the guide curve and ankles. The width at the bottom depends on the amount of folding desired.

To create the panel curves, follow these steps:

1. Choose **Create** → **NURBS Primitives** → **Square**. This is a quick way to start as it satisfies both conditions for panel curves; that is, it is a closed loop and coplanar.
   a. Set **Rotate X** to 90.
   b. **Scale** X to one-quarter the length of the skirtAttach-Curve.
2. Adjust the length, and tweak the shape of the curves to look similar to Figure 1.4. The panel has a bit of a bell shape. This will be significant later when you enable cloth simulation: gravity will pull the fabric down, giving a nice folding pattern along the bottom of the skirt.

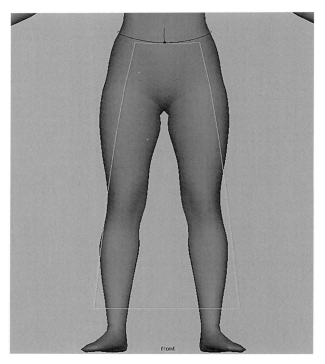

Figure 1.4: *An example of the skirt's front panel curves*

It is easy for your curves to become non-coplanar. To reduce this possibility, work in an orthographic view, and use the axis handles to move CVs.

3. Rename the group node to frontPanelCurves, and move these curves off to the side.
4. Duplicate frontPanelCurves, and rename the duplicate to rearPanelCurves. Move it so there is no overlap.
5. Repeat step 4, and rename the group to side-PanelCurves.

Managing Panel Curves Using Instancing

You should have three groups of panel curves similar to those in Figure 1.5. Although you can directly align them around the model, you will create instances of each group and place them around the model instead.

Using instancing has a few advantages:

- If there are symmetrical panels, in this case the side panels, you have to update only one template and it propagates through all the instances.
- If you rotate your curves to get a closer fit around the model, maintaining coplanar vertices can be difficult.
- The template can remain in an orthographic state, and the transform node of the instance can be rotated independently.

To use instancing, follow these steps:

1. Create an instance of frontPanelCurves (**Edit →Duplicate**, with the Instance option selected), and rename it to frontPanelCurves_Instance. Move it to the front of the model but not clipping through it.
2. Instance rearPanelCurves, rename it to rear-PanelCurves_Instance, and move it to the rear of the model.
3. Instance sidePanelCurves twice. Rename one instance leftPanelCurves_Instance, and move it to the character's left side. Rename the other instance rightPanelCurves_Instance, and move it to the character's right side.
4. Adjust the relative positions of the instanced curves so that they do not overlap but remain close to the model. If you want to adjust the shape of a panel, tweak the CVs of the original panel curves, which are still orthographic. When finished, your scene should look similar to the layout in Figure 1.6.

To see a completed version of the skirt panel curves, open skirt_curves.mb.

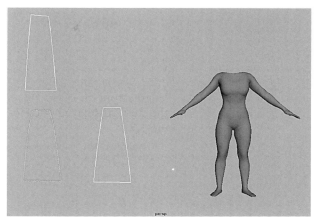

Figure 1.5: All the skirt's panel curves laid out. These will serve as templates for instancing.

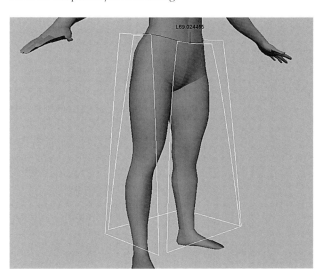

Figure 1.6: Instanced panel curves are placed around the model, and template curves remain in an orthographic orientation.

Creating the Garment

To go from the curves to an actual polygonal cloth mesh, you will create a Maya Cloth garment that is composed of the panels stitched together into a closed cylindrical surface. Follow these steps:

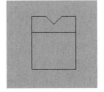

Figure 1.7: The Cloth Panel Icon

1. Select frontPanelCurves_Instance, and choose **Cloth** → **Create Garment**. This command performs two steps. First, it creates a cloth panel node, which is represented by the icon shown in Figure 1.7. Second, it creates a polygon plane that matches the contour of the curves.
2. Rename the garment to skirt_cloth.

Under Inputs for skirt_cloth in the Channel box (see Figure 1.8), you will see several cloth-related items: cpSolver1, cpStitcher1, and cpCache1. These nodes give you control over various characteristics of the simulation and of the mesh itself.

3. The garment's irregular tessellation aids in creating natural folds by reducing any bias inherent in a patterned vertex layout; however, the default density is too low for our purposes. Select cpStitcher, and raise Base Resolution to 65 (see Figure 1.9).
4. Select rightPanelCurves_Instance, and choose **Cloth** → **Create Panel**. Then create panels for the rear and left panel instance curves in similar fashion. A panel represents a piece of fabric in the shape of the panel curves. Each can have its own unique set of properties and tessellation.
5. The cloth will not extend around the model until the panels are seamed together. Select the leftmost curve in frontPanelCurves_Instance and the nearest curve that runs parallel to it in rightPanelCurves_Instance. Choose **Cloth** → **Create Seam**. The cloth mesh should extend across both panels (see Figure 1.10).
6. Continue around the model, creating seams between all the panels (see Figure 1.11). Be sure to close the mesh by creating a seam between leftPanelCurves_Instance and frontPanelCurves_Instance.

Figure 1.8: The cloth garment inputs with the stitcher resolution increased

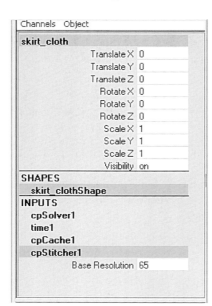

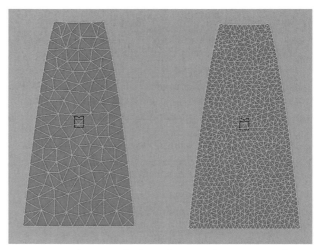

Figure 1.9: The same cloth mesh at resolution 25 on the left, 65 on the right

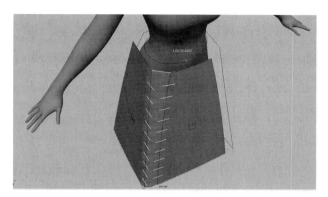

Figure 1.10: The cloth seam used to join the front and right panels

Figure 1.11: The cloth garment extending across all panels and joined by seams

Preparing the Garment for Simulation

When you run the simulation on the garment, the solver calculates the position of each vertex for each frame based on the forces applied to it. Although the skirt will settle in the general vicinity of the model's waist, the goal is for the top of the skirt to wrap around at a specific location, along the skirtAttachCurve. Fortunately, Maya provides methods to manipulate the cloth with great accuracy. In this section, you will create a series of transform constraints that will guide individual cloth vertices to their proper location on the skirtAttachCurve. Once you run the simulation, the skirt should wrap and settle nicely around the model. This process is labor intensive, but you will employ some MEL scripts to accelerate it.

Creating Guide Locators on the Skirt's Waist

First, you need to create some guide locators to designate the destination of each cloth vertex on the guide curve. Follow these steps:

1. Use the scene file you have been working on or open `skirt_garmentBuilt.mb`, which has been prepared for this step.
2. Open the Script Editor and source `attachLocators.mel`.
3. You may need to edit the script if the names you gave for your cloth mesh and attach curve do not match the names in these steps. If so, edit the first two lines of code in the script.

   ```
   string $attachCurve = "skirtAttachCurve";
   string $clothObject = "skirt_cloth";
   ```

4. Select the top row of vertices in the cloth mesh, and execute `attachLocators.mel`.

You should see a lot of locators, as in Figure 1.12. One set lies directly on the cloth vertices and another set directly on the attach curve. A transform constraint is associated with each locator snapped onto the cloth vertex, which forces the cloth vertex to follow the path of the locator to which it is constrained. If you animate the locator from its existing position on the cloth mesh to a position on the attach curve, the vertex will follow suit at simulation time.

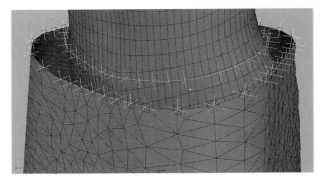

Figure 1.12: `attachLocators.mel` *places locators on the top row of the cloth mesh and on the attach curve.*

Constraining the Skirt to the Guide Locators

The locators on the attach curve are uniformly spaced around the skirtAttachCurve, and there are an equivalent number of locators on the cloth mesh and on the curve. Now it is time to connect the locators such that the transition onto the attach curve will be smooth.

Before you start, let's hide a few things to reduce the possibility of making mistakes.

1. In perspective view, rotate so that you can look down over the locaters.
2. Disable the cloth simulation as scrubbing along the Timeline can inadvertently trigger the simulation. In the Cloth menu set, choose **Simulation → Disable Solver**.
3. Turn off polygon and NURBS surface display for the perspective view.
4. Beginning from the front of the skirt, select a locator that is on a cloth vertex. Shift+select a locator on the attach curve that is the shortest and straightest path from the selected cloth locator (see Figure 1.13).

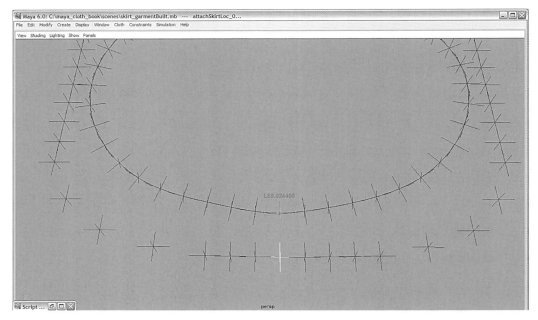

Figure 1.13: Running `attachLocators.mel` *generates two sets of locators. The cloth locator is selected, followed by the attach curve locator.*

5. Choose **File → Open Script → keyLocator.mel**. Select the code and drag it onto the shelf to create a button. (MM drag in Linux and Windows; Option-drag on Mac.) Executing this script by clicking the button snaps the cloth locator onto the attach curve locator and sets a keyframe to animate it.

6. Select the adjacent set of locators, cloth locator first, followed by the curve locator. Press G to repeat the last command, and repeat this sequence for all the locators. Using the hot keys speeds this process.

If all went well, when you scrub the Timeline from frames 1 through 5, the locators will move from their position on the cloth mesh smoothly to the attach curve. When the simulation runs, the top row of cloth vertices will follow these locators to their designated spot on the attach curve.

Making the Model a Collision Object

In order for the skirt to drape around the model, you must tell the solver that the garment should collide against this object. To do so, follow these steps:

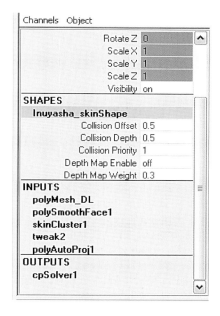

Figure 1.14:
Collision Object
attributes. The
output goes to
the cpSolver1
node.

1. Select Inuyasha_skin and choose **Cloth → Create Collision Object**.

2. Look under the shape node in the Channel box. You should see several collision-related attributes, as in Figure 1.14. Set **Collision Offset** and **Collision Depth** to 0.5. These values tell the cloth solver how much distance to keep between the garment and the collision object. Measured in centimeters, 0.5 is enough of a buffer to prevent the collision object from poking through the skirt but is small enough to keep it from looking puffed out around the collision model.

Assigning cpSolver and cpProperty Attributes

The **cpSolver** and **cpProperty** attributes largely define the shape of your cloth and how it reacts to forces. The **cpSolver** node affects the garment on a global basis and is the single-most important control over Cloth. It should be one of the first items you adjust when developing a new garment. Each panel has an assignable **cpProperty**, allowing flexibility on how a garment should react at specified panel region.

These attributes play an important role in improving the stability of the garment. Because the garment you develop can be used in a diverse range of animations, establishing solid settings will pay big dividends throughout production.

The cpSolver Attribute

Access the solver by choosing **Simulation → Solvers → cpSolver1 ❒**. You can also select the cloth mesh and click the cpSolver1 Input in the Channel box. Now follow these steps:

1. Set **Frame Samples** to 2. This dictates how many subframe calculations the solver makes before updating the cloth's shape at the next frame interval.

Determining a good sampling rate is based on garment complexity, its intended use, and a bit of trial and error. A flat, hanging curtain might be fine with a frame sample of 1 but if it is flapping against gale force winds, a much higher value is required. Keep this number as low as possible while maintaining stability through a typical motion; simulation times increase noticeably with higher numbers. For a typical human character, you might want to set a value that works successfully on a walk. When the motion becomes extreme, you can keyframe the sample rate higher, which provides a more accurate solution and thereby reduces the number of collision problems and poke-through issues.

2. Set **Solver Scale** to 2.5. This is an internal representation of the cloth's size. Raising the solver scale tells Maya to treat the cloth as a larger piece of fabric, although physically its dimensions appear unchanged.

This change in size influences how the cloth folds and reacts to fields and properties (see Figure 1.15). One way to give the impression of stiffer cloth is to use a lower solver scale. Since a smaller amount of cloth is solved versus what is visually represented, it will have less mass and tend to drape less. Because this value has a ripple effect though the other attributes and properties, try to work with the solver scale early in development and establish a standard value. One side-effect of changing the solver scale is that your cache in memory will be deleted. Remember to save your scene file before changing solver scale if you want to keep the current simulation.

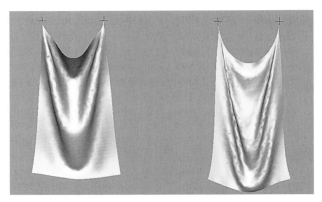

Figure 1.15: Identical cloth with the left at Solver Scale 1, the right at 2.5

3. Keep **Relax Frame Length** at 5.

Because the seams stretch between panels during the initial garment creation, the cloth will abruptly collapse during the first few frames of the simulation. The **Relax Frame Length** helps the solver during this period by making the garment extra stretchy, allowing the stress to disperse more evenly. Extremely large or complex garments may need a longer run-up period. Allow the simulation to continue long after the relax period to let the cloth settle using its normal property values. After the relax has completed and the solver's initial state has been saved, set this attribute to 0.

4. Turn on Output Statistics. Frame solve duration and overall elapsed time are displayed every frame. On long, complex simulations, this is sometimes the only way you know that Maya is functioning correctly (see Figure 1.16).

Figure 1.16: Example output statistics

```
SOLVER TIME for cpSolver1, frame 2.000: 26.958, total: 26.958
SOLVER TIME for cpSolver1, frame 3.000: 13.360, total: 40.318
SOLVER TIME for cpSolver1, frame 4.000: 13.459, total: 53.777
SOLVER TIME for cpSolver1, frame 5.000: 11.967, total: 65.744
SOLVER TIME for cpSolver1, frame 6.000: 12.138, total: 77.882
SOLVER TIME for cpSolver1, frame 7.000: 11.637, total: 89.519
```

The cpProperty Attribute

To access properties, choose **Simulation** → **Properties** → **cpDefaultProperty** ❏, or select a cloth panel and click the cpProperty node under INPUTS. Set the following values:

1. Set U and V Stretch Resistance to 150. For the skirt, increasing this value gives more stability by reducing the chances of the cloth getting caught under the foot. It also reduces the rubbery feel associated with low stretch resistance.

   A certain amount of stretch is necessary for the simulation to work smoothly; however, if the stretch and shear values are too low, there will be noticeable texture stretching, as you can see in Figure 1.17. This is really distracting when any flat garment, such as a bed cover or tablecloth, is being pulled.

2. Set **Shear Resistance** to 135. This value is often adjusted in parallel with stretch resistance. Shearing occurs when cloth vertices begin to move in opposite directions, as in a tearing motion.

3. Set **Density** to 0.03. By increasing the mass of the garment, density gives a greater feel of weight by carrying more momentum when it moves. The look of the folds are also affected (see Figure 1.18).

4. Set **Air Damping** to 0.001. A low value reduces the effect on the cloth as it moves through space. It tends to hang down and feel heavier, whereas a high value creates a more flaglike effect.

You can assign each panel a custom property by choosing **Simulation** → **Properties** → **Create Cloth Property**. To assign a property to a specific panel, select the panel and choose **Simulation** → **Properties** → cpPropertyName to display a list of all currently available properties.

Figure 1.17: The same cloth with stretch resistance at 50/50 and shear resistance at 45 versus stretch at 150/150 and shear at 135

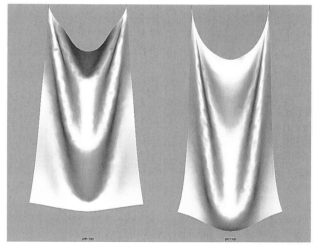

Figure 1.18: The same cloth simulated at a density of 0.01 on the left and 0.03 on the right.

The best way to understand the effects of the **cpProperty** attribute is to alter its values, run a simulation, and watch the results. To this end, we have provided several QuickTime movies, each showing a side-by-side comparison of a single property simulated at the default value and with an altered value. You can find these in the images/cpPropertyExamples folder on the CD.

Running the Simulation

You are ready to begin your first simulation! Take a deep breath, and follow these steps:

1. Set the Timeline to frame 1.
2. Turn the solver back on. Choose **Simulation → Enable Solver**. It is on by default but was previously turned it off when you constrained the skirt to the guide locators. Also, turn on Polygon and NURBS Surfaces display if no geometry is visible.
3. Click Play.

It will take several seconds to start, but eventually you will see the simulation drawing the cloth in toward the model. Notice that the hips and legs do not penetrate since you made the skirt a collision object. Let the skirt settle for about 100 frames. Now is a good time for a coffee break.

Be sure that the Timeline encompasses the start frame. Otherwise, the simulation will not begin. You will see the playback progressing without the solver having any effect.

Once you've finished simulating, the motion should look similar to garmentSettle.mov. When you scrub the Timeline, the cloth should update immediately as Maya saves the simulation data into a cache. If you want to save your results, save the scene file.

Setting Up Cloth for General Animation

If you are working on a film or a project of any length, chances are you will be using the same character and cloth garment for several scenes. Building panels, stitching the garment, and relaxing it for every animation would be a lot of repetitive work. The good news is that once you have a relaxed garment, you can save its state with the solver attached to it. The next time you open the scene file, you can start solving with the garment in the same fitted, relaxed position. Because you allowed the cloth to settle over a long period of time, there won't be any abrupt motion as witnessed during the initial relax. Save this scene file as a template and propagate copies of it for use in specific animations.

Saving the Relaxed Garment State

1. Use your scene file or open skirtAttach.mb. If there is no cache data, resimulate.
2. Pick a frame where the cloth has settled, somewhere between frame 100 and frame 150, select the skirt, and choose **Simulation → Save As Initial Cloth State**.

Set the Timeline back to frame 1. Notice that the cloth no longer has the boxlike shape of the panel curves but looks like the skirt at the frame where you performed the Save As Initial State. Any new simulation will begin using this shape as a starting point for the first frame's solve. If the cache is deleted or the timeline is set at or before the solver start frame, the garment defaults to the initial state. One consequence of this action is that the cache becomes invalid and should be deleted.

3. Choose **Simulation** → **Delete Cache**.

From this point forward, the simulation will begin from the relaxed state. If your character does not begin animation at the location where the garment was fitted, you can move it to the character's new position. Align your garment to the character's position and choose **Simulation** → **Update Cloth State**, followed by **Simulation** → **Save As Initial Cloth State**. **Update Cloth State** changes the data stored in the cache to reflect the new garment position.

Mesh Constraining Cloth to the Model

In this skirt example, in addition to saving the cloth state, you also need to constrain the relaxed skirt to the collision model. This allows the cloth to move with and react to the character's motion.

Earlier we used transform constraints to pin the skirt along the attach curve, but once the character begins to move, it will be out of alignment because the transform locators were not animated to the character's motion. By using a mesh constraint, you can assign the top of the skirt to follow the waist of the model. But, first, let's do some cleanup.

1. In the Outliner, expand the hierarchy of skirt_cloth. Delete all the transform constraints that were created by the attachLocator.mel script.
2. Delete all the locators named attachSkirtLoc_*.
3. Delete all the locators named XFORM_attachSkirtCurve*.
4. Select the top row of the skirt's vertices, Shift+select the character mesh, Inuyasha_skin, and choose **Constraints** → **Mesh**.

This constraint maintains the offset between a cloth vertex and the model's surface as it animates. The result will look as if the top of the skirt is attached to the model. The character is now ready for animation.

Animating the Skirt

After you develop the skirt, you can test its motion in a variety of simulations. Open skirt_jump.mb to test the garment in an animated jump off a box. Although the skirt simulates well in a standing pose, you will need to adapt the **cpSolver** and **cpProperty** settings to deal with the abrupt motion and more extreme posing.

Disable the solver and scrub the Timeline. It helps to look at the motion and see what issues lie ahead. Keep an eye out for problem areas, including quick or jerky motion, extreme bending of joints, and interaction with objects. Enable the solver, and allow the garment to simulate.

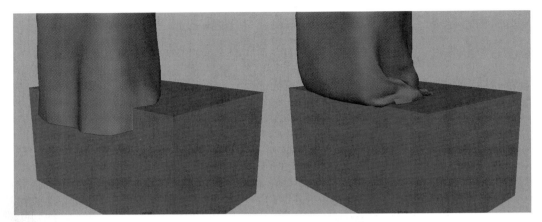

Figure 1.19: The box before and after being made into a collision object

At frame 16, our character crouches down in anticipation of the jump, but the skirt clips through the box (see Figure 1.19). Convert the box into a collision object by selecting it and choosing **Cloth** → **Create Collision Object**. Set the offset and depth to 0.5. When you scrubbed through the animation, you might have noticed a similar crouch on the landing at frame 40. This may not be an issue if the legs are off camera, but, in this case, add a ground plane collision object.

Truncating the Cache

Because of the penetration, you will need to resimulate the portion where the skirt clips through box. Fortunately, adjusting your settings in the middle of a simulation does not mean starting over. You can delete the offending portion of the cache and start solving from that point. Follow these steps:

1. Scrub the Timeline to the last good frame, about frame 8.
2. Choose **Simulation** → **Truncate Cache**.

You can only truncate the end portion of a cache. Any good frames following will be lost, but this is usually not an issue. Once the simulation starts to go bad, it will not usually recover on its own.

Inconsistencies between the cache and your setup can occur when using the truncate feature. For example, if you truncate the cache at frame 15 and set a new property value, every frame now simulates with that new value; however, the cached frames were simulated based on the old value. If you simulate fresh from the start, the results will differ. If the character animation is locked and final, save a copy of the cache file because the result may not be reproducible. Otherwise, simulate clean from the start frame to ensure that you can resimulate your garment with consistency.

Updating cpSolver and cpProperty Values

Click Play to continue the simulation. The skirt should now collide against the box. Continuing the simulation to frame 26 reveals a new problem in the form of some severe penetration of the cloth through the collision surface (see Figure 1.20).

You can fix this by increasing frame samples or lowering the time step. Both attributes work together to establish the amount of subframe sampling. Sampling in smaller chunks improves the cloth's position and velocity accuracy. The negative side-effect is simulation time increases. To minimize the cost, animate the frame sampling during high-stress times. For the jump, try animating frame sampling from its default value of 2 at frame 18 up to a value of 6 or more at frame 23.

In addition to the increased sampling, the skirt should be stiffer during this period to prevent the cloth from stretching and tangling. Set keys for the values as shown in the following list. It helps to ramp up your settings a few frames before the motion hits its extreme. In this way, the properties reach full strength smoothly. The same is true for easing out of these values during the landing.

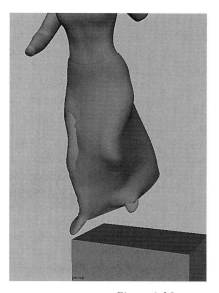

Figure 1.20: Penetration at frame 26 caused by inadequate frame sampling

cpProperty	Frame 18	Frame 23	Frame 40	Frame 45
U/V Bend Resistance	10	50	50	10
U/V Bend Rate	0	0.2	0.2	0
U/V Stretch Resistance	350	750	750	350
Shear Resistance	300	600	600	300
Density	0.3	0.15	0.15	0.3
Thickness Force	5	5	5	5

Increasing Bend Resistance reduces unwanted self-collisions by making it more difficult for the vertices to fold in on themselves. As the resistance increases, the folds tend to become wider and flatter (see Figure 1.21). Since the characteristics of the cloth change, it's best to animate these values up during extreme motion where a value increase will not be readily apparent.

Bend Rate works in conjunction with Bend Resistance in that its effect becomes progressively stronger as the bend angle increases.

Stretch and Shear Resistance are increased across the board to make the skirt less rubbery. Low stretch and shear resistance tends to give cloth a springy effect that can result in distracting motion.

Lowering Density gives the cloth less mass, which reduces the effect of forces on the cloth during the jump.

Thickness is the distance maintained between vertices and other cloth objects as well as when it folds in on itself. The thickness force is the factor of

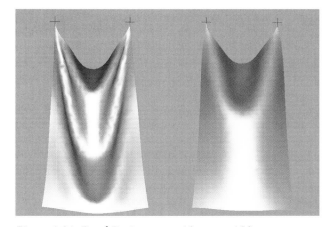

Figure 1.21: Bend Resistance at 10 versus 150

Figure 1.22: The Paint Properties tool. Painting on the cloth mesh creates a map that becomes a multiplier. The darker region indicates that density is reduced.

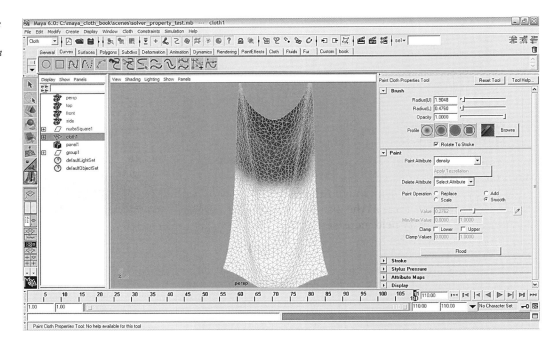

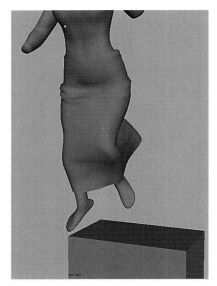

Figure 1.23: The skirt at frame 26 after applying new solver and property values

how strongly the cloth attempts to maintain this offset. This attribute also minimizes the effect of self-collisions.

Once property attributes are set, you can use the Paint Cloth Properties tool to vary the values on a per vertex basis. Select the cloth mesh, choose **Simulation → Properties → Paint Cloth Properties Tool** ❒. The available attributes, which are shown in Figure 1.22, are in the Paint section.

Since some of the cpProperty values have been altered globally, for example, Thickness Force, you need to delete the cache and start the simulation fresh (see Figure 1.23).

As the character begins to fall about frame 30, the skirt begins to ride up the character's legs. Pulling the skirt below the knees will help keep it from pinching into the back of the legs as they bend during landing. Increase the solver's gravity to increase the downward force on the skirt by using the following settings:

cpSolver1	Frame 25	Frame 30	Frame 35
Gravity	0, −980, 0	0, −3000, 0	0, −980, 0

The default is −980 in the Y axis, which is the Maya default for normal gravity. The axes are based on world space coordinates.

Creating a Gravity Constraint

Another way to add gravity is through a field constraint. Using the solver's gravity affects the entire garment. Sometimes you want a greater level of control over where the force is applied. In this case, it can be useful to have this field at the bottom hem. Follow these steps:

1. In the Dynamics menu set, choose **Fields** → **Gravity**.
2. Select the area of the skirt where you want to apply the field (see Figure 1.24), Shift+select the gravity field, and choose **Constraints** → **Field**.

Animate this field to add extra force. Increase **Magnitude** to 2000, and set the direction vector to –1 in the Y axis to force the hem down. Attenuation reduces the amount of force as the distance between the cloth and the gravity field increases. Set this value to 0 to maintain a uniform force throughout the animation.

View the final results in skirt_jump.mov on the CD.

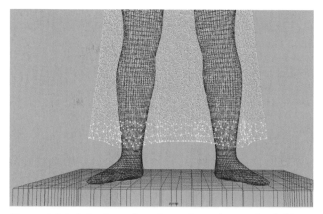

Figure 1.24: Selection of vertices where the gravity field applies. A larger selection will have a greater overall effect on the garment.

Interacting with Collision Objects

Building a garment is only one aspect of working with Maya Cloth. You also want the garment to interact with other objects in the scene. If the character kneels, the cloth should rest on the ground plane. If the character sits, the cloth should conform to the shape of the chair. One character's garment might affect the garment for a second character. Cloth allows virtually any NURBS (Non-Uniform Rational B-Spline), subdivision, or polygon surface to be made into a collision object.

To make a surface into a collision object, follow these steps:

1. Select any object or create a NURBS or polygon primitive.
2. In the Cloth menu set, choose **Cloth** → **Create Collision Object**. Under the Shapes node, some new attributes appear:

Collision Offset This is the distance in centimeters, offset away from the collision surface, that the solver will repel cloth. It creates a buffer to reduce the possibility of the surface penetrating the cloth.

Collision Depth The depth is the distance within the surface where the solver continues to apply a repelling force. Once cloth has gone past the collision depth, the solver no longer repels. If the depth gets too large, an overlap is created where the vector of the repelling force becomes unpredictable.

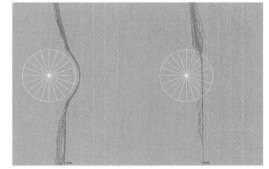

Collision Priority If two collision surfaces are simultaneously influencing a section of cloth, instability in the form of vertex popping can become prevalent. The lowest value is the highest priority collision object (see Figure 1.25).

Figure 1.25: The cylinder has collision priority 1, and the cube is priority 2 on the left image. The priorities are switched on the right.

*Figure 1.26:
Collision object
attributes in
relation to the
geometry surface*

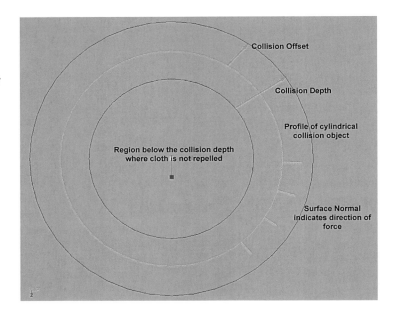

*Figure 1.27:
The left sphere's
resolution is too
low. The right
sphere has fewer
poke-through
issues as a result
of its higher
tessellation.*

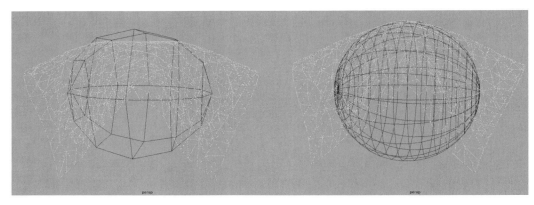

The direction of force from the collision surface is determined by its normal. If the cloth gets sucked into the collision object, rather than being repelled, view the normals and reverse their direction if they are pointed the wrong way (see Figure 1.26).

To view normals, select the object. For polygons, choose **Display** → **Polygon Components** → **Normals**. For NURBS, choose **Display** → **NURBS Components** → **Normals**.

To reverse the direction of the normals, select the object. For polygons, choose **Edit Polygons** → **Normals** → **Reverse**. For NURBS, choose **Edit NURBS** → **Reverse Surface Direction**.

One cause of cloth/collision problems is a mismatch in resolution. When the collision object has too low a resolution, the cloth will have penetration issues, and when dragged over the collision object, it will tend to pop (see Figure 1.27).

As much as low resolution can cause difficulty, complex collision surfaces can be equally problematic. Hands and feet with their multiple digits and relatively small surface areas can also poke through cloth. They can also intersect, causing other collision problems.

In most cases, it is quicker and more stable to replace hands and feet with simpler collision objects. You can fashion a polygon sphere that encompasses the entire hand and use that as the collision object. Avoid collision objects that have sharp edges or if big gaps appear between surfaces. These are also candidates for replacement with simpler collision objects. Also, you can generate new, simpler surfaces by lofting and attaching surfaces together.

Often, collision objects are unavoidably animated to the point where cloth is stretched beyond its designed limits. Imagine a character's pants while the character is riding a horse. Each thigh is applying an outward force while the back of the horse is pushing the cloth up. For these extremes, you can increase the amount of fabric to be simulated by using the cpProperty's U and V scales.

Affecting Cloth Motion Using Constraints

Constraints are versatile tools that provide a great deal of added functionality and are invaluable in cases where the solver does not readily provide a solution. Each constraint has a unique capability to control the motion of a garment. Constraints work on a per vertex basis, which means they exert a fine level of influence. You've already used several types of constraints in the tutorial for both construction and animation purposes. You used a transform constraint to guide the top of the skirt onto the skirtAttachCurve; you created a mesh constraint to keep the skirt pinned onto the character's waist during animation; and you added gravity field constraint to give extra downward pulling force on the hem.

Constraints are commonly used to create the sensation of additional forces being applied to the cloth, including creating effects such as the wind blowing or some force pulling on the cloth. Another category of constraints allows for part or all of the garment to attach to other objects or to pass through them without collision. Used in this way, constraints can be an immense aid during difficult solves.

Quite frequently constraints are used for applying additional forces on the cloth. This might be the wind blowing against a sail or some force pulling on the cloth, such as picking up a napkin. There are constraints to allow objects to be parented onto a garment. This makes adding details like buttons or jewels a simple affair. Garments can also be attached to each other using a cloth constraint. If you had a vest over a shirt, adding this type of constraint helps keep the garments together, increasing the sense of friction and texture. A final, essential constraint allows selected vertices to pass through collision objects or through itself without repelling force.

These collision constraints are an immense aid during difficult solves where cloth gets pinched or stretched too far. All constraints work on a per vertex basis, which is a major benefit since it gives finer control over the constraint's influence. This level of granularity gives you much more artistic control and can make the difference in creating a convincing performance.

These are only a few of the possibilities achievable, limited only by the requirements of the animation and the cloth animator's ingenuity. Let's take a closer look at the different kinds of constraints.

Transform Constraint

You can use transform constraints when a set of cloth vertices must travel to a certain location or follow a particular path. Imagine tossing a towel into a basket. By constraining a small set of vertices, you not only guide the trajectory but also dictate timing and speed. The solver calculates the motion for the section of the garment that is not affected by the constraint. Pay particular attention to the timing such that the cloth feels like it is being driven by a natural force, e.g., the character's arm tossing the towel. Otherwise transform constraints can give the distinct look that the cloth is being pushed or pulled in an unmotivated fashion.

Open buildTransformConstraint.mb and click Play. The cloth falls due to the lack of any constraints or collision objects. Gravity is the only force acting upon it. To create a constraint, follow these steps.

1. Set the Timeline to frame 1 and delete the cache.
2. Select the upper-left vertex and Shift+select locator1.
3. In the Cloth Menu Set, choose **Constraints** → **Transform**. A small box appears, indicating that vertex has a constraint on it (see Figure 1.28).

Displaying constraints can slow your computer's refresh rate. An easy way to hide constraints is to turn off locator display in the view port by toggling **Show** → **Locators**.

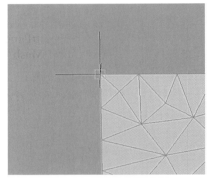

Figure 1.28: Inside the box is an example of a vertex constrained.

4. Create another constraint on the upper-right corner using locator2. As the cloth simulates, the constrained vertices follow the locators. In the Outliner, expand the hierarchy for cloth1. There will be two constraint nodes. Select transform-Constraint1 and look at the Channel box. Under the shape node are attributes for the constraint (see Figure 1.29).

> **Constraint Weight** Sets the constraint on and off. Any value over 0 indicates the constraint as turned on.
>
> **Is Soft** Off, the default, which means the constrained vertices stick to the transform object with no amount of play. Turning Is Soft on allows for smoother cloth motion. The side-effect is that the constrained region and transform object can separate.

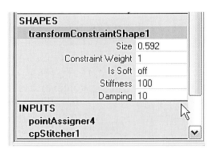

Figure 1.29: Transform constraint attributes

Stiffness Sets the strength of attraction to the transform object when Is Soft is on.

Damping Attempts to reduce the springy effect that occurs as the cloth vertices pull away from the transform object. This also only is relevant when Is Soft is on.

Mesh Constraint

Mesh constraints are similar to transform constraints in that the vertices affected are directly controlled by the object constraining them; however, a mesh constraint only works with collision objects. The end result is that the garment follows the collision object's motion. This is particularly useful for form fitting sections or where the garment is cinched on. If a sleeve is taut near the shoulder but the cuff area is loose, mesh constraining the top of the sleeve will ensure that it does not slide excessively. This idea can be expanded to cases where cloth motion must be reduced for stability reasons. If a simulation begins failing due to the character moving too quickly, constraining a section of the garment to the body for a few frames can help reduce its activity. Just be sure to hide the constraint off camera or use it in cases where the character fills very little screen space. In the opposite case where the garment is up close and static, using mesh constraints can lock down popping vertices.

Let's build a quick mesh constraint:

1. Open `buildMeshConstraint.mb`.
2. In the Outliner, select leftPanelCurve and Ctrl-select collsionCylinder.
3. Choose **Constraints → Mesh**.

The cloth should hang down under the cylinder. The mesh constraint attributes are similar to those of the transform constraint (see Figure 1.30).

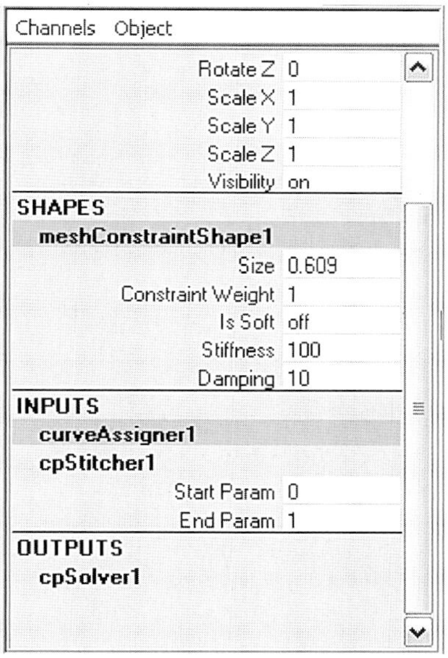

Cloth Constraint

Cloth Constraints bind one cloth garment to another. If your garments are layered, it may be worthwhile to consider solving the garments in sequence, with the first garment simulated by itself and the second garment mesh constrained to the output of the first garment. The advantage is reduced solver complexity, but the down side is that the garments do not interact.

If the garments are of equal weight, then a cloth constraint is the appropriate choice. It is also useful in special cases where two garments must be bound together. An example would be a piece of fabric being torn in half. You could create a cloth constraint to join the two halves together and animate the constraint weight from on to off, then use a series of cloth constraints to have the halves separate one vertex at a time or create the constraint using a panel curve and animate its start and end param values.

Channels	Object	
	Rotate Z	0
	Scale X	1
	Scale Y	1
	Scale Z	1
	Visibility	on
SHAPES		
meshConstraintShape1		
	Size	0.609
	Constraint Weight	1
	Is Soft	off
	Stiffness	100
	Damping	10
INPUTS		
curveAssigner1		
cpStitcher1		
	Start Param	0
	End Param	1
OUTPUTS		
cpSolver1		

Figure 1.30: Constraining a panel curve is a convenient way to constrain the edge row of vertices. Under Inputs in the Channel box for the constraint node is a curve assigner. Setting the Start and End Param values enables you to specify a partial section of the curve to constrain.

Let's take a look at a cloth constraint:

1. Open `buildClothConstraint.mb`.
2. Select the left edge of vertices of cloth2, which are adjacent to cloth1 and Shift+select cloth1.
3. Choose **Constraints → Cloth**.
4. Under the constraint's shape node, turn Stitch on.

The simulation for cloth2 is driven by the motion at the end of cloth1. The stitch feature attaches the two garments. This supersedes the **Stiffness, Damping,** and **Offset** attributes (see Figure 1.31).

Figure 1.31: Two cloth garments held together using the cloth constraint

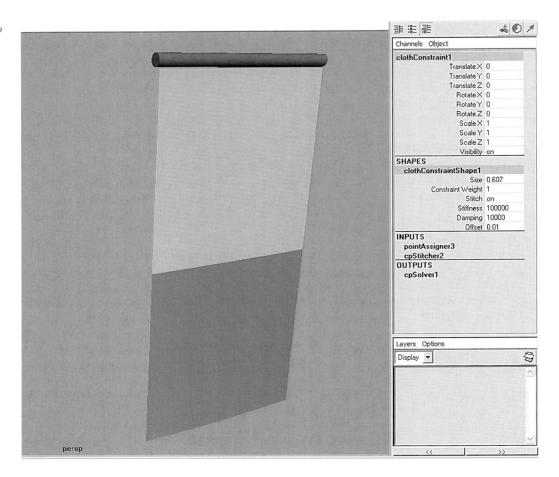

Field Constraint

The Field Constraint is really a whole set of constraints leveraging off existing elements from the Dynamics package. Each of these fields can uniquely influence the shape and motion of the cloth and is extremely useful when you want to animate the cloth beyond what the solver gives you by default. Up to this point, gravity and the collision objects have been the primary forces driving the garment's motion, but additional forces generated from fields can also play a role. Through the field you can specify the amount of force and its vector over the constrained region of cloth. This constraint is less direct than a manual technique like a transform constraint, but it tends to yield smoother, more natural motion.

As an example, if you want to get the feel that the cloth is being blown by the wind, one way to start is by adding a uniform field:

1. Open `buildFieldConstraint.mb`.
2. In the Dynamics menu set, choose **Fields** → **Uniform** and set the following values:

    Magnitude: 75   // Raise the force to an appreciable level
    Attenuation: 0   // Keeps the force constant over distance
    DirectionX: −1   // Sets the world space vector for force

3. Select a group of about a dozen vertices in the middle of the cloth, and Shift+select the uniform field.

4. In the Cloth Menu set, choose **Constraints** → **Field**.

You should see the cloth being pushed in the region of the constraint. Try animating the magnitude of the field or perhaps constraining a larger or different region of the cloth and see how the results differ.

Collision Constraint

Collision constraints allow constrained vertices to pass through collision objects to other cloth meshes or allow the vertices to intersect. Allowing self-intersection can be useful in folding areas such as in the underarm region of a shirt. Sometimes, collision objects are animated to the point where cloth gets stretched beyond its designed limits. Adding a collision constraint to allow the cloth to penetrate in a section that is off camera can give enough looseness for the cloth to solve effectively. Let's try that:

1. Open `buildCollisionConstraint.mb` and click Play. You should see the cloth simulate over the sphere collision object.
2. Choose **Simulation** → **Delete Cache** and return to frame 1.
3. Select the lower half of the cloth vertices and choose **Constraints** → **Collision**.

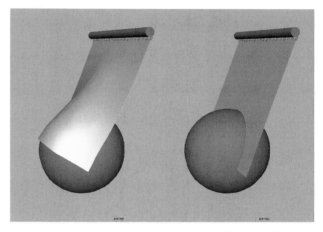

Upon simulation, the cloth should pass right through the collision sphere (see Figure 1.32). If you look at the shapes node of the collision constraint, you will see that both cloth and rigid collisions are turned off. You can animate these independently. Often you will want to allow self-intersections (cloth collision off) but still respect the collision objects (rigid collisions on).

Button Constraint

The Button constraint can be used for adding any rigid objects, such as pins, lapels, nametags, badges, and, of course, buttons. Note that these objects cannot be collision objects because this would create a cycle where the collision object would affect the cloth solve and the cloth solve would affect the position of the collision object. Because the solver cannot factor in the button object, clipping can occur if the garment were to fold heavily. The easiest way to manage this problem is to manually rotate and possibly translate the button object under the cpButton transform node.

Figure 1.32: A cloth garment with a collision constraint placed on the bottom half of the cloth vertices (right)

Unlike the cloth constraint, the button constraint allows rigid objects to be parented onto the surface of the cloth under the cpButton transform node. This gives you extra control to animate the constrained object on top of the motion provided by the constraint. One application is it to rotate the button object to prevent clipping with the cloth. Follow these steps:

1. Open `buildButtonConstraint`.
2. Select buttonSphere, and Shift+select cloth1.
3. Choose **Constraints** → **Button**.

The sphere should follow the cloth. By default, the constraint maintains the offset between the constrained object and the cloth. Choose **Constraints** → **Button** ❑, and turn off Preserve Translation and Preserve Rotation, which will snap the constrained object to the surface of the cloth. You can apply an additional offset within the option box.

Avoiding Cloth Problems During Character Animation

One of the most effective ways to help the simulation along is to take extra care during animation. The forces generated by collision objects are strong and tend to overwhelm everything else. For example, it is virtually impossible for a field to be strong enough to force the cloth through a collision object. Therefore, it is imperative that the animation of collision objects works in a predictable fashion.

A common problem is that the character is often animated to the camera, which means that any part of the character off camera is not given much attention. This can cause nonanimated limbs to crash through the body or be left in odd positions. There is also the temptation to fix a character's animation when hidden behind a wall or other occluding object. It is not uncommon to speed up or slow down a character's motion or perhaps rotate the character completely around to get back on the correct path. This may look fine from the camera's angle, but the solver factors in these forces, which will cause the cloth to react unexpectedly.

Self-intersection in a collision object is another area where animation changes can make life a lot simpler. Although the goal is always not to limit the performance of a character, a pose can be so extreme that the solver will have difficulty simulating without introducing instability. The cylinder in Figure 1.33 is similar to an elbow or a knee bent too far. You can see the eyelet-shaped area where the collision surface reverses the direction of force within a small distance. If the cloth gets caught in this region, the abrupt direction change manifests itself in the form of the popping cloth vertices.

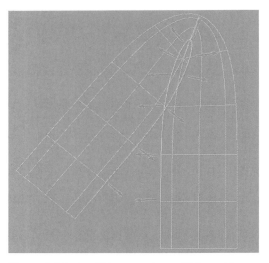

Figure 1.33: A self-intersecting collision object

Manually Updating Cloth

At times, everything looks fine except for one bad frame. In this case, you can manually manipulate the cloth geometry after the simulation and choose **Simulation** → **Update Cloth State** to update the position information in the cache for the current frame. Use this command as a last resort. If you resimulate, these tweaks will be lost.

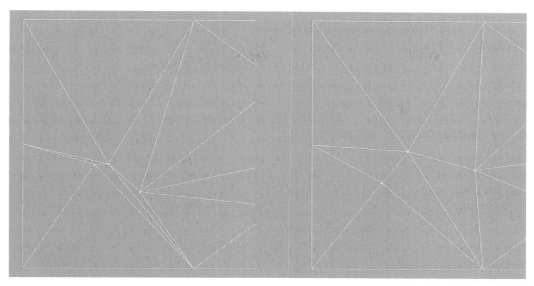

Figure 1.34: The result of polygon averaging on selected vertices

Polygon averaging can help if a small handful of vertices continually pop in and out. It calculates a vertex's position based on its neighbors. Be sure to use this in small doses as averaging over large areas will cause the cloth to reduce in volume. To polygon average the vertices:

1. Select the popping vertices.
2. In the Modeling menu set (press F3 to open it), choose **Polygons** → **Average Vertices** (see Figure 1.34).

Use averaging as a post process step as the averaging information is not saved in the cache. The node remains an input to the cloth even after deleting the cache. Remove polygon averaging before running a new simulation. To do so:

1. Select the cloth mesh and open the attribute editor.
2. Select the tab for the polyAverageVertex node, click the Select button and click Delete.

If you have several nodes and you want to remove all of them, run the following MEL code.

```
string $node, $polyAvgNodes[]
=lsType("polyAverageVertex") ;
for ($node in $polyAvgNodes){
if ($node != "<done>")
delete $node;
}
```

Saving Your Work

After you simulate the garment, the cloth updates in real time without recalculating because the cache is stored in memory. This information is saved on disk through a Maya file format that has the .mcc extension. By default, the .mcc file is stored in the same folder with the same name as the scene file. In previous versions of Maya, the cpSolver had an attribute that listed the path to the cache file. Maya 6 has the expanded notion of a cpCache node. The most important thing to keep in mind is that the cache is written to disk only when your scene file is saved. In other words, if you choose **File** → **Exit**, all the simulation data is lost. A computer-related mantra, which is definitely true for cloth, is to save early and save often. You can manually save the cache or back up a copy under a different filename. To save a file, follow these steps:

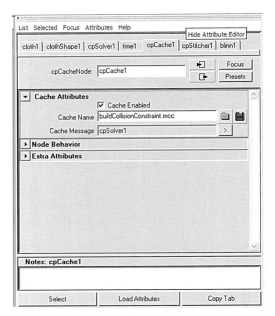

Figure 1.35: The cpCache node

1. Select the cloth garment, open the Attribute Editor, and select the cpCache node.
2. Set the cache name and click the disk icon to save (see Figure 1.35).

In older versions of Maya, you can save the cache through a MEL command:

```
cpSolver -saveCache "filepath/filename.mcc"
```

Maya automatically loads the cache listed in the cpCache node when the scene is opened. You can also load an alternate cache file through the cpCache node by clicking the folder icon shown in Figure 1.35.

And now on to some noncloth things you can do with Maya Cloth.

Alternative Uses for Maya Cloth

Up to this point, you have learned how to create a cloth garment by constructing panel curves and seaming them together. You also learned how to create a workable collision environment for clothing animation. Sometimes though, in a 3D production, the work of a clothing animator does not just center on skirts and other garments; it can also involve props, accessories, and even jewelry.

Cloth simulation is a great way to deform anything that behaves in a similar manner to cloth. You can animate flags, banners, vines in a jungle, and even earrings with the help of Maya Cloth. You can even go as far as animating the cord of a video game controller with Cloth. So, the next time you are animating curtains, cords, towels, or even the fringe that hangs off older lampshades, consider a cloth simulation.

Now, it is time to take your new knowledge of Maya Cloth a step further and see how to use it for nongarment deformations in a production pipeline. Specifically, we will focus on creating a bracelet for our female model and setting up its deformations using cloth simulation.

Building the Bracelet Garment

We'll now build a cloth garment that will be used to deform the bracelet around the left wrist of our character. Follow these steps:

1. Open `bracelet_sim.ma`. You will see our character standing in the neutral position at the origin.
2. We will deform the bracelet model you see around the left wrist. Select a part of the bracelet, and press the F key to center it in your view.
3. Choose **Create → NURBS Primitives → Square**.
4. Select the new NURBS square's group node, and press the W key to invoke the Translate tool.
    a. Turn on point snapping. MM drag over a surface in the view window. The NURBS square you previously created should snap to the surface your mouse was over.
    b. Turn off snapping, and make sure the only thing selected is the NURBS square group node.
    c. Rotate and scale the group node until, from the top view, a rectangular box is completely encompassing the bracelet.

Your top view should look similar to Figure 1.36.

Check the perspective view, and make sure the NURBS square is above the highest point of the bracelet by at least a few units in the Y direction. Now follow these steps:

1. Select the group node of the NURBS square.
2. Choose **Edit → Duplicate □**.
3. Choose **Edit → Reset Settings**, and then duplicate the square.
4. Move the duplicated group node down in Y so that it is below the bracelet.

Your perspective view should look similar to Figure 1.37.

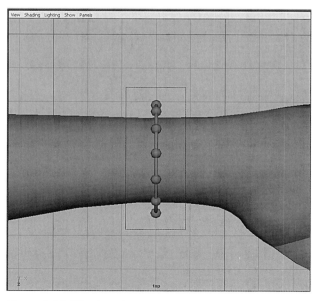

Figure 1.36: The top view

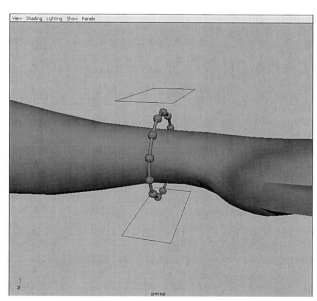

Figure 1.37: Two NURBS squares used to generate cloth panels

Now, in much the same way you built the garment earlier in this chapter, you will build this garment. Follow these steps:

1. Select the top group's curves individually.

Selecting the curves individually is more of a suggestion than a necessity. Based on studio experience and workflow, problems have been encountered at the simulation stage when groups were selected instead of individual curves.

---

2. Choose **Cloth** → **Create Garment**.
3. Select the bottom nurbsSquare2 group's curves individually.
4. Choose **Cloth** → **Create Panel**.

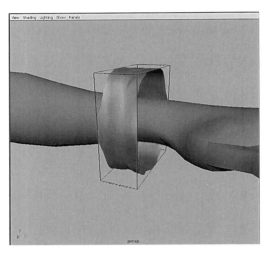

You have just created two panels of a garment that now need to be seamed together to create the final garment that will become the bracelet. Follow these steps:

1. Select the corresponding seam curves along the thumb edge of each square.
2. Choose **Cloth** → **Create Seam**.

Repeat these steps for the other (pinky) side of the garment. You should see a low-poly surface appear within the box that the seamed curves form. Your view should look similar to Figure 1.38. This surface is the cloth garment that will soon deform this character's bracelet.

Figure 1.38: The low-poly bracelet

Solver, Property, and Stitcher Resolution Settings

Now that you have created the actual cloth surface, you have to make sure your settings are appropriate to get the best simulation possible and that your collision environment is ready for your garment.

First, let's get the resolution of the cloth set correctly. Follow these steps:

1. Select the cloth mesh.
2. Highlight cpStitcher in the Channel box.
3. Enter **250** for the resolution.

You want the resolution to be high enough to get a good simulation, but not so high as to slow down your Maya session. The best way to find this number, until experience tells you, is by trial and error. A resolution of 250 will be great for the quality of the simulation and should not slow Maya significantly.

Next, we need to enter some better values for the cloth properties of the panels. Follow these steps:

1. Select a panel node.
2. In the Channel box, highlight cpDefaultProperty.
3. Enter the values shown in Figure 1.39.

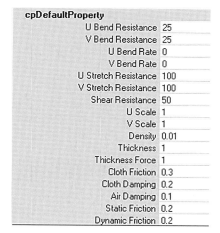

cpDefaultProperty

U Bend Resistance	25
V Bend Resistance	25
U Bend Rate	0
V Bend Rate	0
U Stretch Resistance	100
V Stretch Resistance	100
Shear Resistance	50
U Scale	1
V Scale	1
Density	0.01
Thickness	1
Thickness Force	1
Cloth Friction	0.3
Cloth Damping	0.2
Air Damping	0.1
Static Friction	0.2
Dynamic Friction	0.2

cpSolver1

Start Frame	1
Frame Samples	5
Time Step Size	0.018
Solver Scale	3
Gravity0	0
Gravity1	-980
Gravity2	0
Relax Frame Length	0
Output Statistics	on
Velocity Cutoff Min	0
Velocity Cutoff Max	0
Velocity Cutoff Damping	0

Figure 1.39: Good starting properties for cloth

Figure 1.40: Good starting solver properties

The cpDefaultProperty is the cloth property node connected to both panels of the bracelet garment. The default settings are a good starting point, but will rarely give you an acceptable cloth solve. Again, with experience, these values will become second nature. Until then, starting with the values in Figure 1.39 will get you a lot closer to making happy cloth than the defaults.

Now, the cloth solver needs its settings tweaked to give us a better simulation environment. Follow these steps:

1. Select the cloth mesh.
2. Highlight cpSolver in the Channel box.
3. Enter the values shown in Figure 1.40.

Again, the default settings for the solver will rarely give the best of conditions for simulating your cloth. Figure 1.40 shows the settings that make a great starting place when dealing with models of this scale in Maya.

The final step before beginning any simulations is to make sure your collision environment is ready for your new garment. Follow these steps:

1. Select the polygon model of the female character.
2. Choose **Cloth** → **Create Collision Object**.
   a. Set **Collision Offset** to 0.2.
   b. Set **Collision Depth** to 0.1.

These settings control how the cloth collides with the mesh. Once again, these default settings will not always give you the desired results. You might need to raise these numbers until your simulation is the distance above the skin you want. Especially in this case, when dealing with a garment that should be close to the skin, you will have to massage these settings.

Simulating and Relaxing the Bracelet

Now that all our settings have better default values, and our collision environment is ready, it's time to simulate and relax the garment for propagation to files for animation.

Click Play to begin the simulation. You should see the expanded cloth mesh begin to collapse around the wrist of the character and move around as it settles to a near stop. After the bracelet settles, it should look similar to Figure 1.41.

If simulation stops or appears to quit, make sure your Playback preferences are set to Play Every Frame.

The Time Slider should be at the end of the Timeline now. Rewind the simulation and save your file. You should now have a file called `bracelet_sim.mcc` in the scenes directory of this project. Remember, this is the cache file that Maya saves after a cloth simulation.

Now, scrub the Timeline to the last frame, and you should see the cloth garment back around the wrist and settled. Because you do not want to have to resimulate and resettle this garment for every file it will appear in, a few final steps are necessary.

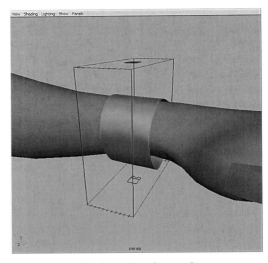

Figure 1.41: The bracelet after settling

1. Save the file as `bracelet_simmed.ma`.
2. Select the cloth mesh.
3. Choose **Simulation** → **Save As Initial Cloth State**.
4. Rewind to the first frame.
5. Choose **Simulation** → **Delete Cache**.
6. Save the file.

Your garment development process is finished. Now we can move on to animating the cloth and deforming the bracelet model.

Animating the Bracelet

Open the `bracelet_animated.ma` file. This file was created by importing the `bracelet_simmed.ma` file from the previous section and animating the character without simulating any cloth.

You can disable the cloth solver in a file either by selecting the solver in the Attribute Editor and choosing **Simulation** → **Disable Solver** or by simply hiding the cloth mesh.

With the cloth mesh hidden, play the file and watch the animation. From frame 0 to frame 98, the character moves from a neutral position to the first position of the animation. At frame 101, the character begins the action of pointing with her left hand. See Figures 1.42 and 1.43.

Observing Motion and Simulating the Cloth

One of your most important tasks when first assigned a scene for which you will be animating the cloth is to watch the animation and look for any areas where the cloth might have a hard time solving. These areas include, but are not limited to, pinching collision surfaces, extremely fast animation, and intersecting collision surfaces.

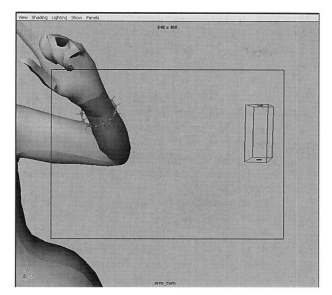
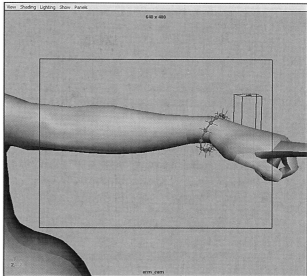

Figure 1.42: The beginning of the point animation   *Figure 1.43: The follow-through of the point animation*

In this scene, the character moves into the point pose quite quickly, creating a situation that should be flagged as a potential problem. Click the Play button to begin simulating the cloth object. You might encounter problems, but most likely the simulation will complete successfully.

Now that you have a baseline of settings to simulate with, you must decide exactly how the bracelet should move and react. In other words, ask yourself questions such as the following:

- How should cloth like this act?
- How can I add anything to the scene through the cloth animation?
- What information do the directors want to see from this scene?

The answers to these questions will steer you toward making the bracelet animation great and getting it approved. If you see the need for changes, adjust the cloth properties or add constraints. Animate, simulate, and playblast until you get the results you need. When you have finished working, remember to rewind the animation and save the file. You should now have a file called `bracelet_animated.mcc` in the scenes directory of your project.

Deforming the Bracelet Model

After the cloth has been properly simulated and a cache file has been saved, the next step is deforming the actual bracelet model, which consists of a strand surface and multiple beads. To accomplish this, you use a wrap deformer on the strand surface. A MEL script handles sticking the beads to the strand surface throughout the animation.

> Using Maya's wrap deformer is an excellent way to animate a high-resolution garment model based on the simulation of cloth. This works on skirts, vests, pants, shirts, jewelry, accessories, and props.

To set up the wrap deformer, first select the surfaces you want to deform and then select the influence object. Follow these steps:

1. Select the tubular strand surface of the bracelet.
2. Shift-select the cloth mesh.
3. From the Animation menu set, choose **Deform** → **Create Wrap**.

Click anywhere in the Timeline to see the strand surface following the cloth mesh and being deformed appropriately. Playblast the animation to see your results in real time.

Constraining the Beads

Though the strand should be moving quite nicely with the cloth, there is still one problem to solve. The beads, which should stay with the bracelet, are not moving along. They were not included in the wrap deformer for a reason. If the beads were included earlier, they would be moving along, but would be deforming inappropriately. They would squash and stretch based on the cloth, instead of being hard. To solve this problem, you can use a MEL script called UVGlue.mel, which you will find on the CD that accompanies this book. Follow these steps:

1. Open the Script Editor.
2. Choose **File** → **Source Script**.
3. Navigate to the mel directory of the Chapter 1 files and select UVGlue.mel.

This script works by having the user select a surface point on a NURBS surface and executing the script with the UVGlue command. Follow these steps:

1. Rewind to the first frame of the animation.
2. Select any bead on the bracelet.
3. Set your view so that the whole bracelet is visible.
4. Hide the character geometry, as well as any other geometry obstructing your view of the bracelet.
5. Make a display layer for the beads.
6. Set the beads layer to be templated.

This will allow you to select the strand surface points that line up with the beads without actually selecting the beads themselves. Your view should look similar to Figure 1.44.

Now make sure that the strand is the only thing selectable in your view window. Follow these steps:

1. Right-click over the strand geometry to open its marking menu.
2. Select Surface Point.
3. Left-click the strand surface in the middle of the top bead.

You should see two yellow lines cross each other at that point on the surface with a yellow point at their intersection. Your view should look similar to Figure 1.45.

You have just selected a surface point on the strand surface that should line up with the center of the bead on the strand. Now, with that surface point selected, follow these steps.

1. Left-click in the Command line, or press the back tick (reverse apostrophe) key.
2. Type **UVGlue**.
3. Press Enter.

Upon successful completion of the script, a locator is created at the selected surface point. Repeat these steps for the rest of the beads around the strand. When all the locators

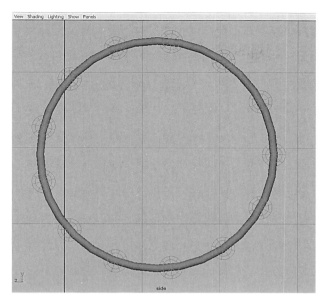

Figure 1.44: The templated beads

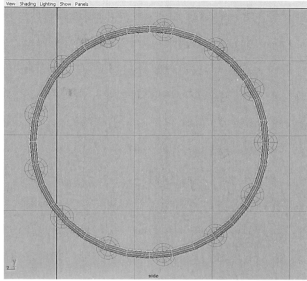

Figure 1.45: The selected surface point

are created, untemplate the beads' display layer. Make sure you are at the first frame of the animation, and follow these steps:

1. Select a bead, and Shift-select the corresponding locator.
2. Parent the bead to the locator by choosing **Edit** → **Parent**.

Repeat these parenting steps until all the beads are parented to their corresponding locators. Unhide the character geometry; switch to a perspective view that shows your work to the best advantage, and playblast the animation. If everything was successful, the beads should follow along through the animation.

What About Changes?

Inevitably, the first work you do on an animation will not quite meet the expectations of the leads, the directors, or yourself. In this case, the bracelet is completely driven by the cloth simulation. So, to handle changes, the only thing you need to do is resimulate the cloth. To simplify this process, hide the bracelet geometry. Make sure you unhide the cloth mesh and delete the cloth cache so that your new cloth properties take effect. Continue to edit properties and resimulate, making sure to unhide your bracelet now and again to check the deformations. This process will continue until you get your animation approved.

Always Learning

This chapter introduced you to using Maya Cloth for everything from garment creation and simulation to deforming jewelry. Cloth simulation can be a versatile tool when you face animating something out of the ordinary, but be patient: Sometimes animating cloth can be like animating a marble with a straw. If you follow the directions given here, and use the settings we provided, you will jump into your shots prepared and ready to go. The next time you face animating the end of that feather duster or the most beautiful ball gown ever, don't forget Maya Cloth.

two

Non-Photorealistic Rendering Techniques

John Kundert-Gibbs
with Jerry Gardiner, Brian Cumming, Rebecca Johnson, and Timothy A. Davis

Although photorealistic *rendering and animation have been the "holy grail" of computer graphics for several decades now, recent trends in both taste and technology have been pushing other CG rendering techniques. Collectively called NPR (for Non-Photorealistic Rendering), these techniques allow for a broad range of aesthetic and narrative effects that complement and extend the capabilities of photoreal rendering. In this chapter, we will implement two very different NPR styles, one of which mimics a hand-drawn "comic book" style of pen-and-ink drawing and the other that imitates impressionistic painting style.*

Photorealism and Non-Photorealism

With numerous big-budget movie successes, starting with *Jurassic Park* and continuing with recent blockbusters such as *The Lord of the Rings*, *Spiderman 2*, and others, photorealistic rendering has become so successful that general audiences have a difficult time distinguishing CG characters from their real counterparts. However, producing photorealistic effects is still expensive and time-consuming and does not necessarily mean box office success (as movies such as *Final Fantasy: The Spirits Within*, *The Chronicles of Riddick*, and others have shown). Photorealism also limits the range and style of a story: a movie such as *Spiderman 2* needs to present an illusion of reality even though characters use webs and giant metal arms to do battle. Films that are rendered by photorealistic techniques, but work in a more stylized mode—such as *Finding Nemo* and *Shrek 2*—allow for stories that include talking fish and donkeys, fantasy creatures, and even surfing turtles. By creating stylized looks, NPR techniques have great freedom to explore narrative and aesthetic modes that are not easily available to stories rendered with photorealism. Additionally, NPR techniques produce a markedly different response in the viewer: consider how a person reacts to a photograph of a

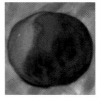

relative versus a painting, a charcoal sketch, or even a stick drawing of that same person. The narrative freedoms and aesthetic effects of NPR techniques are well worth considering as you conceptualize a new animation.

A great number of NPR techniques have been explored over the years, from mimicking traditional painting styles to 2D "cel" shading. Within this range of styles, the general aim has been to allow (or force) the computer into the role of artist—letting it make aesthetic decisions about line and color placement, stroke size, and such. Although this approach is laudable, it is complex and subtle to get computers to act appropriately in the role of artist. Thus, a different approach involving (human) artists more intimately with the final product is also a valuable method, one that, although more labor intensive for those involved, allows for greater control over the look and feel of the final product. As a means of exploring NPR techniques in Maya, we will present an example of both methods in this chapter.

In the first method, virtual models are hand textured by artists who use adjusted UV projections on the models, plus their understanding of line and form, to create lines of appropriate direction and thickness on the surface of the models. Further, these textures are blended via shading networks, allowing for line density modulation to show relative luminance on the surface of the model. This method produces frames that look like they could be hand-drawn, while maintaining the benefits of working within a 3D production environment. The second method uses MEL scripting to automatically apply Paint Effects brush strokes to surfaces in object space, creating a look similar to that of an impressionistic painting. Although highly automatic, this method gives users great control over the application and look of strokes, thus enabling good control over the look of the final rendering.

Samples from each style are shown in Figure 2.1 and the opening page of this chapter.

Figure 2.1: Still frame from the animated short "Demons Within," showing the comic-book rendering style.

Each NPR technique has aesthetic and technical advantages, as well as disadvantages. Due to their differing impact on the viewer, each of these techniques is used to create a different effect, helping to create a "world" for the animation of which it is a part. While the former technique creates a stark world with contrasting details that is well suited for comic-book style action sequences, the latter creates a soft world in which edges and colors blend and that is well suited to the calmer, more domestic scene created with this technique.

Integrating Hand-Drawn Textures with 3D Models

Our first NPR technique is an attempt to re-create the look of a hand-drawn "line art" comic book in animated form. Our motivation for developing this technique is an animation involving an "over the top" comic book battle between good and evil—a perfect setting for which to develop a line-art rendering style. Pulling from such influential sources as Japanese anime and American graphic novels that have been influenced by Japanese animation techniques, we use the computer to render models that are textured with pen-and-paper drawings, producing, essentially, a flip book of comic panels. This technique creates a graphic, handmade look, while allowing the benefits of computer animation via a blend of motion capture and keyframing, control over lighting, proper perspective, and the ability to adjust rendered images for aesthetic or technical reasons. Unlike either hand-drawn animation—which is labor intensive and difficult to alter—or fully procedural computer animation—which often looks too regular and smooth and can be difficult to control—this "hand drawn" method blends the best of both techniques to create exciting, visually appealing animation that can be created by a relatively small team in a reasonable amount of time.

Anime is a term encompassing a number of styles coming from a Japanese tradition of animation in which the line of a drawing is strong, the characters somewhat stylized, especially around the eyes, which are usually very large and rounded (Western eyes to the Japanese observer), and coloring can be very simple or non-existent. The subject matter is also an important defining element of anime: often it involves giant robots, demons, samurai, and such. Two popular examples in the U.S. of anime are *Akira* and *Dragon Ball Z*.

Creating and Applying the Hand-Drawn Texture

The process begins with UV mapping. For this chapter, we'll texture a human male figure as an example. Our main concern when mapping is to minimize distortion of the texture. This is accomplished by keeping the polygon faces in the Texture Editor proportional, as they are on the model. For example, if a face on the model's chest is one-half the size of the face below it, the same proportions should hold true for the corresponding faces in the Texture Editor. Also, a polygonal face should keep its relative shape when viewed in the Texture Editor. If, for example, a particular face is square on the model, but in the Texture Editor it's a rectangle three times longer than its width, the texture is going to be somewhat distorted when it is applied to the model. Distortion causes stretched lines on the texture and destroys the illusion of the hand-drawn look.

Maya provides four ways to map UVs: automatic, cylindrical, spherical, and planar. Any mapping method is fine, and for complex objects it is often helpful to use multiple

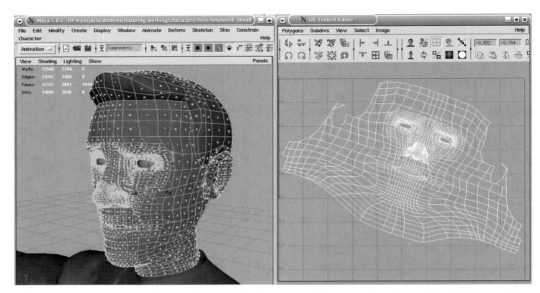

Figure 2.2: The polygonal faces making up the character's face are selected, avoiding the hair and ears. A cylindrical mapping is applied, and with some tweaking, the result is shown in the UV layout on the right.

methods for different parts of the object. For instance, by grabbing the polygonal faces of a character's face, you can apply a cylindrical mapping to good effect. (See Figure 2.2) You then select the faces for the hair and map them separately, using automatic mapping.

Mapping logically grouped faces on a model, even if using the same method on each group, significantly reduces distortion and makes for less work in the Texture Editor. A cylindrical mapping obviously works well for legs and arms. You might use automatic mapping on the faces of the front of the torso and automatic or even planar mapping on the back. Of course, neither of these methods yields a perfect layout at first—some cutting, moving, and tweaking are always necessary—but it helps to start as close to a good solution as possible. Figure 2.3 (Left) shows the UV layout of the character's boots after automatic mapping is applied. Maya has divided the faces into a lot of small, connected pieces, but this is not a bad starting point for a complex object. Figure 2.3 (Right) shows the finished layout. By moving and sewing connecting seams, we were able to minimize the distortion and get most of each boot in a single piece, thereby avoiding a lot of seams.

Complex objects that are one solid piece of geometry, such as this human figure, can benefit from layering sets of UVs on top of each other. Instead of crowding everything side by side into the grid of the Texture Editor, common elements (for example, parts of the pants or the upper torso) are grouped together. The polygonal faces that compose each group are given their own colored shader, which acts as a placeholder. In Figure 2.4, we've divided the figure into seven groups: the face, hair, arms, legs, boots, vest, and leftovers (hands, teeth, mouth interior, undershirt).

These groups are mapped separately from each other, and, when completed, the UVs of each group are scaled to fit the texturing space from 0 to 1 in the U and V parameters (or the upper-right quadrant of the Texture Editor workspace). It is important that the scaling

Figure 2.3: Left: UV snapshot of the character's boots, after automatic mapping Right: A good deal of work to get a nice final layout

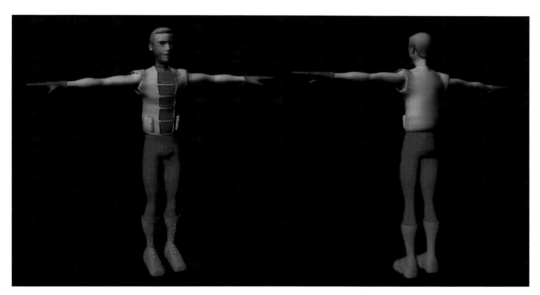

Figure 2.4: Seven areas were chosen for this character. All the faces for each particular area were selected and assigned a colored shader. By the end of this process, each area will have its own texture file.

be fairly proportional across all pieces in the Texture Editor; otherwise, drawn lines of the texture will appear with different widths at different parts of the body. When mapping and scaling are complete, the groupings are placed on top of each other until the final result looks like a garbled mess, as shown in Figure 2.5.

Although the situation in the Texture Editor now looks hopeless, you can access any of the groups through its assigned colored shader. (In the Hypershade, right-click the shader and choose Select Objects With Material.) Or you can create a quick select set for the UVs or faces that a group comprises. This allows access to the different groups, but once they are

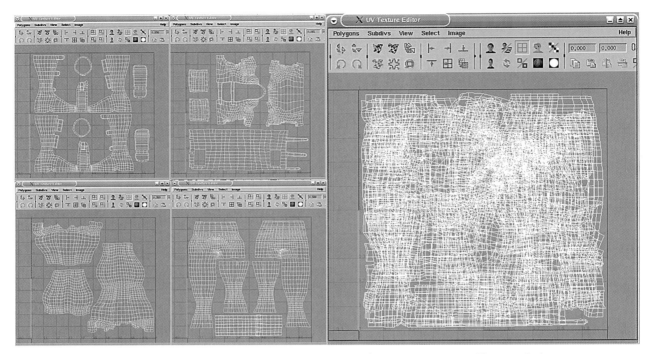

Figure 2.5: Left: Four of the seven UV groups, (boots, vest, arms, and legs) with the mapping completed. Right: All seven of the mapped groups are placed directly on top of each other.

layered, you must use Isolate Select mode to be able to work with any particular group on its own. Using the Isolate Select mode is relatively easy. Follow these steps:

1. Select the UVs of the group that you want to work with, and click the Add Selected icon on the Texture Editor toolbar, as shown in Figure 2.6.
2. Click the Toggle Isolate Select Mode button. Now all of the other UVs should disappear, leaving only the group that you added to the set.
3. Make any necessary adjustments to the UV group, select all the UVs, and click Remove Selected to empty the Isolate Select mode.
4. Toggle the Isolate Select mode off.

Eventually, a different file texture will be applied to the faces of each grouping. Layering the UVs for the human model allows for much more detail since 7 to 10 textures, as opposed to 1 or 2, are applied to one figure. You can apply one giant texture to a model and achieve similar results without layering UVs, but pen-and-ink drawing techniques are limited in how thin a line they can produce. Thus, for the scale of the texture drawings to remain the same size, a large scanner would be necessary or a patchwork of multiple scans. Both methods present a multitude of their own problems.

In the mapping stage, plan out seams on the model's texture that are naturally produced by separate pieces in the Texture Editor. By strategically adjusting the UVs so that seams fall where a drawn line will occur (see Figure 2.7), any seam will be virtually invisible. It is not always possible to create seams where lines would naturally fall, however, so other seams are manipulated to manifest in hidden or seldom seen areas like on the back or under the arms of a character.

Toggle Isolated Select Mode

Add Selected

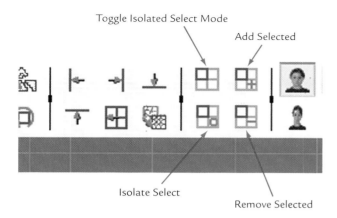

Isolate Select

Remove Selected

Figure 2.6: The controls for the Isolate Select mode are on the Texture Editor toolbar.

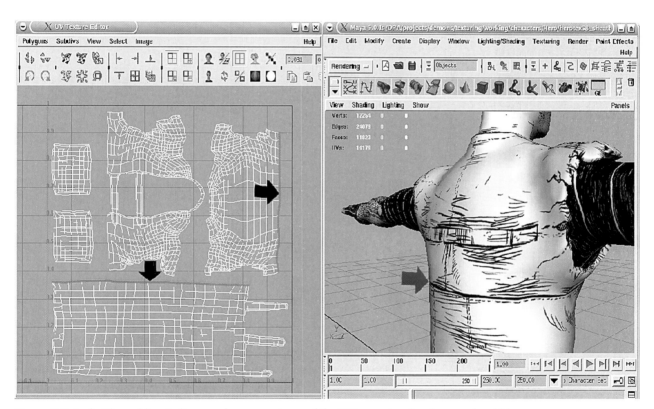

Figure 2.7: Left: The red line indicates where two pieces of the UV mapping for the vest should be connected but are not; therefore, a seam would occur. However, this is a planned seam. Right: A line is drawn on each of the pieces where the red line is, and it merges into one solid line on the model, as indicated by the blue arrow.

Once mapping is complete, it is necessary to create a UV snapshot for each of the layered UV groups. If a UV group is selected, through use of a shader or quick select set, and UV Snapshot is activated (by choosing **Polygons** → **UV Snapshot**), the snapshot will actually show all UVs on the model. To bypass this problem, copy the UV group into a new temporary UV set. Follow these steps:

1. In the Texture Editor toolbar, choose **Polygons** → **Create Empty UV Set** to create an empty UV set.
2. Click ❐ to name the new set.
3. Select the UVs of the group for which you want a snapshot.
4. Choose **Polygons** → **Copy UVs to UV Set**, and then choose the set you just created.

Now you can make the snapshot. Don't try to delete the UVs in this temporary set and then copy the next group of UVs into the set; this will cause problems. Instead, make a new empty set for each of the UV groups and repeat the process until all the snapshots are output. At this point, it's best to delete the temporary UV sets.

5. From the Texture Editor toolbar, choose Image → UV Sets, and then choose a temporary set that you created.
6. Choose **Polygons** → **Delete Current UV Set**.

The left side of Figure 2.8 shows a snapshot taken from one of the UV groups of our character. In an image manipulation program, the luminance of the snapshot should be inverted. The levels are adjusted so that the black lines are brought down to a light gray; making these lines nearly invisible makes it easy to remove them upon rescanning after drawing in the lines. Black marks are then added to each of the four corners. These are registration marks and are important later to match up the drawn image to the original snapshot.

As shown on the right Figure 2.8, the image is now ready to be printed. A printout with the UV lines just barely visible is most desirable and requires some adjustment to the

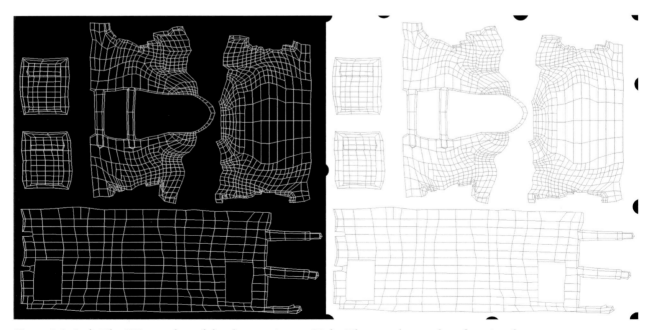

Figure 2.8: Left: The UV snapshot of the character's vest. Right: The snapshot ready to be printed.

"levels" step. A high dpi (dots per inch) is beneficial to get cleanly printed lines. The size of the printed UV mapping is important in controlling how large the drawn lines appear on the object. To stay fairly consistent with line width, the size of the printout should be relative to the size of the object being textured. For instance, in "Demons Within," we printed an 8-inch square for larger objects (machines, doors, people), a 2-inch square for smaller ones (cans, cigarette boxes, and so on), and anywhere in between for medium-sized objects.

The texture is drawn directly on the printed UV map using the barely visible lines for guidance. A line drawn on each edge of the same seam appears to be a solid line on the model. It's useful to do a quick test drawing at this stage and apply it to its assigned UV group for reference (see the left side of Figure 2.9).

Once the drawing is complete (see the right side of Figure 2.9), it needs to be scanned back into the computer. Scan an area slightly larger than the printed and drawn portion of the texture. It is essential for proper placement that the scanned texture be as accurate as possible in alignment and rotation. However, the scanned drawing will probably be slightly askew. You can use a little-known Photoshop method to adjust this. Follow these steps:

1. Magnify the scanned image until the pixels are evident and the view is at the very top of the upper left registration mark (the dark mark made earlier).
2. Apply the Measuring tool to the precise corner of the mark, and "measure" the image over to the corner of the top-right registration mark.
3. Choose **Image → Rotate Canvas → Arbitrary**, and you'll see that the exact angle to perfectly square the selection is already provided.
4. Carefully crop the image to the outer edges of the registration marks. The image is scaled down from a high dpi for scanning to, usually, 1024 × 1024.
5. Adjust levels on the scanned image to get rid of the light printed reference lines, and darken the drawn lines if necessary.

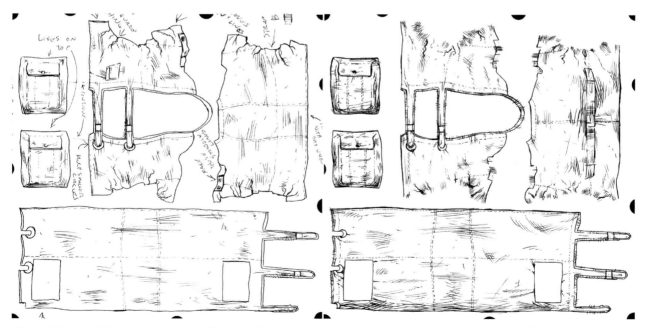

Figure 2.9: Left: This rough texture will be applied to the model for testing purposes. Right: The final hand-drawn texture for the vest.

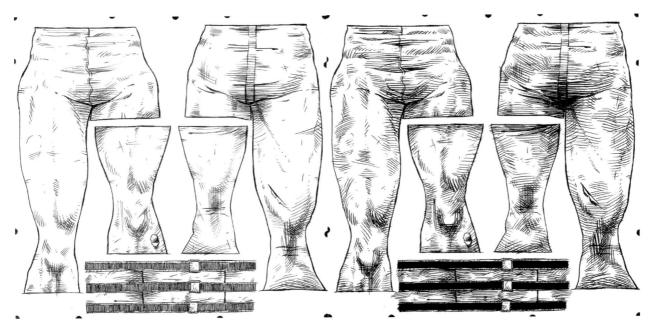

Figures 2.10: Left: The "lit" version of the texture. Right: The "unlit" version, drawn directly on top of the "lit" version.

Our shader network, described later in this chapter, gauges the amount of light striking any portion of an object. The shader blends between two different textures, depending on the amount of light that portion of the surface is receiving. One of the textures—the "lit" version—is drawn as if the object were receiving bright light. (Fewer, lighter lines are drawn.) The other "unlit" version is drawn as if the object is in shadow. (More, heavier lines and cross-hatching are drawn.) Thus, if the object is in shadow, more lines are seen (the unlit texture), but they disappear as the object moves into the light (the lit texture). After the lit texture is scanned in, the unlit is drawn either directly over the lit version (preferable) or over a printout of the lit version. The unlit copy must be scanned in, rotated, and cropped to fit perfectly over the lit image. The dark "in shadow" texture should build upon the lines already there, setting up a natural transition between the two. See Figure 2.10 for an example of lit and unlit versions of our character's pants.

The texture is ready to be applied to the object. Unfortunately, there is usually some error due to printing and scanning. Generally, you have to shift a certain number of UVs into place, but only edge UVs. The slight errors that accumulate during the scanning and drawing process are rarely enough to warrant needing to move interior UVs. The edge UVs, however, are more sensitive because they constitute a line along with the edge of another piece. Off-the-mark edge UVs can produce ugly results. Once all the textures are applied to the UV groups, some nice results can be achieved.

Creating a Shader for the Hand-Drawn Texture

In traditional "line art" comic books, as an object is exposed to different lighting, various degrees of hatching are used. To simulate this effect, our main texturing goal is to blend different textures as the objects are mapped to pass through changes in lighting. The textures of a strongly lit object should appear mostly white with little hatching, while the textures of an object in shadow ought to be darker and heavily hatched; anything in between should be an interpolated blend.

As luck would have it, Maya provides a shader node called Blend Colors that allows us to solve this problem quickly (assuming the tedious work of texture creation has already been done!). First, create two materials and map the "lit" and "unlit" textures to them. Call them lit_shader and unlit_shader, respectively. At this point, assign each of these shaders, in turn, to your model and make sure that they are mapping correctly on the model. Once we set up the shading network to blend the two textures, Maya has a hard time processing the result and displaying it to us in real time. Instead, the texture will show up as a splotchy mess in the interactive view because Maya is trying to sample the two source textures and do the best blending job it can while still maintaining good interactivity. If problems with textures or how they are mapping are apparent, it is best to fix these problems before attaching the blended shader to the model.

Once you are ready to continue, you will need three other nodes for your shader: Blend Colors, Surf. Luminance, and Surface Shader. Open the Hypershade and be sure the Create tab is selected (far left of the window). Blend Colors, which is in the Color Utilities twirl-down section of the Create tab, takes two color inputs (Color1 and Color2) and calculates a blended color (Output) based on a third, numerical input (Blender). Surf. Luminance, which stands for Surface Luminance, is a node that provides, as the Maya documentation says, "the part of a lit surface and the degree of light it receives from lights in the scene." You can also find Surface Luminance in the Color Utilities section of the Create tab. The Surface Shader node, found in the Surface section of the Create tab, is useful for determining the color (among other things) of a material based on the output of some control value. In this case, we will simply use it to hold the blended values from our Blend Colors node. For further help with any of these nodes, see the Maya documentation.

Surface Shaders are really handy. As the Maya documentation states, "You can connect an object's Translate Position to a Surface Shader's **Out Color** attribute to determine the object's color by the object's position." The possibilities are endless!

After creating each of these nodes in the Hypershade graph, place them all in the work area (the bottom-right panel of the Hypershade), along with the lit_shader and unlit_shader created earlier—five nodes in all. If the nodes are not in the work area, MM drag them into the work area yourself. The Surface Shader node will be available when the Materials tab at the top is selected, and the Blend Colors and Surface Luminance node will be available when the Utilities tab is chosen. To remember which nodes do what, rename them now. Call your Blend Colors node blender, your Surface Luminance node surface_luminance, and your Surface Shader node result_shader. See Figure 2.11 for an example of how your Hypershade might look before continuing.

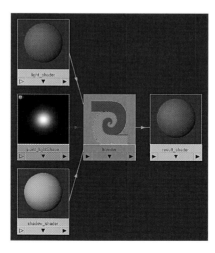

Figure 2.11: The initial Hypershade network

Now it is time to connect some attributes and build the shader network. To attach the output attribute of one node to the input attribute of another, MM click (and hold) the node that contains the output attribute, drag to the node that contains the input attribute, and release the mouse button. A contextual menu will appear with some options Maya suggests for connecting these nodes. Rather than select any of these default choices, choose Other and explicitly specify the connection settings in the Connection Editor. The possible output attributes are listed on the left, and the potential input attributes are listed on the right. By clicking one attribute in each column, you can create a connection between them; the output value you select drives the input value in the connected node. After selecting the output value (on the left), you might notice some of the input values gray out (on the right). This means that the data type of the attribute on the left is not the same as those that are grayed out. For example, a numerical attribute (a float value) cannot connect to a color attribute (an attribute containing three float values). The output value will drive the input value, so it makes sense that a single number could not be responsible for driving a color.

Although it seems nice that Maya grays out values that cannot be connected, it is actually quite deceiving. Sure, you can't connect a number to a color because they are different data types. But you could click the + next to the color attribute, revealing its RGB channels and connect the output value to one (or more) of the color input values.

Now we can build our complete shader network. We have four simple connections to make in order to finish our shader. Follow these steps:

1. Connect the **Out Color** attribute of unlit_shader to the **Color1** attribute of the Blend Colors node called blender.
2. Connect the **Out Color** attribute of lit_shader to the **Color2** attribute of the Blend Colors node.
3. Connect the **Out Value** attribute of the Surface Luminance node called surface_luminance to the **Blender** attribute of the Blend Colors node.
4. Connect the **Output** attribute of the Blend Colors node to the **Out Color** attribute of the Surface Shader called result_shader. See Figure 2.12 for an example of how your Hypershade might look now that your shading network is finished.

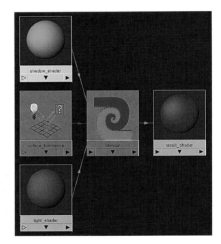

Figure 2.12: The finished Hypershade network

If you make a mistake when connecting attributes, delete the connection and try again. To delete an existing connection, select (click or drag a box around) the arrow connecting the two nodes and press Delete on your keyboard. To view the data that is being passed through an existing connection, place your mouse cursor over the arrow to display the attributes responsible for the connection.

Once your shading network is complete, the last step is to assign the surface shader node to any of the objects in your scene that are supposed to have it. At this point, lighting and animation can proceed to produce the final animation.

Adding Edge Lines

A common property in most comics is that the figures and objects are distinguished by their edges. However, in our CG "comic book," because the characters are round and seen from all directions, it's impossible for their textures alone to simulate continuous outlines around them. The last step to complete the look for "Demons Within" is edge detection.

The method we've developed requires two renderings of the scene. The first rendering is the normal, quality render for the shot. For the second rendering, the edge version, the scene must be altered to create a white image with black outlines around the characters. To begin, follow these steps:

1. Resave the scene, then delete all of the lights in the scene, as well as all objects in the scene that don't pass in front of character.
2. Create one spotlight with an intensity of 3.0 and a cone angle of 170 degrees. We want this spotlight to shine directly from the camera, so change the spotlight's **Rotate** and **Translate** attributes to be the same as the camera's.
3. Parent the light to the camera so that it will always shine in the direction that the camera is looking.
4. In the Hypershade, create two pure white Lambert materials and apply one to the characters. On the other one, increase the **Ambient** attribute to 2.0 and apply it to the objects that pass in front of the characters.

The highly ambient objects will not produce a black outline, but they will "cut out" outlines around the characters, providing the correct look.

5. Open the Attribute Editor, and in the Environment section, change the background color from black to white. Render the scene.

The resulting images, shown in Figure 2.13, will appear to be white with gray lines defining most outer edges. You can adjust the width of the line somewhat by raising or lowering the intensity of the one spotlight in the scene.

Now you must apply the edge images to the regular renders, which can be done in a 2D compositing package such as Shake. First, open the edge images. Currently, the edges are probably too light, and we want to darken them while retaining a pleasing smooth look. A good way to do this in Shake is to create an iMult node and attach the edge images to both input connections. Now create another iMult node and attach the result from the other iMult to

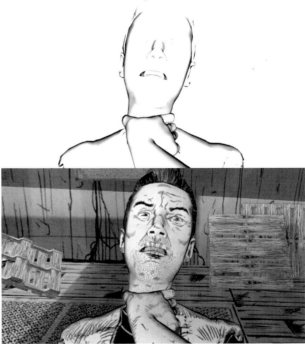

Figure 2.13: Sample images used to create edges for the characters. Top: Original image. Middle: Edge lines render. Bottom: Final composite.

Figure 2.14: Left: A frame without rendered edges. Right: The same frame with edges.

both input connections. This is usually dark enough, but you can repeat the process as needed. Now open the regular scene images. Create one last iMult node, attach the scene render on the right input, and attach the iMult showing character edges on the left. Now create a File-Out node and render the scene.

The final look for this style is complete. Figure 2.14 shows a frame from "demons" before and after edge detection was added. Figure 2.15 shows a frame from the final "Demons Within" animation. (A clip from the movie showing this still frame is included on the CD-ROM.)

There are myriad possibilities to further this process. For instance, by increasing the ambience of all objects in the scene, the image loses all the gray 3D shading and becomes flat, more closely emulating a hand-drawn sketch. Or, by creating four or five textures for each object with slightly offset line placement and width, you can cycle the textures throughout the movie, creating a "wiggly line" look similar to that in A-Ha's video "Take on Me." Edge detection, such as is found in Apple's Shake, would work well with this idea. For "Demons Within," we chose to go with a moodier look, with more range between black and white. The warehouse was lowly lit with slit lights. The texture for the background structure was given an **Ambient** attribute of 0.15, the props an **Ambient** attribute of 0.3, the figures, 0.45, and their eyes, 0.6. Adding this amount of **Ambient** attribute to the textures themselves keeps the result relatively flat looking, but, due to the tiered ambient system, objects are more distinguishable from the background and one another. By using hand-drawn, sketchy textures, the final animation has more of an organic feel. As opposed to precision technical pens, regular Bic pens were used to create the drawings. The occasional clump or irregularity of line only adds to the natural handmade look that we were trying to achieve.

Figure 2.15: Final results of applying hand-drawn textures to the model's shader network

Creating Impressionistic-Style Images

While our first example aims to emulate stark, graphic pen-and-ink techniques for a high-energy animation, our second NPR example focuses on producing a painterly look with bright, blended colors and thick "paint" strokes. The hand-drawn method features artists sketching out textures, while the impressionist method outlined in this part of the chapter uses the computer itself to make decisions about such elements as brush strokes and lengths. Thus, this latter method proves a nice complement to the former. The impressionist style of rendering is interesting not only because of its output (the rendered images) but because it presses the computer into an "artistic" role.

Artists express mood, feeling, and ideas through their works. For a painter, such statements are produced through choice of color, size and placement of strokes, and use of specific stylized characteristics. A true work of art, therefore, is rarely created by accident. The design and structure of a piece requires skill and foresight that do not easily reduce to a simple set of rules or algorithms. As a result, art created with the assistance of a computer is difficult to achieve, and controversial. If we consider the computer a tool in the (human) artist's repertoire instead of a "substitute artist" itself, using the computer's great power to perform tedious and repetitive tasks may be seen as a way for people to explore different ways of producing artistically challenging and interesting works. The computer may not be able to create art, but it can help tremendously in exploring new areas of artistic endeavor.

Rendering in an impressionist style is a good way to explore semiautonomous computer production. To aid the computer artist in creating stylized renders and, ultimately, animations, we have created a tool called Impressionist Paint that works in conjunction with

Maya via a series of MEL scripts. The purpose of this tool is not to replace the artist, but rather to empower the artist. Therefore our tool allows the user to make artistic decisions and guide the work on a higher level, while the computer takes care of tedious and repetitive tasks, such as shading and stroke application.

Impressionist Paint takes, as input, a scene that has been modeled using NURBS surfaces, textured, and lit in Maya. The tool uses particle systems to populate each NURBS surface in the scene with random starting points, specified by individual particles, for brush strokes. The tool then creates spline curves, with random offsets in UV space, that the brush strokes follow. Users can directly edit the placement, size, or direction of these strokes if desired. This painting process can be repeated to produce layers of strokes on the objects. When stroke generation is complete, the width of each stroke is adjusted, based on the distance from the camera, before final rendering to create an image consistent with what might be produced with a traditional paintbrush on a 2D canvas.

The Impressionist Paint Process

To create a system capable of producing an impressionist style, we must first understand how an artist creates an impressionist painting. At first glance, the freedom displayed in impressionist works would seem to defy a systematic approach; however, impressionist painters do adhere to certain rules when creating their pieces:

- Use of nonuniform brush strokes
- Emphasis on painting light on objects
- Application of primary colors
- Reliance on visual color mixing
- Avoidance of black and harsh outlines
- Overlap of paint strokes across objects

Accordingly, the Impressionist Paint tool needs to address these impressionist characteristics when rendering images. The process for using Impressionist Paint is shown in Figure 2.16. To create an animation, the target scene must first be modeled, textured, and lit. Since our system works in conjunction with Maya, this step follows the usual early stages of the production pipeline. One restriction for the current incarnation of the Impressionist Paint tool is that models must be NURBS objects, though no technical barriers exist to adding polygonal models or subdivision surfaces. The textures applied to the models can be raster texture maps, solid shades, or procedural textures, such as ramps or noise functions. This freedom to create complex textures allows for a great variety of eventual stroke colors.

After creating the basic scene elements, one opens Impressionist Paint, which is shown in Figure 2.17 and selects options for rendering the scene in an impressionist style. Within

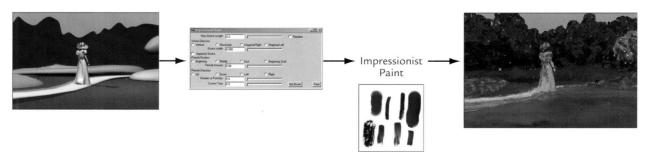

Figure 2.16: The work flow for Impressionist Paint

this window, one can select options for controlling the way Impressionist Paint "paints" the models. The first field, Max Curve Points, specifies the maximum number of spline points for each curve, which is replaced by a brush stroke during rendering. If the Random box is checked, the system randomly sets the number of spline points to a value between 4 and the maximum selected. This feature lets you indirectly adjust the length (and length variation) of the brush strokes.

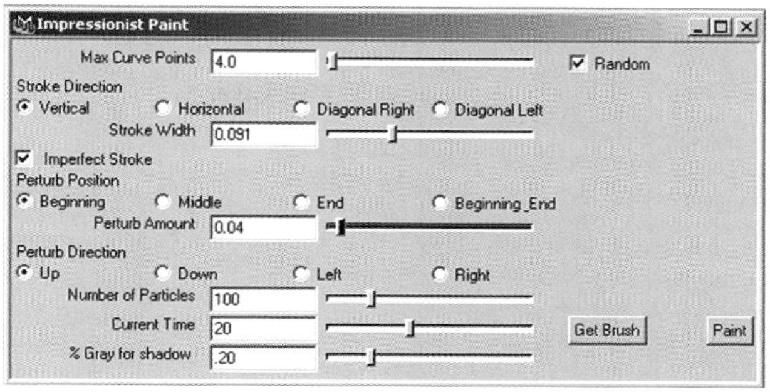

Figure 2.17: The custom interface used to control Impressionist Paint

In the Stroke Direction field, one specifies the direction of the paint strokes *in texture space*. In this way, the brush strokes can enhance shape by following the contour of the object; alternatively, Stroke Direction can be set to minimize form. Additionally, the texture applied can be oriented in any fashion before applying strokes to achieve the desired stroke direction. The process can be repeated by reusing Impressionist Paint to obtain layered strokes or strokes of multiple directions.

The Imperfect Stroke fields allow each stroke to be perturbed at a specified position (Beginning, Middle, End, or all) by the requested Perturb Amount in the Perturb Direction (Up, Down, Left, Right—relative to the spline orientation and direction). Low perturb values result in relatively straight brush strokes, while high values designate more highly curved strokes. The Number of Particles and Current Time fields control the density of the stroke coverage: the higher the values, the greater the number of strokes created. The final slider, % Gray for Shadow, represents a threshold value for computing shadows (discussed later).

Clicking the Get Brush button allows selection of one of many predefined or custom paint brushes. Different brushes applied to the same scene can create images that have completely different styles. For the impressionist scenes tested, we select oil paint brushes, a set of which is shown in Figure 2.16.

After adjusting the fields, the paint button is pressed to begin the painting process. The Impressionist Paint scripts take over at this point, and automatically create the brush strokes. Afterward, one can add, edit, or delete strokes individually or collectively. Once a satisfactory set of strokes is in place, the scene is rendered to produce final output. Another Impressionist Paint script is activated during Maya rendering to finalize paint strokes and adjust stroke size based on the distance between each object and the rendering camera.

Although using Paint Effects "out of the box" can come close to replicating the work done by Impressionist Paint, Paint Effects does not properly handle several critical areas. First, it does not allow width, size, or color variation across strokes. Second, it does not allow control over placement and curve path of the strokes. Finally, while Impressionist Paint paints shadow brush strokes in images, Paint Effects uses CG-generated shadow; the latter looks very computer driven, while the former appears painted. Impressionist Paint, therefore, allows a much greater level of control over "painting" the final image than Paint Effects alone would.

Implementing Impressionist Paint

The scripts that implement Impressionist Paint are written in MEL. Figure 2.18 provides a visual description of what the scripts do. When the Paint button is clicked in the GUI (see Figure 2.17), the system of scripts creates strokes for each object individually. First, particles are emitted from each object's surface to identify the starting points for the curves (strokes). Next, spline curves are created at each particle location according to the specified parameters.

Figure 2.18: The stages of creating rendered strokes

Modeled, textured, and list object   Emit particles   Create stroke   Render strokes

Figure 2.19: Particles carry color information from the base object.

The paint strokes that are generated follow the spline curves with the selected brush pattern. Each of these strokes obtains its color value from the texture color at the particle emission point on the object's surface, thus affording great flexibility in shading objects (see Figure 2.19). One can also set a separate color for the end of the stroke, with a gradual blend from start to end. Once initial stroke placement is complete, additional particles are emitted to calculate shadows and highlights on the object.

The strokes are then scaled based on their distance from the camera, which relates directly to the perspective size of the object in screen space (see Figure 2.20). To keep strokes from becoming so small that an artist could not possibly have painted them, strokes that appear deeper in the scene are scaled to larger sizes that cover a greater area of the object. This scaling technique is in keeping with real painting techniques: for example an artist might paint a large house with a single stroke or two if the house is far off in the distance in the painting. Impressionist Paint combines object and image space information to obtain the look of the final stroke.

Since strokes are painted in object space and are associated with the object throughout its lifetime, Impressionist Paint achieves temporal coherence across animation frames: the strokes do not "dance" from one frame to the next. (If such an effect is desired, however, strokes can be reapplied on each frame.) One may also detach paint strokes from 3D objects—a situation that occurs when strokes are assigned in image space and do not appear to be fully attached to the objects—with this method.

To animate the scene, therefore, one simply animates the objects, allowing Impressionist Paint to perform the rendering, similar to the way rendering occurs in the standard production cycle.

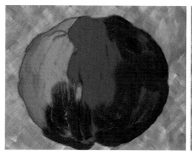

Figure 2.20: Stroke width changes according to distance from the camera.

Incorporating Shadows

The effect of shadow placement on each object within the scene can be altered by creating object shadows once or on a per-frame basis. The first method promotes faster render times, which is beneficial if the character or object does not undergo substantial lighting changes. For a simple animation, one can save time by calculating the shadows only once. In this case, the script is run on the first frame of the animation. The shodw light/dark file texture that is created provides a map for 360 degrees of lighting and remains accurate until the object moves drastically from the object's original position where the shading occurred. This shadow creation technique fails to consider extreme changes in lighting conditions; as mentioned, the shadows are calculated only one time, at the beginning of the animation. For a more complex animation in which objects pass in and out of shadow, one should calculate shadow strokes on a per-frame basis. Although the former method reduces render time, the latter is more accurate for objects under variable lighting conditions.

The derivation of the shadow color and placement is similar for both constant and per-frame shadowing. To calculate shadow (and highlight) strokes, a special particle is emitted from the object. The emitted particle RGB color is first converted to the Hue Saturation Value (HSV) color model, which provides a simpler way to manipulate the color properties. In additive color space, using the complementary color of the particle color produces white instead of black for shadows due to additive color mixing principles. To avoid lightening the final color, the shadow color is computed as the average of the original color and its complementary color. The average color falls halfway between the opposing colors and, when mixed with the original color, forms a hue that mimics the look of the mixture of the complementary color and the original color using subtractive color mixing. The new hue must be darker to create a convincing shadow color; therefore, the value of the shadow particle is used to derive the new color value since its luminence provides the correct value. The HSV color is then converted back to RGB color and used as the shadow color. When the shadow stroke blends with the original stroke, the shadow color resembles the color an impressionist painter might use to create a shadow.

The shadow stroke is created using the shadow particle position and the color derivation to create a colorful shadow. The particles for the starting point of the shadow stroke fall in different locations than the original strokes; the strokes overlap, therefore adding to the painterly feel of the rendered image. These two layers of strokes also provide unique color combinations that avoid the harsh precision of computer-generated shadows. Highlight color strokes are determined in much the same way, only adding to, rather than subtracting color from, the base color.

Figure 2.21: The final rendered image

Final Renders

We have created several animations with Impressionist Paint thus far. Three images from one animation, which demonstrates our scaled stroke width, are shown in Figure 2.20. A frame from a more complex animation is shown in Figure 2.21. This image demonstrates several features of the Impressionist Paint system. First, although the scene appears fairly complex in terms of shading, it is derived from a reasonably simple scene, as shown in Figure 2.16. When using Impressionist Paint, we only specified the basic shapes and shading for our objects; the MEL scripts did most of the remaining work automatically.

We also found that some basic techniques for generating paint strokes worked especially well for creating painterly natural phenomena. For example, just as individual leaves are not laboriously painted for a tree or a shrub in an impressionist work, our system creates less distinct (more impressionistic) forms for a bush rather than highly detailed leaves. As shown in Figure 2.22a, we began with a simple model of a bush. Adding strokes to the object creates the appearance of individual leaves (see Figure 2.22b), but the underlying geometry is too pronounced. By applying a small displacement to the strokes from the base geometry, we obtained a more realistic bush (see Figure 2.22c). From this object, we emitted another particle set (see Figure 2.22d) and instanced a single painted red sphere to each particle to create the flowers seen in Figure 2.22e. To create a less uniform appearance, each

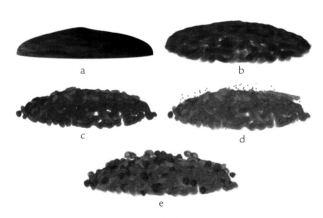

Figure 2.22: (a) original model; (b) model with brush strokes; (c) model with displaced brush strokes; (d) particles emitted from object; (e) geometry attached to particles.

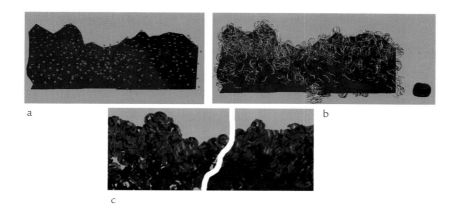

a   b

c

Figure 2.23: (a) Tree line with particles; (b) tree line with instanced geometry (single object shown right) and attached curves; (c) tree line with strokes and underlying geometry hidden (left) and visible (right)

flower was transformed based on the direction and velocity of its associated particle. A similar approach was used to create the tree with yellow flowers in Figure 2.21.

The tree line against the sky shown in Figure 2.21 represents another natural object that we were able to create fairly easily with our system. The underlying geometry for the tree line is a basic planar shape, from which a set of particles were emitted, as shown in Figure 2.23a. A simple piece of irregular geometry, covered with curves, was attached to each particle in a nonuniform way (see Figure 2.23b). Once these objects have been painted, they create an interesting painterly effect for trees that resembles what an impressionist artist might produce. Figure 2.23c shows the tree line with and without the underlying geometry visible.

Although work still remains to perfect the Impressionist Paint tool set, it is, in its current form, a powerful tool that allows users to create convincing images in a style reminiscent of impressionist works from the late Nineteenth Century.

The Impressionist Paint tool is still in development, and thus is not provided on the book's CD. You may contact the authors for further information concerning the tool.

Always Learning

Although very different in technique and results, both the hand-drawn and impressionist render styles discussed in this chapter are successful in creating a mood appropriate for the scene being produced. The hand-drawn technique produces graphic, high-contrast images akin to those produced by traditional pen-and-ink methods and thus well serves the comic book battle between characters. The Impressionist Paint tool uses computer automation to achieve a look similar to impressionistic painting, producing an appropriate look for the garden scene rendered with it.

Both techniques are continuing to evolve: there are still a number of technical hurdles to overcome to perfect each of these NPR methods. However, each has achieved a level of sophistication and polish that allows it to be used in creating finished products that have the appropriate aesthetic for the scenes they were created to render. You can use each method described in this chapter to create similar animations, or you can use these methods as a basis for further development of NPR techniques. Whatever you choose, be sure to consider using NPR for your next animation!

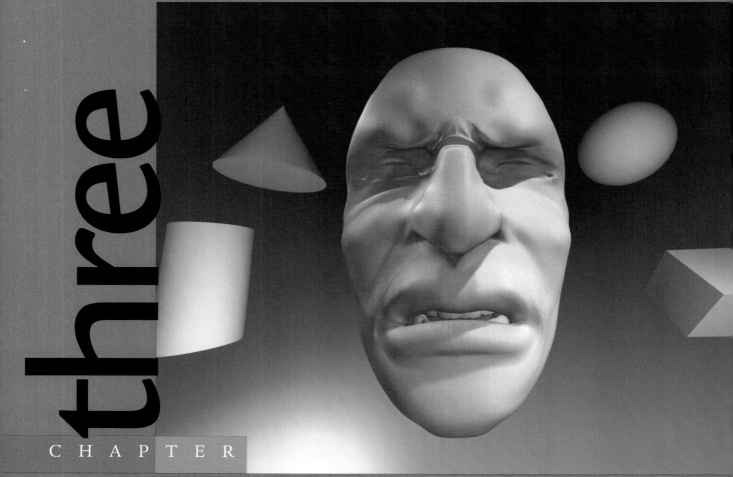

three

Realistic Camera Movement

By Keith Reicher

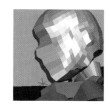

With the surge *of all and partly CG feature films, many CG animators have become good at the techniques involved in mimicking and exaggerating the motions and rhythms of life. Technology has also played a role, as current CG setups have more controls and enhancements than ever before. The resulting productions have improved in the past few years, evident in such movies as* Shrek 2, Finding Nemo, *and* Shark Tale.

In this chapter we are going to create some motion effects that come naturally when handling a real-world camera, but that can be tricky to create in the CG universe. We will start with a simple dolly-and-pan movement, move on to the more challenging camera shake, and then try an extreme handheld effect that is true to live-action documentary-style filmmaking. Finally, we will use Maya Live to transfer a real camera's motion into the virtual world.

CG Cinematography

You probably already have a solid knowledge of CG cinematography basics. For our purposes here, I'm going to give some background information to get us all using the same language. If you're already a camera jockey, you might want to skip this section and go straight to the how-tos later in the chapter.

Most CG feature films use keyframed animation rather than motion capture. Keyframed animation lets the animator exaggerate a character's movements, and it is this exaggeration that translates better in CG movies, making it more lifelike and interesting to watch.

But although character animation is often an exaggeration of true life, exaggeration isn't something you should strive for when it comes to animating CG cameras. Overdone camera movements often distract the viewer from the action in the scene and thus from the story being told. Animating CG cameras needs to stay true to the motion of real-world cameras, and since we've seen countless live-action movies and peered through our own digital camera viewfinders, most of us have a subconscious understanding of what is realistically acceptable and what isn't. Staying true to natural camera movement is a significant challenge for the CG camera animator.

In live-action film production, the cinematographer (also referred to as the director of photography or, simply, the camera person) works with the director to set up the shots and determine camera placement, angles, and movements for a scene. In a CG production, layout animators do the same by working closely with directors to translate hand-drawn storyboards into a 3D world. Operating a virtual camera within this 3D world is similar to using a real-world camera, and, just as in real-world filmmaking, it takes a good eye, creativity, and skill to conceptualize and execute great compositions for a CG animation. A lot of professionals develop their own knack for filmmaking by watching as many movies as they can, observing and analyzing the cinematic techniques used and thinking about why one choice was made over another. Since the methods of film cinematography are easily translated to digital cinematography, your knowledge of film will greatly improve your animations. Let's take a look at some of the basic cinematic terms as they relate to real world filmmaking and operating 3D cameras in Maya:

Dolly To *dolly* is to move the camera horizontally, either forward or backward, along one camera axis, typically the X or Z axis in Maya. When you dolly a camera, you either follow an action occurring within a scene or reveal something within the scene. On the set, a dolly shot can also be referred to as a tracking, trucking, or traveling shot. For example, dollying a camera across a landscape conveys that the camera is physically moving across space. You will notice that in many films in which a character sets out on a quest, the direction taken (called screen direction) is from left to right, and so is any dolly movement to accompany the journey. When the character makes the return trip, they are usually seen traveling right to left, with the dolly movements being reversed as well. Take a look at how screen direction and camera movement are used in some of these movies: *Lawrence of Arabia*, *Dances with Wolves*, *The Prince of Egypt*, and *The Lord of the Rings* trilogy.

Boom At times you will hear a director tell the Director of Photography (DP) to boom up or down. The *boom shot*, also known as the *crane shot*, is used in live-action filmmaking for any nonaerial shots in which the camera is raised off the ground and moved through the air in an up or down motion. The boom, or crane, is actually the hydraulically operated mechanical arm to which the camera is connected. The boom shot is usually used for establishing shots (which many times you will see at the beginning of a movie) or for shots in which the camera moves away from the environment and actors (which has become common when ending a movie.) Of course, with our CG camera we are not hindered by booms, cranes, and hydraulics. We can simply translate the camera vertically, or along the Y axis.

Pan Panning, an abbreviation for *panoramic shot*, is simply rotating the camera around a vertical axis running through the camera from a fixed point, whether it is around a tripod or a camera operator. (In Maya, this axis defaults to the camera's Y axis.) You can use a pan to show the point of view of a character looking across a valley as they stand high atop a mountain. The panning reflects their looking either left or right, while not moving from their position.

Tilt A *tilt* is a vertical pan since the camera is pivoted up or down around a horizontal axis perpendicular to the lens from a fixed point, rather than rotated from side to side, as in a pan shot. (In Maya, this axis defaults to the camera's X axis.)

Roll To *roll* the camera is to rotate it around a horizontal axis parallel to the lens. (In Maya, this axis defaults to the camera's Z axis.) Also referred to as a Dutch angle, oblique angle, or off-angle shot, this is used for disorientation or in shots that are supposed to convey a feeling of peculiarity. The roll can be animated over time within a shot to point out the growing danger in the scene. Alfred Hitchcock's movies are filled with shots that use roll to accentuate the disturbing nature of a scene.

Zoom No camera movement occurs with a zoom. Instead, this type of shot involves an increase or a decrease in the focal length of the camera, allowing an apparent distance change between the camera and the subject being filmed. As opposed to the dolly shot, the zoom allows the relationship of background and foreground elements to change based on camera focal length; so the zoom is used under different circumstances from the dolly. Before amateur video cameras became widely used, the zoom shot was rare; now, however, it gives a somewhat amateur feeling to a shot. In Maya, you can create a zoom by setting keyframes over time in the focal length attribute of the camera. You will learn more about focal lengths later in the chapter.

Maya Camera Types

You can create three types of cameras in Maya. Each can be used for various situations in your animations. To create a camera, choose **Create** → **Cameras** and choose **Camera (one-node camera)**, **Camera and Aim (two-node camera)**, or **Camera, Aim, and Up (three-node camera)**. After you create a camera, you can still change its type in the camera's Attribute Editor under the Camera Attributes section.

Camera (one-node camera) The one-node camera is the default Maya camera usually used for rendering still images or in animations if a camera does not move, which is often called a "locked-off" camera. Since the one-node is the transform node that stores the camera's rotations and translations, you can still move and rotate this camera as you would any other Maya object. Thus, if you plan to do simple camera translations or simple pans and tilts, you might also choose to use this camera. The perspective camera in Maya is a one-node camera. Figure 3.1 shows a one-node camera and how it appears in the Outliner.

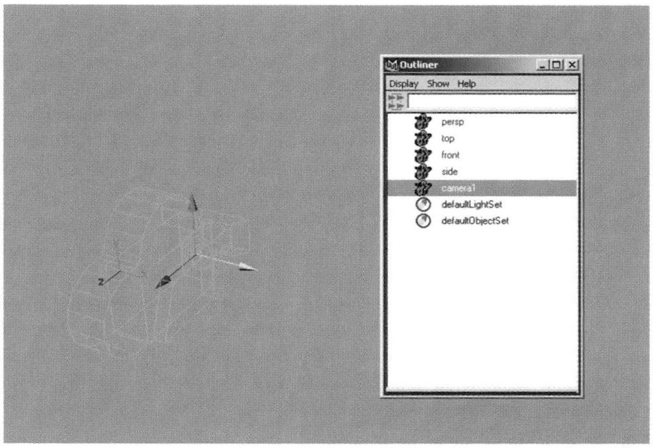

Figure 3.1: A simple one-node camera and how it appears in the Outliner

Camera and Aim (two-node camera) The two-node camera consists of the camera node and an aim node. When translating the aim node of this two-part "object," the camera rotates along the X and Y axes, remaining fixed in the direction of the aim. In this way, you can pan the camera left to right by moving the aim point back and forth along a

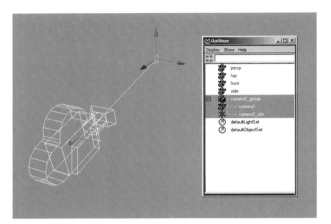

Figure 3.2: A two-node camera consisting of a camera node and an aim node used for panning and tilting

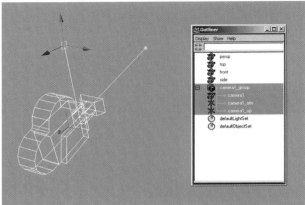

Figure 3.3: A three-node camera consisting of a camera, an aim, and an up node used for rolling the camera

horizontal axis. In order to tilt the camera up and down, translate the aim node vertically, or along the Y axis. The two-node camera is useful when you need to follow the action in a shot. It is more convenient than the one-node camera because all you need to do is position the aim point where you want the camera to look, whether it's focusing on an actor's movement or looking at a car passing on the street. To accomplish this with a one-node camera, you would need to rotate the camera both on the X and Y axes independently, and sometimes that can get cumbersome. Figure 3.2 shows a two-node camera and how it appears in the Outliner.

Camera, Aim, and Up (three-node camera) A three-node camera is used for more sophisticated camera movements. Animating the up node is the same as "rolling" the camera or rotating it on its Z axis. This is good when you need to create a Dutch angle shot or shots in which the camera needs to bank around obstacles such as in a carchase sequence. We will be working later with the up node to create a handheld camera effect. Figure 3.3 shows a three-node camera and how it appears in the Outliner.

Now that you are familiar with the types of cameras in Maya, let's try an exercise using a two-node camera.

Creating a Dolly-and-Pan Shot Using a Two-Node Camera

A big advantage of using a two-node camera is that you can achieve subtle effects by translating the camera and the aim nodes simultaneously. Let's take a scene in which an actor exits an elevator, walks across the lobby, and then walks through an apartment door. The camera is positioned in the lobby at a distance so that we can maintain a wide shot of the actor and establish the environment. Our objective is to follow the actor's path by panning with her while at the same time dollying the camera in the opposite direction so that the actor remains in view rather than being hidden by a wall as she crosses the set.

Begin by loading `dollyPan_start.mb` from the CD.

1. Choose **File → Open** and navigate to Chapter 3 on the CD then to `dollyPan_start.mb`. The camera will be in its starting position, framing the elevator doors as well as part of the lobby. Figure 3.4 shows the camera's starting position.

2. In the Outliner, select the camera1_aim node from the camera1_group node. In the Channel box, highlight the translation attributes, right-click them, and choose **Key Selected** to set a translate keyframe at frame 1.

3. Move the Timeline to frame 240, and in the top view, translate the camera1_aim node to approximately the end position of our actor. Set a keyframe at frame 240 for these translation values. If you play back the animation at this point, the camera will rotate (or pan) to follow its aim node, thus following the actor.

4. Now, we want to dolly the camera in the opposite direction so we can get a clear view of where the actor is walking. In the Outliner, select the camera node. At frame 1, set a keyframe for the translation attributes of the camera to set its initial position.

5. Now move the Timeline to the last frame. In the top view, use the Move tool to translate the camera to the opposite side of the hallway. Set a keyframe for the camera node's translations, here at frame 240.

6. If you play back the animation, you will notice that the camera1_aim is way ahead of the actor. We will want to delay the movement of the camera for about 50 frames to wait for the actor to move into the camera's initial aim position. To do this, bring the Timeline back to frame 1. With the middle mouse button, scrub in the Timeline to frame 50. Scrubbing in the Timeline with the middle mouse button will not play any of the keyframed animation that you set. This makes it easy to duplicate keyframes over time. Set a keyframe for the translation attributes of the camera and the camera1_aim nodes.

7. Play back the animation to see where we can tweak the camera move. You will notice that about frame 130 our actor begins to outpace the camera1_aim. It is always good

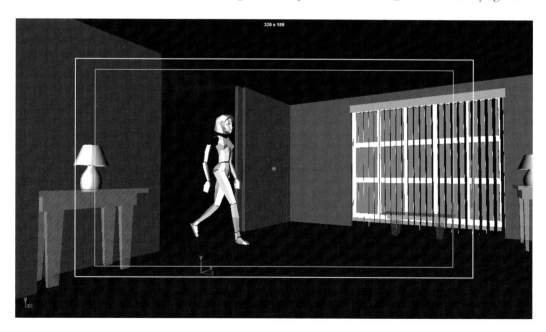

Figure 3.4: A wide or long shot at the beginning of the scene establishes where we are and sets the tone for what is to come next.

Figure 3.5: At frame 130, the actor outpaces the camera.

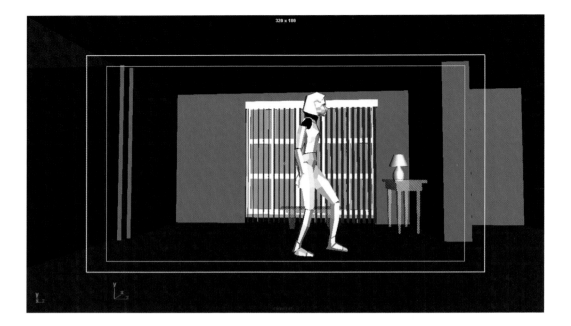

for the actor or action to outpace the camera slightly to mimic a real-world camera and camera operator. As you can see, however, our actor is a bit screen right at this point, and we are leaving a lot of room to the left of the actor (or screen left), as shown in Figure 3.5. At about frame 130, simply adjust the camera1_aim in the top view by translating it along the Z axis a bit closer to the actor and setting a keyframe.

8. Now let us put an ease-out onto the camera to avoid an abrupt stop at the end of the motion. (You can look at the curves in the Graph Editor to see how the camera motion stops abruptly.) Cameras that start and stop abruptly are obvious signs of a CG-animated camera. We don't need to worry about the ease-in because this was already created when we delayed the camera for those 50 frames. In the Outliner, select the camera1 and camera1_aim nodes and open the Graph Editor (choose **Window** → **Animation Editors** → **Graph Editor**). Marquee+select the end keyframes, and choose **Tangents** → **Flat**, or click the Flat Tangents icon in the Graph Editor.

9. As a final camera tweak, let's change the end time for these keyframes. With the end keyframes still selected, change the time from 240 to 230 in the Graph Editor. The camera nodes will now ease out to a stop, and the actor will continue to walk for the 10 frames to the end. There are no hard-and-fast rules for when to stop camera motion, but it just looks and feels better to stop the camera before the actor stops walking. These subtle camera tweaks can sometimes create a world of difference in your shots.

One other subtle tweak to adjust this camera motion is to add a slight "bump" at the end by overshooting the camera motion and then letting it settle back to its desired position. Simply drag the tangent handles for the final keyframes up a bit, which causes a slight overshoot to the motion. For more control, you can add extra keyframes at the end of the camera motion. You'll want to be subtle with this adjustment, however, or you'll get an amateur look to the camera motion.

Camera Lenses and Focal Lengths

Before we tackle some more hands-on camera work, let's take a look at camera lenses and how they affect our shots. Although we still refer to the camera lens as if it's an interchangeable physical object in the 3D environment, we don't change lenses as we would in the real world. Translating a specific type of lens from the real world of cinematography to the digital realm is as simple as adjusting the focal length of the Maya camera. The longer the focal length of a lens, the smaller its field of view (FOV). (In Maya, the FOV is referred to as the angle of view.) You adjust the focal length of the camera in the Camera Attributes section of the Attribute Editor.

The following are different lens types and the reasons for using them:

Fish-eye lens You create a fish-eye lens by adjusting the focal length to a short 15mm or less. This results in an extremely wide angle of view, hence exaggerating the distance between the foreground and background planes of the shot. Using a fish-eye lens is perfect if you're looking to create a sense of space (as in a panoramic shot) or even of distortion, as in Figure 3.6, which is set to 10mm.

Wide angle lens The focal length of a wide angle lens is typically anything less than 30mm. A shot taken with a lens that has a wider field of view can capture more of the scene's elements or objects than a regular or normal lens. For live-action filmmaking, this is convenient for shooting in a narrow or closed location. The shot in Figure 3.7 was taken with a wide angle lens.

Normal lens To closely mimic the perspective of the human eye, you use a standard or normal lens with the focal length set to about 50mm, as in Figure 3.8. Some cinematographers have used normal lenses in films to achieve the illusion of real-life normal perspective in certain abnormal or horrific situations. In the 1979 movie *Being There*, directed by Hal Ashby, a 50mm lens was used for most of the film to create a normal viewing perspective of Peter Sellers as a simple-minded gardener who, having

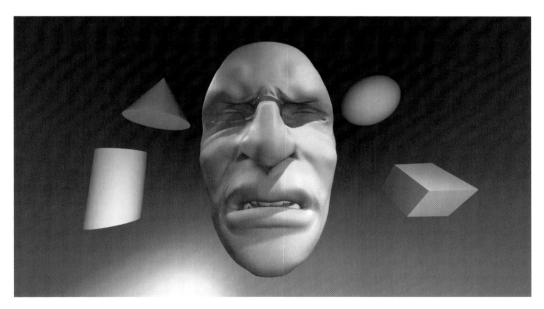

Figure 3.6: A 10mm focal length drastically distorts the image because of its extreme wide angle of view but makes for an interesting effect.

Figure 3.7: This image uses a wide angle lens of 24mm.

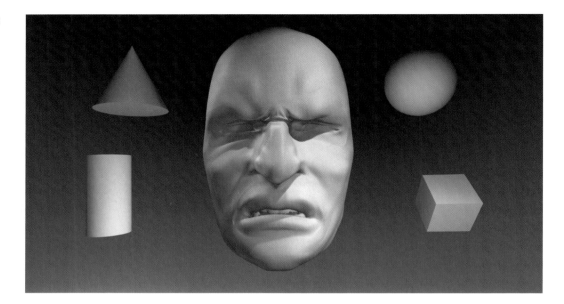

Figure 3.8: At 50mm, this normal lens is a close match to the perspective of the human eye. Notice how much more space is between the head and the primitive objects than in the previous lenses.

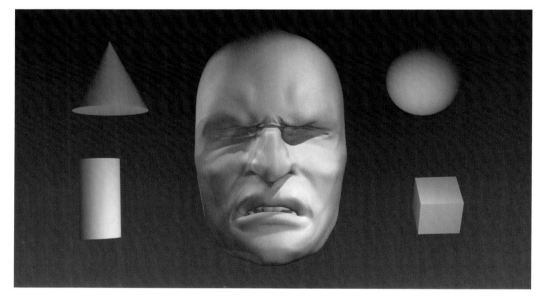

spent a lifetime in seclusion, is suddenly thrust into an abnormal situation as he gets his first exposure to reality beyond his sheltered existence.

Telephoto lens   Anything between a focal length of 100mm and 150mm begins to fall into the category of longer lenses, but usually anything beyond 200mm is considered telephoto. These lenses reduce the depth of field, which can be an advantage as you can focus right in on your subject, producing a crystal-clear image, while the foreground and background surrounding it become out of focus. Figure 3.9 has a focal length set to 200mm. Notice how flat the head and primitive objects are as compared with the previous focal lengths. Telephoto lenses tend to flatten the distance between the subject and the camera, making objects appear closer than they actually are.

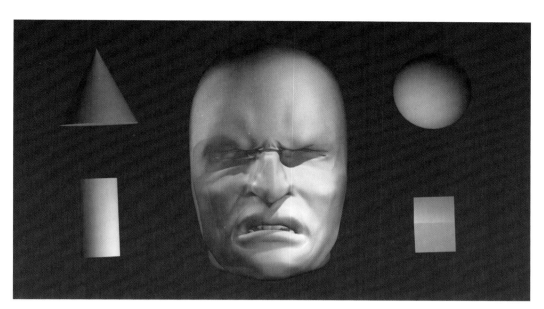

Figure 3.9: A 200mm telephoto lens decreases the distance from the camera to the subject, resulting in a flattened image.

Creating a Dolly Zoom

In this next exercise, let's animate the focal length and position of the camera to create an effect that is used often in motion pictures.

The dolly zoom, also known as tracking zoom or zolly, is the combination of dollying while zooming the camera, but in opposite directions. This shot keeps a character or an object in about the same position within the camera frame, while altering the perspective of the background. This effect usually conveys unease, strife, or alarm as a character's understanding of their universe changes drastically. It has been used in such classic films as Alfred Hitchcock's *Vertigo* (conveying James Stewart's fear of heights), Steven Spielberg's *Jaws* (to reflect Roy Scheider's shock as he realizes a boy is being attacked by a shark), and Martin Scorsese's *Goodfellas* (to communicate the shift in the lives of Ray Liotta's and Robert Dinero's characters as they are about to betray each other).

Let's create this dolly zoom effect by moving a one-node camera while altering its focal length.

1. Open the dollyZoom_start.mb scene file on the CD. Here we have some animation of a character who stops and turns to look over his shoulder. We will dolly zoom toward the character as he turns. First, choose **Create** → **Cameras** → **Camera** to create a one-node camera, and move the camera into position to compose the shot. You can use these values for the camera node and set a keyframe at frame 1 for a composition similar to that in Figure 3.10:

   Translate X: –0.89
   Translate Y: 3.67
   Translate Z: 5.0
   Rotate X: 4.0
   Focal Length: 40

Figure 3.10: "I have a bad feeling about this!" We start this shot with a somewhat normal lens of 40mm as our CG actor hesitates for fear of impending danger.

Ready for Wide-Screen

Back in the age of VHS video, it was somewhat rare to rent a movie that was in a wide-screen format. Most people preferred full screen, pan and scan because they thought the black bars that accompanied letter-boxed movies were actually cropping the movie. Little did they know that it was the pan and scan doing the cropping. "Good times," I say. "Good times."

Now in the age of DVD and high-definition wide-screen televisions, it appears you can't get enough of the wide-screen format. In fact, many 3D artists are rendering their demo reels and animations with the anamorphic 16:9 aspect ratio. And, yes, I am guilty of that too as you can see in the rendered clips and tutorials in this chapter. The 16:9 aspect ratio is most often used for film and is now used with wide-screen TVs.

In each of these exercises, in the Render Global Settings window, I have set the resolution to 320 × 180, which gives you a device aspect ratio of 1.78 (which is actually the result of dividing 16 by 9). Now, when you choose **View** → **Camera** → **Settings** in the camera view panel and turn on Resolution Gate, the rendering area of the camera view is displayed in the 16:9 aspect ratio, which is helpful when setting up and composing your shots. Also, turning on Safe Action is useful since the Safe Action area guarantees that the action in your scene displays on screen as long as everything remains within this area.

2. Scrub to frame 60 in the Timeline. Take note of how the camera frames the character; the head is just skimming the top of the Safe Action area. At frame 60, zoom out by changing the focal length to 16 and set a keyframe. Now, on the Z axis translation, dolly the camera forward to about the same position where the character's head is just touching the Safe Action area. This is to maintain the character's position within the camera view throughout the duration of this tracking zoom camera effect. Set a key at frame 60.

3. Let's give some ease-in and ease-out on the focal length zoom as well as the Z translation. With the camera selected, open the Graph Editor, select the **Translate Z** and **Focal Length** attributes, and marquee+select their keyframes. Click the Flat Tangents icon to flatten the curve at both ends.

4. Now create a slight roll in the camera by setting a keyframe on the Z rotation with a value of −2 at frame 1 and then rotating slightly in the opposite direction to 2 and setting a keyframe at frame 60. Apply the same technique as before to the keyframes to create an ease-in and ease-out of the curve. Your end frame should look like Figure 3.11.

Figure 3.11: "I think now would be a good time to...RUN!!" The quick shift in focal length with a dolly forward to compensate creates disorientation and unease for our actor as the background is exaggerated while maintaining the foreground spatial relationship.

You can see the final results in the `dollyZoom_end.mb` scene file on the CD or watch the final rendered movie file `dollyZoom.mov`.

Re-creating Advanced Camera Motion

When re-creating the natural camera movements of a real-world camera, the CG camera animator must keep in mind certain physical aspects of handling such equipment. For one thing, a film camera has mass and weight. It takes some effort to get a heavy object to start moving, and it requires effort to stop or change the course of a heavy object once it is moving. Therefore, CG cameras should not start or stop on a dime. They require a certain amount of ease-in and ease-out motion when being animated.

Another way to keep cameras from appearing too computer created is to bear in mind who is operating the camera. Some of what makes real-world camera footage appear authentic is the often slight delay of the camera person's hand as they try to keep the action framed in the shot. It's the lack of these little human nuances that cause an audience to recognize CG camera shots.

With these suggestions in mind, let's delve into two popular techniques in filmic camera motion: camera shake and handheld cameras.

Creating Camera Shake

A huge twister has swept through town, whisking away trees, houses, and even a couple of automobiles. We are going to animate a camera shake as a couple of cars are dropped out of the sky in front of us. An effective way to create a camera shake is through the pan and tilt of the camera. We are going to do this with a two-node camera. We will animate the X and Y translations of the camera's aim for the shake and then later the camera1_group for any global camera translations and rotations.

1. Open the `camShake_start.mb` scene file on the CD. If you play back the animation, you will see two cars falling from above onto a ground plane.

2. Create a two-node camera, and enter the following values into the camera1_group's translation attributes:

    Translate X: 0
    Translate Y: 0
    Translate Z: 5

These settings place the camera in a position that nicely composes the action of the falling cars. Let's make the field of view a little wider by changing the focal length to 28. At frame 90, you should now have something that looks like Figure 3.12.

3. Let's have the camera follow the first car as it plummets to the ground. At frame 1, select the camera1_aim and translate it up and slightly left toward the car closest to us. The car should be somewhat centered and low in frame, as in Figure 3.13. Set a keyframe for the camera1_aim attributes.

4. Notice that the first car hits the ground at frame 25, so let's move the Timeline to frame 28 and set a keyframe on the camera's aim. The three-frame difference in the tracking motion of the cars as they fall is to give a slight delay in the camera operator's movement since a human is operating the camera and not a computer. A three- to five-frame delay in movements like these is always good in creating realistic camera movements. You don't want to delay too much though in situations like these because you don't want your audience to miss the action. Another thing to keep in mind is that you generally don't want your camera movements to distract from the action in your shots. (Of course, there are no steadfast rules as you will see later when we do handheld cameras.)

5. At frame 28, change the **Translate X and Y** of the camera1_aim back to 0. These adjustments will return us to the framing we had in step 2. Set a keyframe for the X and Y translations.

6. The camera seems to be outpacing the car about frame 15. Raise the camera1_aim a bit to get the car more into frame and set a keyframe.

7. With the camera nicely following the car to its crash landing, it's time to add the shake. Since the car touches the ground at frame 25, set a keyframe on the **Translate X and Y** of the camera1_aim at frames 25 and 27. Our initial camera jolt will occur between these two frames. It might be easier at this point to use the Graph Editor. At frame 27,

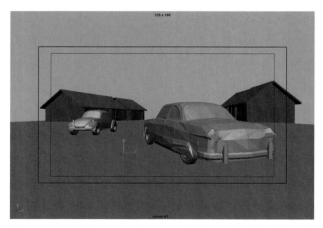

Figure 3.12: The camera's start position with a focal length of 28mm

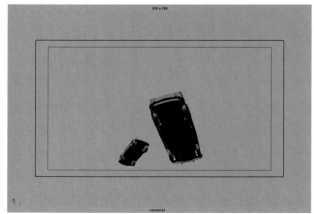

Figure 3.13: The camera's aim node is positioned at frame 1.

select the **Translate Y** keyframe and enter **0.5**. Continue adding the following keyframes and their values for the Y translation of the camera1_aim.

Keyframe	Value
27	–0.5
29	0.3
32	–0.2
35	0.1
39	0.0

8. If you play back the animation, the shake seems a bit slow and bouncy, not reflective of a shake that occurs when a ton of fiberglass and steel comes crashing down in front of you. Let's speed the frequency of the shake up a bit and reduce the magnitude on each keyframe to take out some of the bounciness. Let's move each keyframe back one and drop each value down a little as follows:

Keyframe	Value
26	–0.4
28	0.2
31	–0.1
34	0.05
38	0.0

In the Graph Editor, smooth out the last keyframe at frame 38 by clicking the Flat Tangents icon. Your curves should look something like Figure 3.14.

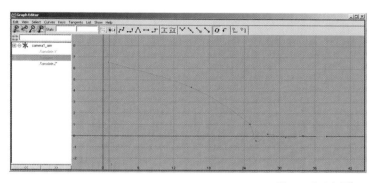

Figure 3.14: The Y translation curve of the camera's aim node as seen in the Graph Editor. This animates the tilting motion of the camera shake.

9. You'll start noticing the pattern of a camera shake. First, take a look at where our keyframes are placed. The initial jolt takes place between frames 25 and 26, a space of one. Our next movement happens between 26 and 28, a space of two. As time moves on, the space between keyframes gets wider until the shake fades out. Our spacing pattern between keyframes ends up as 1, 2, 3, 3, 4. You can also see a pattern in the values of each keyframe. The initial jolt brings the camera down to –0.4 and then up to 0.2. As the shake gradually fades, the values lessen as well, with the camera tilting down to –0.1, then up a bit to 0.05, and finally resting at 0, which was the camera's original fixed state when we composed the shot at the beginning of our exercise.

10. Let's add a bit of panning motion to give this shake an extra level of realism. Since the car is crashing right in front of us, the blast would push the camera away from the impact. We also want to offset the keys from the tilting motion by about one frame, so set your key on **Translate X** at frame 27 with a value of –0.2. Continue setting keys with these values as shown in Figure 3.15. (If you already have keys set on **Translate X**, you can just reposition them to the correct time and adjust their values as follows:

Keyframe	Value
29	0.06
32	–0.1
35	0.02
39	0

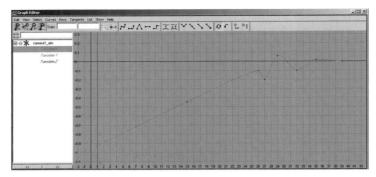

Figure 3.15: The X translation curve of the camera's aim node as seen in the Graph Editor. This animates the panning motion of the camera shake.

11. Now that you are familiar with creating the camera shake, it won't be too difficult adding the shake of the second falling vehicle. Take note that the second car hits the ground at frame 46, so we want our second shake between frames 46 and 48 (the same as the two-frame difference in the first shake). Starting with **Translate Y**, set a keyframe at frames 46 and 48. It should be the same value as the last keyframe from the end of the first shake, which in this case was 0.

12. To make adding the second shake quick and easy, we are going to copy and paste the keyframes from the first car falling. In the Graph Editor, select all the keyframes from frame 26 to 38 in **Translate Y**. Choose **Edit → Copy**. Bring the Timeline to frame 48, if it's not already. Choose **Edit → Paste □**, make sure Time Range is set to Current, and change Paste Method to Merge, as in Figure 3.16. Click the Paste Keys button.

13. Our second shake is in place, but it needs to be toned down because the second vehicle is falling farther from the camera. Let's make the following changes:

Keyframe	Value
48	–0.1
50	.05
53	–.03
56	.02
60	0

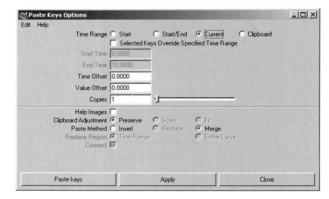

Figure 3.16: You can simplify the process of the second camera shake by copying and pasting keyframes from the first shake.

14. Let's do the same now for the X translation of the camera1_aim. First, set a keyframe on the X translation to 0 at frame 47. Since we want to offset the pan motion from the tilt, let's copy the previous keyframes from 27 to 39 and paste them at frame 49 (making

sure that the Timeline is at frame 49 when you paste). Tone down the amplitude of the shake. The following values seem to work well:

Keyframe	Value
49	–.06
51	.02
54	–.025
57	.01
61	0

15. If you'd like to animate the camera moving into the danger zone, simply change the global translations on the camera1_group. You can initially move the camera1_group back a bit on the Z axis to about 5.5 units. Set a key at frame 1. Also, set a key on the X axis at –0.2, so our moving camera won't eventually intersect the car model. At frame 90, move the camera1_group forward to about 0.5 units on the Z axis and set a keyframe.

16. If you want, you can also add a bit of extra camera shake on the secondary bounces of both cars (just a tiny bit compared with the initial shake). This can help add weight to the bouncing cars.

All CG animation benefits from a little motion blur; otherwise, the images appear too crisp and clean, too CG. For the example movie generated from this exercise, I rendered with the default motion blur settings using the mental ray for Maya renderer. Experiment with how much motion blur works for you in your animations.

The final version of this, camShake_end.mb, is available in the Chapter 3 folder on the CD. You can also navigate to the Chapter 3 → Movies folder to see the final rendered version, camShake.mov.

Creating a Handheld Camera

Although there are a number of options to keep a camera steady during film production, such as a dolly rig or a steadicam, many cinematographers and directors use handheld or shoulder-held cameras instead. The choices are evident in such films as *Saving Private Ryan*, *Collateral*, and *Schindler's List* and can even be seen in TV series such as *NYPD Blue* and *24*. The handheld camera definitely brings a certain documentary style to a film or a specific scene within that film, but most of the time the decision to use this effect has more to do with intention than with style. The jerky movements of a handheld camera heighten the sense of realism in a scene, all while giving the audience a feeling of participation, or "being there," since the camera is essentially acting as a first-person perspective.

In this next tutorial, you will animate a Maya camera as if it were handheld in an extreme situation: running with the camera over a rocky ground terrain. This style of film-making is most prominent in *Saving Private Ryan* but really hasn't been seen much in CG feature films. The handheld camera technique truly mimics the documentary-style news camera footage that we've seen many times, which is probably why it seems more true to life than other types of camera techniques.

Composing the Shot and Global Translations

On the CD, open `handHeld_start.mb`. Here we see our CG actor running over a bumpy terrain. There are some "buildings," as well, in our environment so that we have some motion reference when we create the camera animation. Use a three-node camera for this exercise.

1. Choose **Create** → **Cameras** → **Camera, Aim, and Up**. We will animate three nodes to get an effective handheld feel. The camera1_group node will be animated along the Z axis, forward into the scene. The aim node will be used for the pan and tilt to create the quick and jerky movements of a handheld, and for added realism, the up node will be used to add slight roll into the camera movement with each footstep our virtual camera person takes.

2. Let's get a good starting composition. It would be nice to have our actor coming into the frame from the right side. Since we don't want to alter the position of this character, move the camera1_group into the following position:

   - Translate X: –2.0
   - Translate Y: 2.67
   - Translate Z: 5.0

   Set a keyframe for these at frame 1. Also, change the focal length on the camera node to 28. Let's adjust the camera1_aim, as well, and set a keyframe at frame 1. These values work fine:

   - Translate X: 0.425
   - Translate Y: 0.106

   Since the camera aim and up nodes will be driving the motion of the camera, there is no need to set keyframes for the translation values of the camera1_node.

   When finished, you should have a composition that looks like Figure 3.17.

   The default value of the Z translation of the camera1_aim is –5. You don't need to change or keyframe this because it will remain the same throughout the exercise. Moving the camera1_aim along the Z axis will have no effect on our handheld camera.

   ---

3. With our starting composition set, let's set our global camera translation over the duration of the scene. As in the camera shake tutorial, I like to put the global camera translations into the camera1_group node. This keeps all the camera nodes together, as they are children of this group node. Since we already keyframed the first frame, move the Timeline to the last frame. Translate the camera1_group in the Z axis to about –6, just behind our actor, as in Figure 3.18. Set a keyframe here at frame 200.

Animating the Aim Node: Pan with TranslateX

Now it is time to create the jitter that makes our camera appear to be handheld. We will first animate the side-to-side motion by keying the **Translate X** of the camera1_aim node. This

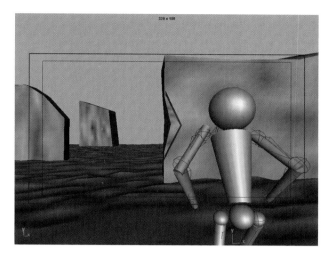

Figure 3.17: Start composition for the handheld camera

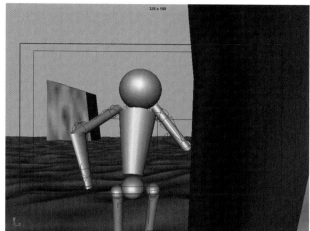

Figure 3.18: End composition for the handheld camera

side-to-side motion simulates our virtual camera person's body weight as they shift from one leg to the other while running with the camera.

1. Starting at frame 1, in the Top View, move the aim slightly to the right to get a bit more of the actor into the frame. Set a key for the camera1_aim's **Translate X**.

A good setup for your view panels is a Three Panes Split Bottom layout with the Graph Editor across the top and the Camera View and Top View across the bottom.

---

2. Move to frame 25. Since there is a slight ease-in as the camera operator begins his run to follow the actor, the camera is just about starting its translation forward along the Z axis at this point. There won't be much bouncing of the camera yet, so, let's just pan a bit with the actor by translating the aim slightly to the left, to approximately 0, and set a keyframe.

3. At frame 50, continue panning left to about −1 and set a key. At this point, our camera person has started to follow the actor, so we will begin our side-to-side motion here. Move the aim back to 0 and set a keyframe at frame 75. On frame 100, set another key with a value of −0.5. It's good to vary the values of each side-to-side movement because we want to avoid any mechanical motion.

4. As you create this side-to-side motion, keep in mind how the actor is framed in the shot. Since this is a handheld camera, try to avoid keeping him totally centered, though somewhat within the camera view. Continue to set keyframes with the following values:

Keyframe	Value
125	0.4
150	−0.4
175	−0.35
200	−0.9

Figure 3.19: To start, we set keyframes every 25 frames on the X translation of the camera's aim, which animates the side-to-side motion as the virtual camera person runs forward.

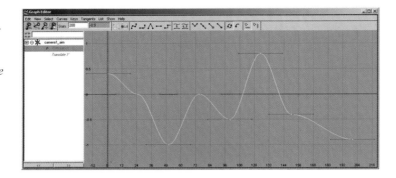

5. If you play back the animation or do a playblast now, our side-to-side motion is a bit too smooth. To create the quick and jerky motions of a handheld camera, we will need to add more keys between the ones we just set. Our objective is to hold these positions longer and create a sharp peak on our animation curve from one extreme to the other. Before we begin setting additional keyframes, first select all the keys in the Graph Editor for the camera1_aim's X translation and click the Flat Tangents icon. This will change the shape of the curve, creating a curve that is less smooth and more bumpy, perfect for the handheld camera we are trying to achieve. You should get a curve similar to that in Figure 3.19.

6. Now we can begin applying the sharp, jerky movements to our camera. Since we already created the side-to-side motion by keyframing every 25th frame over the total time of the camera move, we will start breaking the movement down to every 10th frame. In the Graph Editor, set a keyframe on the X translation of the camera1_aim node at frame 10 using the Add Keys tool. Select this key and drag it down a bit using constrained translation. To do this, select the key, and then hold the Shift key while dragging the keyframe downward. A hook with an arrow will appear telling you that this move is vertically constrained.

7. Now, move forward another 10 frames to frame 20 and add a key. Take notice that the next keyframe is set 5 frames later at frame 25. We will take this as an opportunity to give our camera a good jerk. Grab this keyframe (at frame 20) and move it downward, slightly below the value of the keyframe that is at frame 25. We have now created a quick change in direction for the camera aim that occurs in a swift 5 frames. We will continue to do this along the entire curve, taking into account that as we are creating keys at every 10th frame, we will create a quick, sharp, jerking motion where any keyframes are 5 frames apart.

8. Continue to follow this method for the rest of the curve. Your X translation curve should look similar to that in Figure 3.20 when you finish. Save your scene. You can do a playblast or render your scene to see the results so far. You should have something like handHeld_mid.mb found in the Chapter 3 folder on the CD.

Animating the Aim Node: Tilt with TranslateY

The handheld camera will begin to take shape when we start setting keys for camera tilting motion. You create this up-down motion by adjusting the **Translate Y** attribute of the camera1_aim node. The motivation for the tilting motion is the impact between the camera person's footsteps and the ground on which they are running. Since the tilt motion will need to

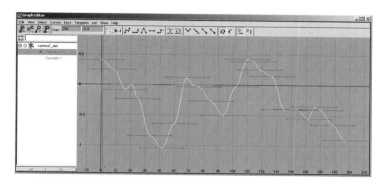

Figure 3.20: The refined X translation curve of the camera's aim node

be even less smooth than the panning motion of the X translation, we will be setting even more keyframes on our Y translation curve of the camera1_aim. Let's begin.

1. First, mute the X translation of the camera1_aim so we can have clear feedback when we set keys on the Y translation. Select the camera1_aim, and in the Channel box, right click **Translate X** and choose **Mute Selected**. The camera pan is now temporarily turned off.

2. Let's do the same with **Translate Y** as we did with **Translate X** by setting keyframes at every 25th frame and then breaking it down further by every 10 frames and then by every 5 frames.

This keyframing technique—first blocking out major motions and then filling in smaller keyframes—is called blocking and is used by character animators to get precise movements for their animations. Some animators even refine down to every other frame. In a sense, we are treating our handheld camera as a character.

---

3. The value of each key should reflect an up-down motion along the length of the curve. As a general rule, you might want to use the X translation curve as a guide. The sharpest tilting movements from the Y translation should somewhat match with the sharpest pan movements of the X translation. This makes sense because if our camera person's hand becomes unsteady at a certain point, both translations will be affected at the same time.

4. Scrub along the Timeline to see if any areas need adjusting. The framing might be too extreme in some areas, and our actor might be either too high or too low in the camera view. Make these adjustments, but don't worry too much about fine-tuning at this point. Here are some values that work well:

Keyframe	Value
1	0.1
25	−0.13
50	0.14
75	−0.2
100	0.22
125	0.06
150	−0.06
175	0.56
200	0.23

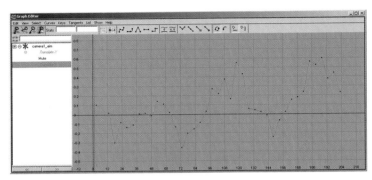

Figure 3.21: The Y translation of the camera's aim animates the tilting motion of the handheld camera. Notice that there are more keyframes here than the X translation curve with keys set every 5 frames.

5. Now we will fine-tune. Simply follow the same technique as before. We'll keyframe every 10 frames, and we'll create a sharp jerk for keys that are 5 frames apart. Afterward, for further refinement, you might want to set a keyframe at every 5th frame and adjust the values. Don't forget to select all your keyframes and click the Flat Tangents icon to create a bumpier curve, as shown in Figure 3.21. Notice how the extra keyframes contribute a good amount of jitter to the handheld effect even in areas that have no sharp, jerk motion.

6. Since we've keyframed the X and Y translation on similar frames, let's offset the Y translation a bit. In the Graph Editor, marquee+select all the Y translation keyframes, choose **Edit** → **Transformation Tools** → **Move Keys Tool** (or press W on the keyboard), and, holding the Shift key, click and drag the entire curve about 3 or 4 frames to the right.

Animating the Up Node: Roll with Translate X

For a final touch, we are going to add some roll to this handheld camera by animating the X translation of the camera_up node. This is somewhat easy because we can simply copy the animation curve of the X translation from the camera1_aim node and paste it into our camera_up curve. This will work because the roll of the camera should occur at the approximate time that the camera pans from side to side.

1. First, marquee+select all the keyframes of the camera1_aim's X translation and choose **Edit** → **Copy**. Next, on the camera_up's X translation, set an initial keyframe at frame 1. Select this keyframe, and with the Timeline set at frame 1, choose **Edit** → **Paste ❏**, making sure Time Range is set to Current and Paste Method is set to Merge. Click the Paste Keys button.

2. If you scrub through the Timeline, you will see too much roll on the camera. We want a subtle effect for a handheld camera, not like we are sailing on the open sea. Marquee+select all the keyframes, and choose **Edit** → **Transformation Tools** → **Scale Keys Tool** (or press R on the keyboard). To scale the keyframes toward 0, hold the Shift key, MM click at the 0 grid line in the Graph Editor, and drag downward as in Figure 3.22. Don't scale too much because we don't want to loose the roll effect completely. Keep your eye on the camera view to see the result of your scaling.

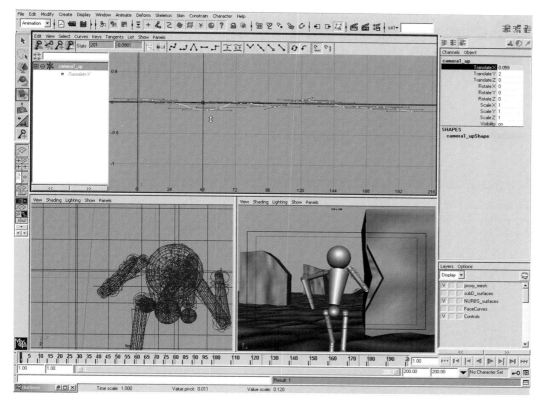

Figure 3.22: Since there is too much roll in the X translation of the camera's up node, you can scale all the keys as a whole to reduce the effect.

3. As before, offset this curve a few frames from the camera1_aim's X translation since their keys currently are set on the same frames. And don't forget to flatten their tangent handles too. You can view the final results in the handHeld_end.mb scene file or watch the final rendered movie handheld.mov, both of which are on the CD.

Capturing Camera Motion with Maya Live

So far you've achieved realistic camera effects by moving the camera around in 3D space. Although CG-based camera motion is the usual method for CG feature animation, you can also capture camera movements from recorded video with the Maya Live module.

In a process called matchmoving, Maya Live extracts live-action camera movement to be applied to a Maya camera, which allows for superb integration of CG objects within the live-action footage. Although Maya Live's controls are sophisticated enough to achieve precise results, we don't need too much precision in the following example. Since we are not going to worry about integrating CG into live-action footage at this time, we don't need to worry too much about the finer details of matchmoving.

Maya Live works only with Maya Unlimited. If you own Maya Complete, you can read along, but you will not be able to step through this exercise.

In this exercise, we are going to use Maya Live to capture some handheld movements from a video that was taken with a digital camera. You can import your video into any video-editing software, such as Adobe Premiere, that allows export of movies as a sequence of images. Since the sequence of images has already been created for you, let's begin.

1. Open a new scene. In the Maya Live module, choose **Scene → New MatchMove**. The layout will switch to a Setup control panel below the Perspective view. In the Perspective view you will see the shotCamera and an image plane, both of which are used in the matchmoving process. In the Setup control panel, click the Browse button next to the Full Res Image field and navigate to Chapter03 → sourceimages on the CD. Choose the first image, handheldPan001. Maya loads the sequence of images and updates the frame range to reflect the number of images in the sequence (140 frames in our case). The first image appears on the image plane that is in front of the camera, but you can scrub the Timeline to play through all the images. For this exercise, we don't need to worry about the other settings on the right side of the control panel concerning filmbacks, film apertures, and aspect ratios. After the initial setup you should have what looks like Figure 3.23.

If there are issues when scrubbing, make sure Playback Speed is set to Play Every Frame in the Animation Preferences menu. Also, on the far left in the Maya Live Setup control panel, click the Cache button and make sure Use Cache is checked so that your images are stored in memory, making it easier to work. You might also want to change Pixel Type to Luminance so that you can get a higher frame capacity stored in the cache.

Figure 3.23: Maya Live creates a shot-Camera as well as an image plane that displays a sequence of images used for tracking points in the matchmoving process.

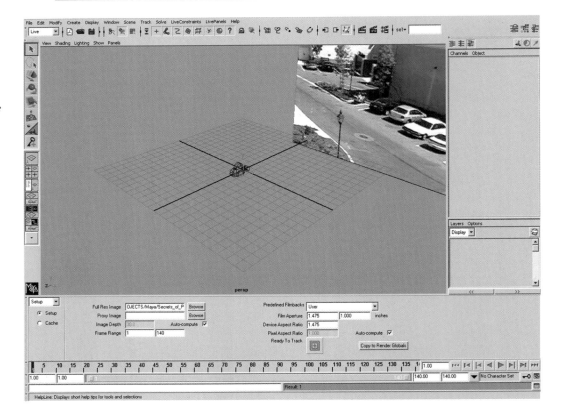

2. Once the setup is complete, choose Track in the drop-down menu on the far left. A new arrangement of windows appears with the Track control panel, including a shot-Camera, pointCenteredCamera, and a Track Summary view panel, as shown in Figure 3.24. If you haven't yet scrubbed through the video, now would be a good time for planning out which areas of the scene we need to track to ultimately achieve the results we are looking for. We are looking for track points that are high in contrast, visible for the duration of most of the shot, and stationary in the world.

3. Our first track point will be the manhole cover in the middle of the street. With the Timeline at frame 1, select Create in the Track control panel to display a new tracked-Point. You can change the name of this in the Channel box for better organization of track points. Rename this point to manhole_cover.

4. To reposition the track box, first click the Track Box tool by the Select None button in the Track control panel. Then, in the shotCamera window, drag the manhole_cover track point roughly to the location of the cover. You can refine the position in the pointCenteredCamera window by clicking the crosshairs within the track box. You can also scale these boxes if necessary. The inner target box defines the pattern that you will be tracking, with the outer box being the search range that is used to search for this pattern. Generally, the default size of the track box is all you need, but in some cases you might need to make minor adjustments. In the case of the manhole_cover point, widen the inner target box to encompass the entire darkened area and some of the surroundings. Simply click the outer edge of the target box and drag to the right, as shown in Figure 3.25.

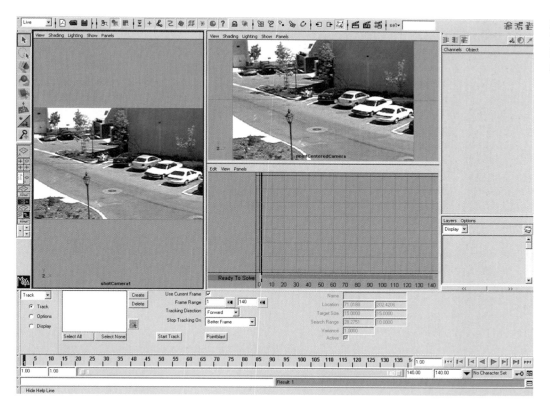

Figure 3.24:
The Track layout within Maya Live.

Figure 3.25: The manhole cover in the middle of the street makes a good tracking point because it is in high contrast with the surrounding area and remains visible for the duration of the video.

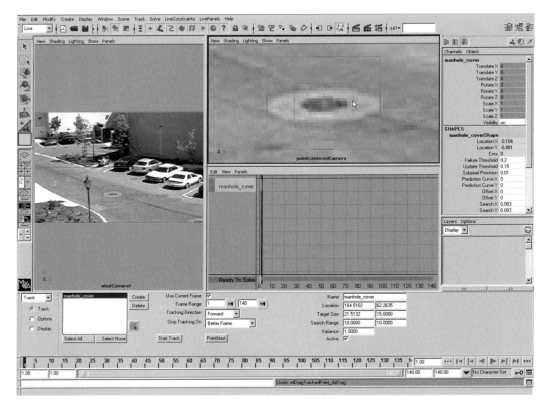

5. Before you begin tracking, make sure Use Current Frame is checked and that Stop Tracking On is set to End of Sequence. Click the Start Track button to start tracking. If the camera movement makes a drastic change and the pattern you are tracking moves out of the limit of the search range, the tracking process will stop. To continue, scrub the Timeline to where it left off, and scale the outer Search Range box.

6. The Track Summary panel gives direct feedback about the quality of how your points are being tracked. Green indicates a good match, yellow is just a warning but is still efficient, and red indicates that the tracking failed. Bits of red don't mean that the tracked point is unusable, but you might want to remove any larger sections of red (click and drag over the red section in the Track Summary panel, right-click, and choose Delete Region) and then retrack for that section by adjusting the track box.

7. Let's create another point and rename it lamppost. Move the track point to the very tip of the lamppost. Here we have a good contrast between the dark edge and the light gray of the pavement below. Click the Start Track button to begin tracking. Notice where the tracking quits as a result of the drastic horizontal change in the camera direction. Again, increase the outer Search Range box to compensate for the change. Be careful not to accidentally reposition the track box, as this may cause problems later when we attempt to solve for the camera movement. Repositioning the track box will be reflected as blue ticks in the Track Summary panel.

Figure 3.26: These points seem to work best for tracking.

8. Continue setting tracking points until the Ready to Solve bar at the bottom of the Track Summary panel is green. Figure 3.26 displays the points that seem to work best for solving for this camera.

A perfectly green Ready to Solve bar is not necessary in order to solve for the camera movement. Use the Track Summary just as a guide, but ultimately you will determine how accurate to the original you need your camera to be. Some like to set a few track points to roughly solve for the camera movement and then increase points accordingly. Try different methods to see what works best for you.

---

license_plate The license plate of the black car next to the motorcycle.

parking_stripe The white mark from the parking stripe on the ground next to the shadow of the far-right, white car. (This mark will disappear a few frames before the end of the sequence.)

drain_pipe The dark mark (drain pipe) on the wall. (This mark will become unreadable a few frames before the end of the sequence.)

white_glare The white glare on the right side of the bumper of the silver car next to the black car.

sign The sign on the wall of the building at the upper left of the frame (a black box above the black car).

Remember to rewind your animation before creating each new marker point. If you forget, it's easiest just to erase the new tracking point and start over.

Figure 3.27:
Tracking results
show mostly
green bars in the
Track Summary
panel. Solving
for this camera
should be easy.

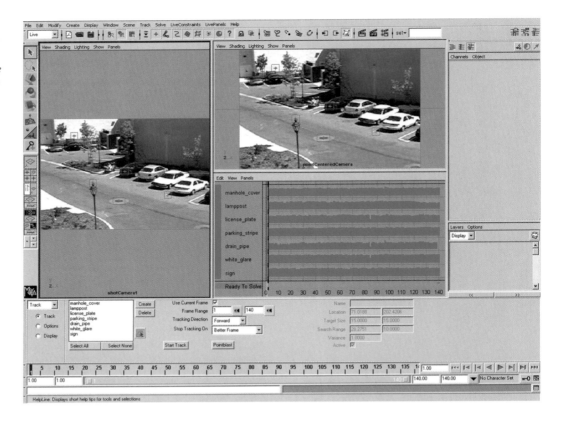

9. Continue with your own scene file or open the `matchMove_tracked.mb` file from the CD. With our track points ready (see Figure 3.27), choose Solve from the drop-down menu in the Live control panel. Click the Solve button under Root Frames to run the Solver program. Choosing the Solve button automatically runs the Solver through all the steps at once, but for more control you can also interactively run through the steps separately by clicking the Start button and then each consecutive button below it. This allows you to make any improvements between each step for a better solve.

10. In a nutshell, the Solver creates locators that are placed in 3D space for each point you tracked. The camera is then keyframed according to the calculations of the camera movement around the locators. You can review how closely the Solver matched the 3D locators with the 2D track points in the Locator Summary panel. If you have large areas of red and yellow, the Solver did not have sufficient tracking information. You might have to go back and add more track points for the frames in question. If all goes well, you should have something like Figure 3.28.

11. We now have a closely matched handheld Maya camera to that of the original camera that shot the video footage. We can export the shotCamera and import it into another scene, to be used to give a handheld camera feeling to an all-CG shot. Delete all the tracking data that imported with the camera. Since the shotCamera has set keyframes in its rotations and translations, create a null node (choose **Create → Empty Group**) and parent the shotCamera to it. You can apply any global translations to the null node while keeping the handheld keyframes intact. To see the final result of this process applied to a "stonehenge" environment, view `matchmove_handheld.mov` on the CD.

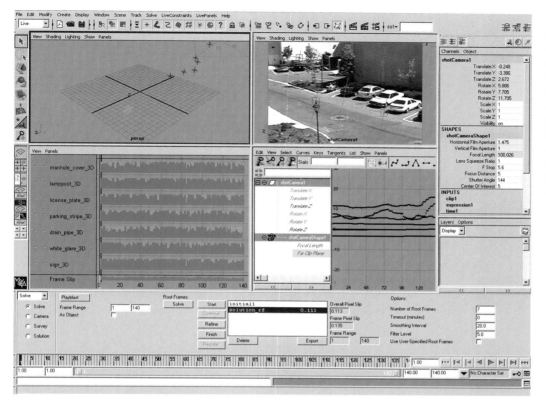

Figure 3.28: The results of a successfully solved camera. The Solver has accurately matched 3D locators with the 2D track points, as you can tell by the mostly green bars in the Locator Summary panel.

Always Learning

In this chapter we explored a variety of techniques for achieving the natural physical movements of the motion picture camera within Maya. There are no steadfast rules for doing this, so it is ultimately you that should experiment and explore to get the results that feel good to you. There is a wealth of reference out there in movies, so pick up some DVDs and watch how each camera moves through the scene. Pay attention to shot composition, the type of lens (normal or wide angle?), and the type of camera effects (handheld or steadicam?). How do certain scenes make you feel, and what is the camera doing at that moment? Listen to the DVD commentary for further insight into the director's and cinematographer's decision-making process. When you're finished with the DVDs, pick up your video camera, experiment with camera motion, and see how your body movement affects the camera, even while trying to remain perfectly still.

In the end, increasing your knowledge of film, cinematography, and the physics of movement will improve your animations. Well, of course, you'll need a good story too.

four

Radiosity and Image-Based Lighting Techniques in Production

Dariush Derakhshani and Jake Carvey

Radiosity, HDRI, *Global Illumination, Image-based Lighting. These buzzwords are familiar; they are discussed in great depth by the 3D community in web forums and magazines worldwide. They also play a major role in the marketing of all the major 3D software packages.*

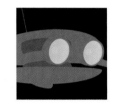

However, we find a widespread misunderstanding of these techniques, especially in the production environment. Many professionals are reluctant to abandon their old bags of tricks, having become proficient at "faking" the same phenomena for years, and many newbies overuse radiosity techniques in situations that plainly just don't need them. Everyone can benefit by taking an in-depth look at some Maya 6 features you may have overlooked for creating natural lighting effects.

A Quick Review

HDRI stands for High Dynamic Range Imagery, which simply refers to pictures that store a wider range of colors and brightness that can be seen on the computer screen. They are created by taking a number of pictures of a scene, with a wide variety of exposures, from very underexposed to very overexposed. This creates several images that essentially show the environment in slightly increasing brightness levels as you move from exposure to exposure. These photos are then combined into a *single* HDR image file that contains the entire captured range of exposure information and, with it, a highly dynamic range of luminance.

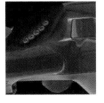

IBL (Image-Based Lighting) is the technique of using images to light a 3D scene, often without the need for additional light sources. An IBL lighting scheme takes an image's brightness values and projects them as lighting values across the scene. It is often used to place CGI elements into live-action filmed environments if the CG elements need to be lit perfectly to the environment. This way color values and varying degrees of brightness of the original shoot are used to directly create the CG lighting necessary for the CG element's eventual integration. In production, IBL is usually supplemented by additional light sources. Any kind of images can be used for IBL, but HDRI is the most common.

These source images are typically created from multiple exposures of panoramic shots or by photographing a highly reflective ball. The ball reflects essentially everything around it, covering most of the scene. You can even create HDR imagery with a cheap chrome Christmas ornament and an inexpensive digital or film camera capable of manual f-stop settings.

RGB values give a normalized brightness range of 0–1 (usually expressed as an integer value between 0 and 255) compared with actual daylight contrast ranges on the order of 0–50,000. It is easy to see the wide gap between real ranges and recorded ranges. It is that really high dynamic range that provides the realism for renderings—very bright reflections and powerful light that can penetrate our scene. It's the subtlety that these images' high ranges supply the lighting scheme that will bring out the nuances of textures and materials that will make a scene vibrant.

Storing all that contrast information requires a much greater range than that provided by standard image file formats which store their information in three color channels, each with 8 bits of information, which means each has a value from 0 through 255. HDR image files must be stored in a floating-point file format, in which each pixel on the screen is described by 16 or 32 bits per channel, resulting in billions of colors, as opposed to the 16 million colors stored in standard 8-bit RGB formats. Typical floating-point file formats are .hdr, floating-point TIF, and floating-point SGI.

You can encode and store HDR imagery in a few ways to save memory and disk space. For example, 16 bits per channel is known as half, and 32 bits per channel is known as float or RGBE compression, in which the fourth channel marked E that is usually reserved for the alpha information, instead contains an exponent that describes the relative brightness of each pixel.

LDRI, or Low Dynamic Range Imagery, describes typical RGB images that contain 8 bits per pixel for each of the three channels—red, green, and blue—and sometimes an additional 8-bit channel for the alpha information, resulting in millions of colors. HDRI, by contrast, stores its information in floating-point format, which can result in billions or even trillions of colors.

Where to Use

You use these rendering techniques in professional CGI production for two basic reasons:

- To achieve photo-realistic results (car commercials, set extensions, digital actors) for either fully CG scenes or CG elements inserted into live-action plates
- To create a specialized rendering style (like the films *Ice Age, Fifty Percent Grey*, and the work PepeLand.com and so on)

Many radiosity renderings seen on the Internet unfortunately have little application for everyday use in a professional production environment. One typical setup is the use of a luminous "dome" to light a completely gray model. This method uses radiosity by surrounding the model with an even grid of lights (usually point lights). This is typically used to show off the sculptural qualities of the model by creating subtle shadows and bringing out surface details and shapes. These setups can also function as a means to an end, to generate ambient occlusion textures, for instance, but are not generally suitable for final production renders. Ambient occlusion shaders are typically used to create areas of light falloff such as at places of intersection on surfaces, along gentle curves, and so forth.

Other artists are turning out beautiful, amazingly accurate renderings that take hours or even days to render. As a result, many of them exist only as stills. It would take far too long to render an entire animated sequence for them to be practical in production.

Nonetheless, in many production situations radiosity and IBL solutions can prove indispensable, and there are plenty of techniques to make it work for our purposes without risking extravagant render times.

Common Applications for HDRI Techniques

Several situations in commercial and film-effects production benefit greatly from the use of HDRI techniques. The following is a list of situations in which most effects artists would use HDRI and IBL.

Vehicles (Especially Shiny Cars) Reflections are highly essential characteristics of metal surfaces. There is not much more to seeing some metal surfaces than reflections and "specular detail." HDRI lets us do away with the typical Phong specularity. (Specularity in real life is actually just the reflection of the light source itself.) What we really want is the ultrabright reflections of the light sources used to illuminate the surface. In studio car photography, the lighting comes primarily from a large softbox that is usually at least 25% larger than the car itself. The softbox not only creates the light to illuminate the car, but gives gentle highlights and reflections, showing the sheen and coolness of the car and showing off the carefully designed curves of the vehicle.

Daylight Scenes The sky itself functions as a giant softbox. The bright light is already diffused and can be directed with bounce cards and the like, although it is important to make sure these cards don't show up in the direct reflections.

In CG, HDRI helps to easily achieve believable fill light to key light ratios and give a nice skylight effect—a broad, soft light source—in addition to adding bounce light from the ground, which is evenly distributed in most cases across the subject. The scene might need a single distant light acting as the sun on sunny days to help illuminate the CG properly, in addition to the IBL setup.

This is effective for matte materials as well as glossy, reflective surfaces.

Mixed Lighting Environments (Exterior and Interior Light) HDR Image-based Lighting techniques can help achieve proper color and exposure balance between bright daylight exteriors and dimmer interiors. Light temperatures can be easily matched and transitioned into and out of.

Directors of photography often use white sheer on the windows on sets to "catch" and soften the light and provide the illusion of exterior sunlight even when shooting at night or on a set inside a soundstage.

Matching Colors and Intensities from Existing Footage This generally involves either HDR images captured on set or using LDR images (the filmed sequence itself, for instance, digitized from video or scanned from film) to provide enough of the right color to effectively blend CGI elements into the scene. Use of LDR often requires several supplemental lighting techniques to gain the necessary contrast and brightness for the CG to mix properly, but can be a fairly effective way to simply and quickly match 3D elements to background plates. IBL here makes for a great fill light and is good for matching color temperature (the level of warmth in light with warm in the oranges and cool in the blues).

Methods and Strategies for IBL

Several IBL rendering techniques can find their place in just about any Maya production pipeline.

Most of these techniques require the use of the mental ray for Maya (a renderer that is included with the latest releases of Maya).

Faking It

3D rendering is all about faking it. Before we had the computing power and programming invention, we had to do without radiosity. Now we have better, faster routines and faster processors to handle them.

You'll find that old-school three-point lighting with supplemental fill lights is the most often used lighting technique for most CG. Here the lighting artist uses the background and any reference images to replicate the light colors and intensities with which to light the CG for integration. The lighting artist adds and arranges numerous CG lights into the scene to best approximate the background. All light parameters (color, intensity, falloff, and so on) are painstakingly adjusted to approximate the overall effects of various light sources, including "bounce lights," which simulate how the source lights bounce off surfaces. You can use an everyday LDR image of the background mapped to a sphere to assist you in analyzing the scene and figure out where the brightest light sources are in the scene and visually trace their paths to your CG elements using their relative color and brightness to adjust your lights to match.

Usually, a generous amount of compositing and color correction is necessary to fit the CG into the plates with finality.

Light Domes

Light domes are essentially grids of lights that are evenly placed, usually inside the surface of a dome and hence the name. A light—point or spotlight pointed inward—is placed at each vertex of the dome, creating an even light and soft shadows in the CG scene. Using an external application called HDRShop with the LightGen plug-in, you can automatically generate a special light dome based on an image of the background. It simply generates colored lights based on the intensity and color information from the image to insert lights where they should be placed in the dome for a fairly effective, yet fake IBL technique. You'll see an example of a light dome in the Droid example later in this chapter in the "Ambient Occlusion" section.

HDRI Reflection

Renders of highly reflective objects benefit greatly from using HDRI reflection maps because of their depth of contrast. This technique can produce excellent renders even without any traditional radiosity because the reflection itself brings out the features of the model and its material.

Furthermore, HDRI with bright sunlight should show up as bright highlights even in shaders with low reflective values since the luminance can have such a wide range, pushing the upper ends. This is important in photo-real car renders because of the highly glossy and reflective enamel surfaces of a car. The nuances of reflection make or break a CG car's appearance, especially if it is to fit into a live-action plate. Most notably is the phenomenon called the Fresnel Effect.

HDRShop

HDRShop is an application developed by Paul Debevec, a major pioneer in the field of HDR imagery. It is freely available for personal use. (See the resources at the end of the chapter for links, or search the Web for HDRShop.)

HDRShop is primarily used for creating, adjusting, and converting HDR imagery. It is not an image-editing application and includes no paint tools. There are some applications available that allow for more powerful paint and editing operations similar to Photoshop's capabilities for use on HDR images. HDRIE and Photogenics are probably the most fully developed. HDRShop is more a specialized utility for conversion and includes simple procedures to manipulate an HDR image.

For example, HDRShop lets us perform various operations such as blurring, adjusting exposure, and converting into various image formats and layouts. One of the most useful of these is the ability to convert among various panoramic formats that contain 360 degrees of our scene.

For instance, to convert a spherical panorama to an angular light probe image, load a spherical image file (known as Latitude/Longitude in HDRShop), and then choose **Image** → **Panorama** → **Panoramic Transformations** to open the Panoramic Transform dialog box:

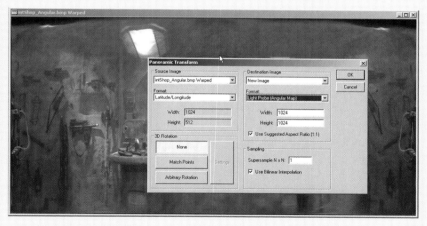

For the source image, set **Format** to Latitude/Longitude. This assumes a 360-degree image laid out as a rectangular image. For the destination image, set **Format** to Light Probe (Angular Map).

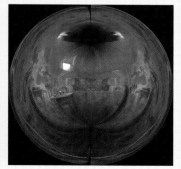

In plain and simple terms, the Fresnel Effect, shown in Figure 4.1, describes the natural phenomenon in which a surface becomes more reflective as it becomes more perpendicular to the line of sight. (Technically this is also tied to the index of refraction of a surface, but that's a whole other ball of wax we don't have to bother with often.) This line of sight is the *angle of incidence* (shown in Figure 4.2) and is described or measured from 0 degrees (facing the camera) to 90 degrees (perpendicular to the line of sight from the camera).

Using the Fresnel Effect

It's extremely important to take the Fresnel Effect into consideration when designing your reflective materials. For the most part, the important thing is to create a decent curve that determines how high the reflection value is at a particular angle from the sight line. We will use a ramp node in Maya to create the curve, and a Sampler Info node to determine the angle of incidence across the surface, as shown in Figure 4.2.

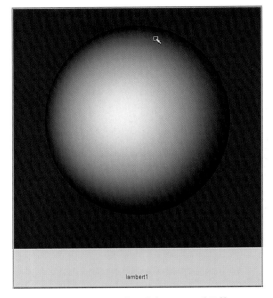

Figure 4.1: *An example of the Fresnel Effect*

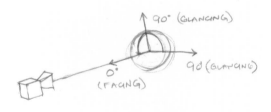

Figure 4.2: *A diagram of the angle of incidence*

1. Create a NURBS sphere, and apply a phongE material.
2. Set **Roughness** and **Highlight Size** down to 0. We want to get our specular reflections from the environment via reflections, not from faked Phong specularity.
3. Click the Texture icon for Reflected Color and choose **Environment Textures** → **Env Ball**.
4. Click the Texture icon for the **Image** attribute of the EnvBall as in Figure 4.3. On the CD, choose `Textures\HDR\brewerySKY_adjust.hdr`. This file is a homemade HDR, shot with a consumer-level digital camera. You'll find many tutorials on the Internet that show you how to create your own HDR images (See the Using HDRShop sidebar earlier in this chapter for more on HDR images). For a sample of such websites, see the "Resources" sidebar at the end of this chapter.
5. Render the scene for a good look. Be sure to select the Maya Software renderer. Because we are using an Environment Ball to map reflections through the shader, you do not need to enable raytracing to see the reflections. The render looks a bit bland and a little computery. This is where the Fresnel Effect comes into play.

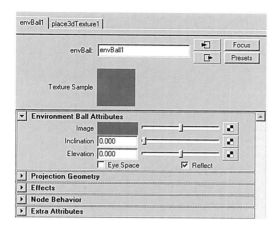

Figure 4.3: Attach Image Texture

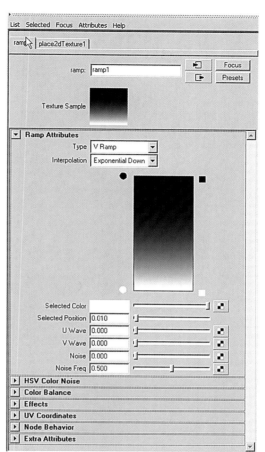

6. Click the Texture icon for **Reflectivity** in your Phong E shader, and add a ramp texture that has black at the top and white on the bottom as in Figure 4.4. Set the **Type** attribute to **V Ramp**, and set **Interpolation** to **Exponential Down**. This gives a reasonable approximation of a typical fresnel curve. For more precision, you'll need to track down the exact fresnel curve for your particular material, but most of the time, you'll just want to eyeball it for what looks best in your scene.

7. Create a Sampler Info node, and connect its Facing Ratio output to the V

Figure 4.4: Ramp Node is added to the Reflectivity to feather out the amount of reflection seen.

Coord input of your ramp. The Facing Ratio node will give us feedback on how the surface we're rendering is oriented to the angle of the camera's view. This way we can apply a Fresnel Effect.

8. It should now be clear what the Sampler Info is doing. The surface of the sphere that faces us directly will have no reflection, while reflection gets gradually more and more intense as it nears 90 degrees.

9. You can now tweak the ramp to get the settings you'd like. Don't be afraid to over-crank the values on the ramp. Click the white color swatch to open the Color Chooser, and then change the V value to 2 instead of 1. You'll see those reflections really scream!

This surface should now work nicely in just about any environment. This Fresnel reflection is also an important factor in creating realistic water.

Using the Fresnel Effect and Matte Surfaces

This technique can apply to matte surfaces as well. Even surfaces that aren't typically shiny exhibit Fresnel reflection. If you stand in the middle of a desert highway, you will notice that the road reflects the sky as it recedes into the distance. Don't stare too long, though; you might end up as roadkill.

Essentially you will need to blur the reflection to maintain the matte look; keep your ramp values low as well. HDRShop has filters to allow you to blur HDR imagery. I find it is much faster to do it this way rather than in Maya.

1. Replace brewerySky_adjust.hdr with BrewerySkyPano_BLUR.hdr, and lower your ramp values significantly. The bottom color value should be about 0.2, as shown in Figure 4.5. This creates a subtle sheen around the edge of the object that can contribute greatly to the realism in your scene.
2. Be sure to export this shader so that you can use it in other scenes without having to set it up from scratch.

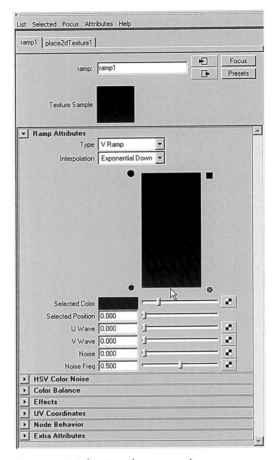

Figure 4.5: Adjusting the ramp values

Creating Reflection-Only Lighting

Now that you're more familiar with how reflections can benefit the look of an image, let's have a go at lighting with them. For a little treat, let's see what we can do to light a surface with just reflection—no lights, no radiosity, just a reflected environment. We've gone absolutely mad!

Automotive photography is frequently approached in just this way. It's often said that you don't ever light a car; you light what's *around* the car. Follow these steps to setup the scene.

1. Load SecurityShip.mb. This is an untextured model that has plenty of curves and a smooth, carlike surface.
2. Examine the materials that were already created for you. There are three shaders: a reflective painted material for the body of the ship, an even more reflective window material, and a matte material.
3. Notice there are no lights in the scene. Turn off **the Enable Default Light** attribute in the Render Options window to prevent any lights from being created for you when you render.

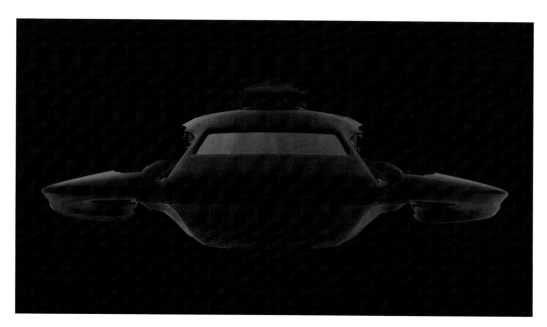

Figure 4.6: The spaceship lit with nothing but environment reflections

4. Render the scene using the Maya Software renderer. Notice how the reflections help to define the shapes; this is definitely enhanced by the Fresnel Effect, as you can see in Figure 4.6.

Now we want to get rid of the environment map since we're about to switch to true raytraced reflections to light our object. Follow these steps:

1. Open your shaders in the Hypershade window and delete the EnvironmentBall node and the nodes feeding into it. If you were to render now, you would see nothing but black.

2. Create a NURBS plane about 25% bigger than the spaceship and place it just above the model. Real-life photographers get the light as close to the model as physically possible without being seen by the camera. In Maya, we can just disable the **Primary Visibility** attribute in the Render Stats section of the Attribute Editor for the object.

3. Apply a surface shader to the plane, and click the swatch for its Out Color. Crank the V attribute up even higher than 1 to brighten the surface.

4. Choose **Anti-aliasing Quality** → **Quality,** and in the Render Global Settings section, select Production Quality. Enable raytracing and render.

You can add panels, with unique shaders, to fine-tune the look you want. If you want to block a certain area from receiving reflection, you can add a black-colored NURBS plane to block the reflecting light. For the example render, we duplicated the overhead light, applied a new surface shader, and made it quite a bit darker, with a slightly bluish tinge. We moved it down underneath the ship to reflect from below.

The renders in Figures 4.7 and 4.8 look really good with nice, slow camera moves or rotation of the subject, especially if several shots are dissolved over one another over time. Just like high-end car commercials, the reflections play over the hard glossy surfaces of the subject, giving smooth flow with nothing more than a simple camera move.

Figure 4.7: The spaceship lit With raytraced reflections

Figure 4.8: Another Example: droid lit with raytraced reflections

Ambient Occlusion

One of the characteristics of many radiosity renders is that areas which are slightly blocked from the light, such as the crease of an elbow, exhibit nice, soft shadowing from all directions. The more "hidden away" an area is, the less light it receives. This usually subtle shadowing is known as ambient occlusion (seen in Figure 4.9) and is one of the aesthetically stimulating characteristics of radiosity-based renderings.

To accomplish this effect, several third-party shaders, generally known as dirt or accessibility shaders, are available. They essentially calculate where ambient light can or can't reach a particular area of a surface.

You can apply this technique in production in two major ways: baking out ambient occlusion or using a separate ambient occlusion pass.

Baking Out Ambient Occlusion

Baking out the lighting brings out these subtle shadows into a file texture and multiplies the shader into the diffuse channel of the object, adding the slight shadowing effect to the shading of the surface directly. This greatly saves render time since it needs to be calculated only once. But the disadvantage is that you can't tweak the effect in the compositing stage to pull it back or make it more pronounced as if it were a separate render pass. This method can also be fairly labor intensive in Maya and requires carefully constructed UV maps to be effective.

> You can also easily duplicate this ambient occlusion effect using a light dome with an array of shadow-casting lights.

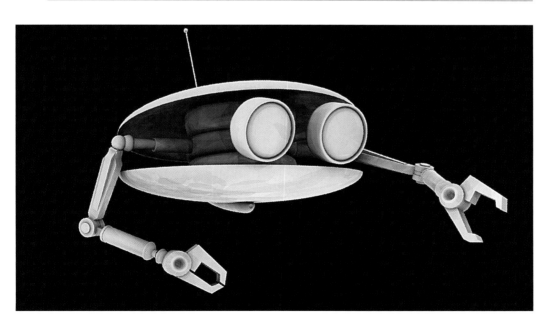

Figure 4.9: A sample of an ambient occlusion pass from the droid example later this chapter

In general, ambient occlusion doesn't change over time for hard-surfaced, inanimate objects. It is merely a representation of areas that are less accessible to light. In many cases, you can bake out ambient occlusion textures and later composite them into the various channels of your shaders (such as diffuse, reflectivity, and so on), while still allowing shadows and other components of your materials to react realistically with changing lighting conditions. This approach can save massive amounts of rendering time, without sacrificing visual quality.

What's intriguing is that this approach provides us with a method for getting a "radiosity look" without having to calculate global illumination on every frame. We can also use standard, fast-rendering lights to complete the scene, while still keeping those nice dark areas in our surface. This technique is popular in producing textures for real-time video-game models.

For characters and objects with broad animation, the changes in lighting can be distracting as certain areas block or shadow other areas. Consequently, when baking ambient occlusion textures for characters, it is wise to pose the character "wide open" so that there is as little blockage as possible when initially calculating the ambient occlusion solution.

Separate Ambient Occlusion Pass

Ambient occlusion can also be rendered as a separate element and combined with other render passes in the compositing stage. This allows for the best flexibility, but higher render times. It is wiser to begin here and then move on to baking ambient occlusion passes to the shaders themselves.

Using ambient occlusion as a separate render pass is often more popular in production, usually because breaking up a scene into separate elements for effective baking can be risky in a proven studio work flow and is often too labor intensive and complex to justify the rendering time it saves in the end. In addition, the loss of flexibility in the compositing stage can sometimes be crippling and not worth the risk.

A Practical Approach—the Droid

For a quick venture into ambient occlusion, we'll render a CGI robot droid in several passes and composite them back together in Phostoshop to show the flexibility of ambient occlusion as well as rendering in layers for different lighting passes. Follow these steps:

1. Open `Droid_Setup.mb`, as shown in Figure 4.10. Cute, huh?

   This scene is already set up with mental ray for Maya rendering, and several raytraced spotlights are arranged in a basic three-point lighting rig. Notice that there is little or no ambient light in the scene. We're going to add that light back in during the compositing phase.

2. Render Camera1 and save the resulting image as `Droid_Beauty.tif`. This is our beauty pass (seen in Figure 4.11).

3. Disable Emit Specular for each of the three lights, and render. Save the image as `Droid_Diffuse.tif`, our diffuse pass (shown in Figure 4.12).

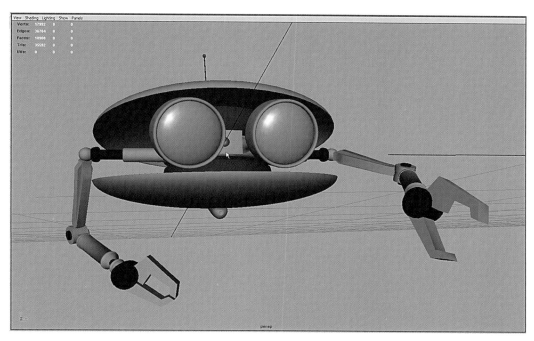

Figure 4.10: The droid open GL view

Figure 4.11: The droid beauty pass

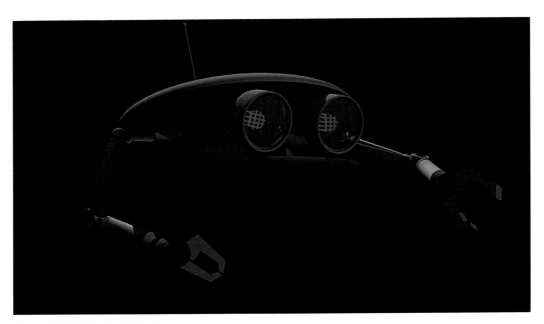

Figure 4.12: The droid diffuse pass

You can use render passes to render out elements of the scene such as beauty passes, specular passes, and so on, but by selecting how each light emits individually (i.e., specular, diffuse, etc.), you gain implicit control of your lights and bypass any weirdnesses that can sometimes occur with render passes and mental ray rendering.

4. Reenable Emit Specular, and disable Emit Diffuse. Render, and save the image as `Droid_Specular.tif`, our specular pass (shown in Figure 4.13).
5. Disable Emit Specular and Emit Diffuse for all the lights. Create a new ambient light. Set **Color** to pure white, **Intensity** to 1, and **Ambient Shade** to 0.00.
6. Choose **Render Global Settings** → **Mental Ray** → **Raytracing**, and then disable raytracing. Render. This generates a raw color pass seen in Figure 4.14.

The robot's incandescent eyes will be bright in all these passes. If this creates problems, you can temporarily darken them in the diffuse and beauty passes.

7. Assign a new Lambert material to the entire droid. Set the color of the Lambert material to white, and set **Diffuse** to 1.0.
8. Delete or disable the ambient light created for the raw color pass.
9. Import the file `lightDome.mb` from the CD. Select just the newly imported lights (Figure 4.15). (There should be 92.)

Figure 4.13: The droid specular pass

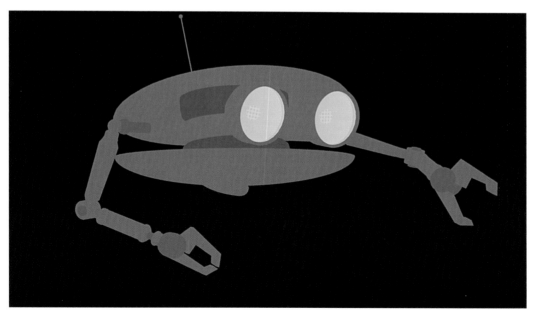

Figure 4.14: The droid raw (ambient) color pass

Figure 4.15:
The imported
light dome

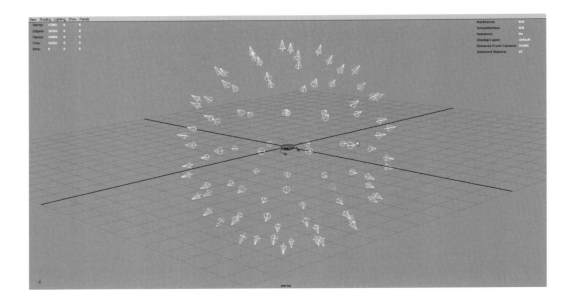

Figure 4.16: The
droid ambient
occlusion pass

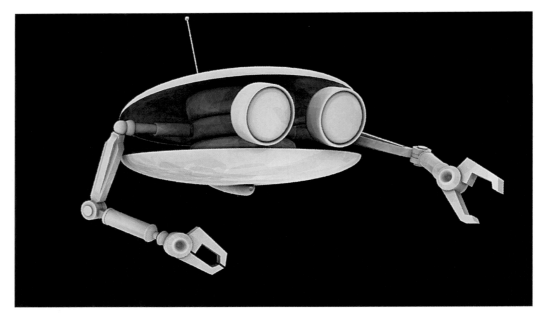

10. Hide the Attribute Editor (press Ctrl+A). In the Channel Editor, you can now make changes to all selected lights at the same time. In the Intensity section, enter the total desired light intensity (let's start with 1.0) divided by the total number of lights (92), which equals 0.011.

11. Turn raytracing back on.

12. Render the ambient occlusion pass (shown in Figure 4.16).

13. Since Maya lights are additive, the dome of lights adds up to a lot more light than you might think. However, the render may still be a bit dark. With all the lights selected, adjust the intensity in the Channel box (to make sure all the light intensities are changed) until the brightest parts of the model are close to pure white.

You might notice that broad smooth areas have artifacts caused by overlapping shadows from the array of spotlights. For most situations, the artifacting is probably acceptable. You can decrease the artifacting by creating a light dome with more lights, you can experiment with shadow softness settings for the lights, or you can switch to depth-mapped shadows, although I find them harder to control, and they eat up tons of memory with so many lights. You can also generate the ambient occlusion pass via Final Gathering without too much additional rendering overhead. Final Gathering is discussed in greater detail later in this chapter.

Compositing the Passes

We can now use the rendered frame(s) from this scene to supplement the ambient or diffusion pass in our compositing package of choice. The difference is primarily in how the layer is combined with other rendering passes. For our purposes, we just want to use it as a way to darken the less-accessible areas of our model. In Photoshop or After Effects, we multiply or overlay this layer over our full RGB render and adjust the opacity of the layer until we're satisfied (see Figure 4.17). In other packages, such as Shake, which take a more strictly mathematical approach to compositing, we will multiply and add together a number of layers to achieve our desired effect (see Figure 4.18).

Whether rendering sequences or baking out an ambient occlusion texture, remember that you can use many techniques to generate the desired result. Final Gathering, Global

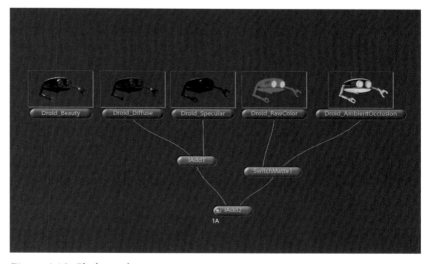

Figure 4.17: Photoshop layers   *Figure 4.18: Shake nodes*

Figure 4.19: The Final Gathering result of the droid rendered and composited with the ambient occlusion pass

Illumination, and similar soft and even lighting techniques can provide varying levels of quality versus speed in generating the ambient occlusion pass; you don't need the extensive light dome. Experiment to see what you can generate with a much faster Final Gathering render for your ambient occlusion pass. Figure 4.19 shows you the final composited Droid with all his lighting passes.

Illuminating Global Illumination

A sphere or plane (or any other surface for the matter) with a self-illuminated (incandescent) surface shader and/or an LDR or HDR file texture is used to create a single lighting scheme similar to a light dome. This scheme evenly lights a scene and creates natural soft shadows on the CG elements. Using a single color on the incandescence of the sphere creates a simple one-color light and is often used for evenly lighting models. The Final Gathering render bounces the light (though only once) off nearby surfaces for a more natural lighting effect. Modelers can use Final Gathering to quickly create soft light and natural shadows to show off their models in even lighting and be assured the model is showcased for its merits right off the bat.

Using an image on the sphere's incandescence creates effective nuances to properly light CG into a particular background. This is perhaps one of the simplest ways to create IBL and is great for quickly adding color and proper values to work CG into a live-action plate. Even when no live-action is required, carefully placing color and brightness in the mapped image can easily enhance the composition and the look of the CG.

Once you create the sphere and map your lighting image, simply turn of Primary Visibility in the object's Attribute Editor so it does not render out. It will then just act as the lighting for the shot.

Fortunately, in Maya 6, you can easily create an IBL node through mental ray. This in essence creates a sphere for you and maps whatever image you choose to it to create the lighting. And since the renderer creates it for you, you need not create a shader and manually map the image or turn off Primary Visibility to exclude it from the rendered image as you would without Maya 6 and mental ray.

Later in this chapter, you'll find a step-by-step example of how to use a Final Gathering lighting solution.

What Global Illumination Means

Photon-based Global Illumination, or GI, takes the theory of Final Gathering another a step further by creating a much more realistic light effect. It creates light rays (photons, actually) that bounce on multiple surfaces to create a natural bounce light in the scene. Whereas Final Gathering is a quick, even lighting solution, GI gives you much more control over the detail and amount of realism, though frequently at the expense of render time.

The big benefit to GI, of course, is that the light in the scene reacts to objects and bounces to reflect light to approximate lighting in reality. It is a bit of an effort to optimize a scene for the best setting for GI lighting; balancing the right settings and values is a highly iterative process, and the more complex your scene, the longer the renders.

Effective GI is obviously more painstaking to set up than a simple Final Gathering render. It is important to manually specify which lights and objects contribute to and/or receive the GI solution through their respective Attribute Editors. Although this may seem like a lot of work as opposed to enabling GI for everything in the scene, the amount of control it provides is invaluable for balancing render times against final render results, and that is half the battle of a production.

Final Gathering (with or without HDR Image-based Lighting) works well for lighting individual subjects that need to be integrated into a scene or for adding an extra level of polish on a GI rendering. But for more complex scene requirements, GI is indispensable. Its photon tracing allows much greater flexibility and fidelity than Final Gathering since Final Gathering allows for only one bounce in an effort to streamline the rendering process. With GI, the sky is the limit. Or at least your rendering schedule is.

Global Illumination is a term that commonly encompasses all types of radiosity rendering; however, mental ray GI is specifically related to tracing the effects of photons as they bounce from surface to surface in a scene. The overwhelming number of tweakable GI parameters can make or break your image and save or cost you truckloads of render time. As you become more familiar with this and other radiosity techniques, you will begin to develop instincts that help you make educated guesses and estimates that will greatly reduce the amount of time you spend developing efficient GI solutions. But as you learn more about this advanced lighting technique, experimentation is key. And since GI settings can be so specific to the requirements of the scene, it's difficult to hammer out a list that will work on more than a few occasions, let alone as guidelines for all scenes.

Practicing Practical Global Illumination

We can demonstrate a few rules of thumb, but be aware that GI is a science of guesswork. Try to organize your experiments so that you can predict the results of your tweaks; concentrate on one step at a time so you can measure your progress. Don't change the color of a shader just when you are honing in on an important GI parameter. Common sense, but it bears repeating.

As a quick test of this process, follow these steps:

1. Import SecurityShip.mb.
2. Create a polygon box big enough to serve as a hangar for the ship, like the one in Figure 4.20. Use a Boolean to hollow out a space inside it. Using Booleans again, cut a large door opening in the side of the box, just even with the "floor." Apply a Lambert shader with a cheery, bluish-gray concrete texture. This light box, so to speak, will be used to bounce around the GI photons that will essentially light the scene. Add some details inside to break up the light—some rafters, a couple of barricades, a frame for the door.
3. Park the ship in this new box as shown in Figure 4.21.
4. Create a single directional light to act as sunlight, and enable raytraced shadows. Make it a warmish-yellow color and set its intensity rather high, to 3 or 4. Rotate the light so that it points almost straight down, and then angle it so it points just into the door opening. Figure 4.22 shows us the lighting setup.
5. Render the scene with mental ray with raytracing enabled. If **Mental Ray** does not appear as a choice in the **Render Using** menu, you will need to enable the Mental Ray plug-in (see the sidebar called Enabling mental ray for Maya later in this chapter for directions on how to turn on mental ray). The interior of the "garage" should be black,

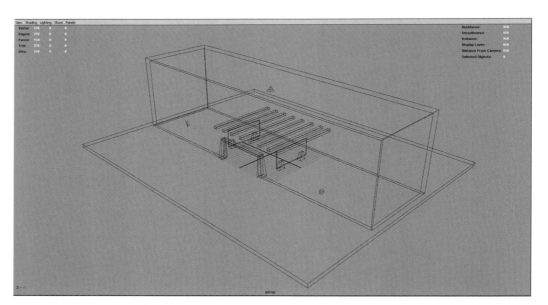

Figure 4.20: A quick-and-easy polygon hangar

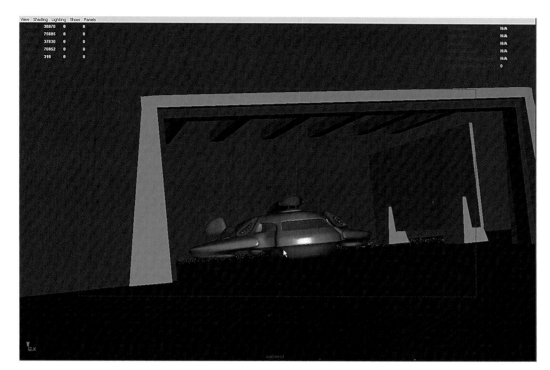

Figure 4.21: The ship in the hangar in the Maya view panel

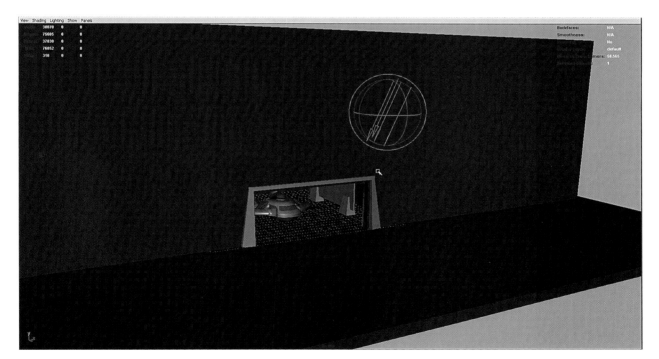

Figure 4.22: The lighting setup in the view panel

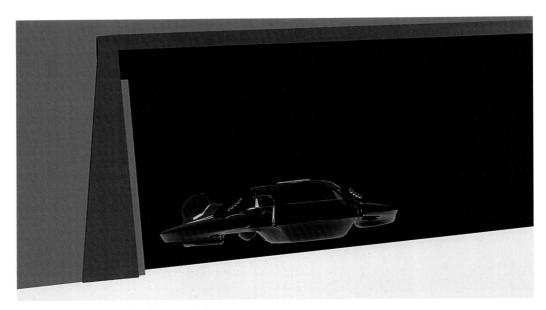

Figure 4.23: Overcranked distant light

and the outside surfaces that are exposed to the sunlight will be overexposed (see Figure 4.23). The ship itself will not be directly affected by the light, but will start to reflect the parts of the environment that are lit.

6. Choose **Render Global Settings** → **Mental Ray** → **Quality Presets**, and then choose **PreviewGlobalIllum**.

7. Change the intensity of our distant light to the default 1.0. Under the mental ray attributes of the distant light, check **Emit Photons**.

Since these settings are closely related to the complex physics that control light in the real world, the results can often seem unpredictable compared with the simple, linear solutions we're used to in many CGI rendering solutions. The most efficient settings are often difficult to find. The best strategy is usually to research as much as possible to understand the inner workings behind mental ray and its GI or at least follow several tutorials until the methods for tweaking the renders become clearer. The mental ray for Maya documentation can be sketchy and cryptic, but many resources are available, both in print and on the Web, that you can use to increase your knowledge of these techniques. Find settings that work for you, and keep them close at hand.

---

8. If you render now, the scene will look like nuclear winter. When tweaking the settings for light, Photon Intensity sets the overall brightness or energy, and Exponent seems to handle how quickly that energy dissipates as it travels through the scene. Higher settings dissipate the energy more quickly; so if your scene ends up way too bright, try adjusting Exponent to a higher number and/or Intensity to a lower number.

Notice the overlapping circles, similar to the artifacting in the ambient occlusion pass for the droid earlier. These represent the photons being fired into the scene. Our task now is

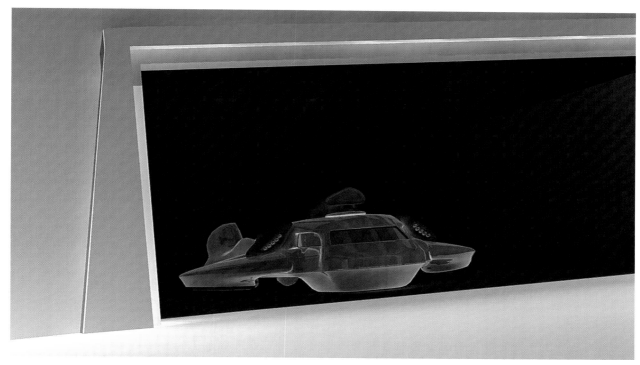

Figure 4.24: Spaceship rendered with Global Illumination and Final Gathering enabled

to find the right balance among several parameters: number of photons, photon accuracy, photon intensity, and exponent setting for our main light.

9. Change Exponent to 2.65 and Photon Intensity to 700. Increase the number of photons to 100000.

10. Choose **Render Global Settings** → **Mental Ray** → **Caustics and Global Illumination,** set **Global Illum Accuracy** to 128, and **Global Illum Radius** to 2.0. The accuracy increases computation time, but results in—guess what?—more accurate distribution. The radius blends individual photons so that there is less artifacting. A well-researched tutorial is available on the Alias website that analyzes these setting in detail.

11. Render again. We're getting there, but a lot of artifacting remains. Not to worry— we're going to take care of most of that with Final Gathering.

12. Choose **Render Global Settings** → **Mental Ray** → **Final Gathering,** and enable Final Gathering. Set **Final Gathering Rays** to 500. Leave the rest of the settings at their defaults. Again, as you become more familiar with the options, you can tweak these settings to balance quality and speed. Figure 4.24 shows the rendered image with Global Illumination and Final Gathering turned on.

You should be able to see how Final Gathering smoothes out the GI photon solution nicely.

This example is still fairly high in contrast, to illustrate the use of a single light in a GI solution. It would obviously benefit greatly from some ambient light spilling in from outside.

Later in the chapter, we'll look at how to use HDR imagery to contribute to the Final Gathering solution.

You might also want to add a light or two inside the hangar to illuminate the back wall or continue playing with the photon attributes of the daylight. Or you might even want to add some Boolean skylights into the roof of the hangar to let some more light in. And, of course, the textures could really use some TLC.

An IBL Real-World Application: Katana

This short exercise uses HDR imagery and mental ray's Final Gathering to quickly create a GI setup to light a Japanese katana sword. We are looking for dramatic, high-contrast lighting for a film production company logo. We will render to a floating-point format to provide the necessary range for creating intense glows and sheens in the compositing process.

You'll need to set up a few things to enable the advanced IBL features in Maya, such as mental ray rendering. Here is checklist to complete before you continuing. Some of these features have been touched on in the earlier exercises. Familiarity with these settings will also be essential as we tackle more complex production situations later in this chapter.

Enabling mental ray for Maya

To use mental ray for Maya, you will need to enable mental ray plug-in if it isn't already. Follow these steps:

1. Choose **Window** → **Settings/Preferences** → **Plug-in Manager**.
2. Check both Loaded and Auto Load for `Mayatomr.mll`.
3. Choose **Window** → **Rendering Editors** → **Render Globals, and then choose** Mental Ray from the Render Using drop-down menu.

Maya's Software renderer does not support the IBL techniques we're discussing, so you will need to use mental ray for your renders.

4. Choose **Common** → **Resolution** → **Presets**, and then choose CCIR 601/Quantel NTSC. This is the standard 720 × 486 D1 broadcast video resolution. You will change this as appropriate for your project, but for the most part, this will be our standard setting for this chapter.
5. Choose **Common** → **Render Options**, and then uncheck Enable Default Light. This prevents Maya from creating its default light in a scene that is being rendered with IBL only.

1. Make sure your render settings are configured properly in the Render Global Settings dialog box, as shown in Figure 4.25. For reference, see the "Enabling mental ray for Maya" sidebar.

2. In the **Quality Presets** drop-down list, select PreviewFinalGather. This enables raytracing and Final Gathering and provides a good starting point for tuning the render (see Figure 4.26). Notice that it also enables the default GI settings, which assist Final Gathering in solving the lighting for the scene. You can often disable GI to speed things up a little bit.

3. In the Final Gather section, set Min Radius to 1.000 and Max Radius to 10.000, as in Figure 4.27. A good general rule of thumb is to set Max Radius to (10% of) the radius of your scene's size (or at least the focal point of the scene) and to set Min Radius to 10% of the Max Radius. If you leave the values at zero, mental ray calculates these values automatically. For simple scenes, this is usually sufficient.

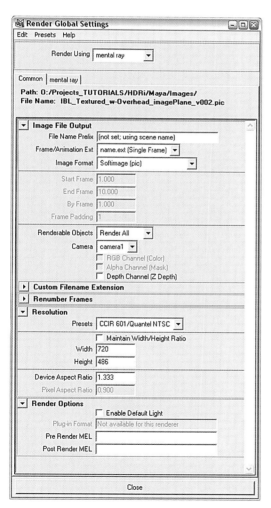

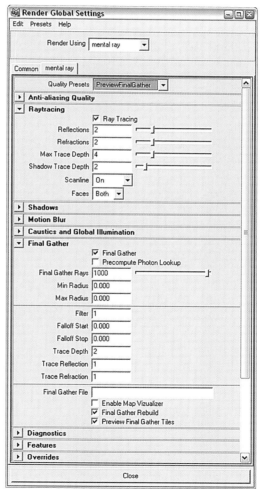

Figure 4.25: Configuring the proper settings in the Render Global Settings dialog box

Figure 4.26: Establishing the correct mental ray settings

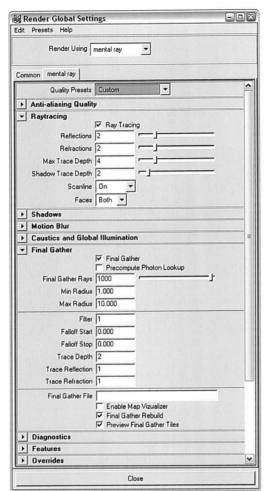

Figure 4.27: Sample Final Gathering settings

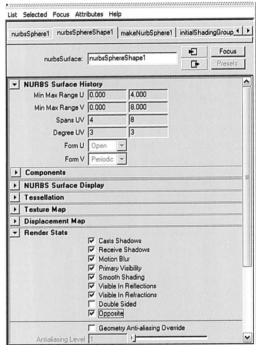

Figure 4.28: Flip the sphere's render direction.

Once you're set up, you can import the model file and begin lighting the scene:

1. Follow the previous steps 1 through 3.

2. Import into your current blank scene the scenes\katana.mb file from the CD. Make sure the file is imported rather than just opened to ensure that the mental ray settings we've just finished stay put.

3. Create a NURBs sphere large enough to surround the katana (3 units should be fine, although if you want to animate the sword, the sphere should be scaled up to completely contain all the movement). This will be the base for our IBL lighting setup.

4. In the Render Stats section in the Attribute Editor for the sphere, disable (uncheck) **Double Sided**, and enable **Opposite** as shown in Figure 4.28. This makes the sphere face inward.

5. In the Render Stats section, uncheck **Primary Visibility** to turn off rendering for this object.

6. Apply a Surface Shader material to the sphere.

7. Assign a file texture to the Out Color of the Surface Shader. This image should be what you'd like to light the katana with, that is, the environment of the katana. You can use the file `hicon_spherical.hdr` (on the CD) as the texture shown in Figure 4.29. This HDRI file will give you a good range of levels to light the katana with, though you can use your own images, of course.

8. In the File Texture Attributes pane, under Color Balance, click the color swatch next to Color Gain. In the Color Chooser, set the **V** value to 3 to help control the level of lighting you'll get from the image.

9. Under the place2Dtexture node for the file texture we just added, set Rotate UV to 90 to orient the image properly on the sphere.

Now make sure you are looking through the camera that was imported with the scene, or create one of your own. It is best to render through a camera rather than just through a perspective viewport when using mental ray. Many additional controls might come in handy as you further explore more of the advanced rendering features of mental ray.

10. Open the Render Globals panel (choose **Window** → **Rendering Editors** → **Render Globals**). Select **Mental Ray** from the **Render Using** menu.

Figure 4.29: The `hicon_spherical.hdr` *file*

Rendering Out in HDR

If you need to render out an HDR image, you can do so through mental ray. In the Render Globals window's Common tab, make sure that under the **Image File Output section, the Image Format** is set to "HDR". And the renderer will write out an HDRI file for you to play with in HDRShop.

However, to ensure that all the information is passed to the floating-point HDR file, go to the mental ray tab in the Render Globals and under the **Framebuffer Attributes section, set the Data Type** to "RGBA (Float) 4 x 32 Bit". This ensures that you are including all the color channels (RGB) as well as the alpha channel (A), that you are using the full floating-point range (Float), and that each of these channels is represented by a full 32-bit channel. If you were to render for opening in Photoshop or After Effects or another application that only supports 16 bits per channel, you would need to choose RGBA (Short) 4 x 16 Bit, but for full-float HDR images, you will need to set this properly to output 32 bits.

11. Render.

If your renders are coming out black for the katana, make sure that Final Gathering is enabled, that you are rendering with mental ray, and that your IBL dome light has an image mapped to it.

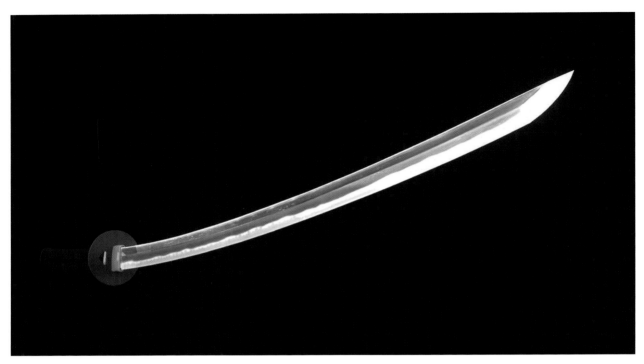

Figure 4.30:
The katana
HDR render

12. Adjust the color gain on the sphere surface shader as necessary to get a nice look, and check a newly rendered image. If things are too blown out, set the value of the color to a number lower than 1 If the scene is mostly black, try setting the **Value** attribute much higher than 1 by just entering the values, since the Value Slider stops at 1. (To change the value of a color, click the color swatch that opens Maya's Color Chooser. The value, or brightness, is controlled by the V field in the Color Chooser). Figure 4.30 shows an HDR render of the katana.

13. Experiment with textures for the sphere for different effects. You can use something funky such as an image sequence of a fire perhaps or an animated procedural texture such as fractal noise. Play with choosing **Color Balance** → **Color Gain as discussed earlier** to adjust the brightness of the render. You can add more geometry into the scene to block or supplement the Final Gathering light from the NURBS sphere. In Figures 4.31 and 4.32, the cylinder has had polygons removed from the ends and the bottom, blocking the light from all other directions. The plane serves to darken a portion of the blade.

Don't forget to disable Primary Visibility for the additional geometry. This ensures that the objects contribute to the scene lighting but won't appear in the final render.

The katana represents one of the biggest uses of HDRI techniques, metal. Since metal is a highly reflective surface (usually) and is greatly affected by its environment, using IBL is a fantastic way to light your metal surfaces. You can experiment with placing the katana in several environments and play with the images used in the IBL.

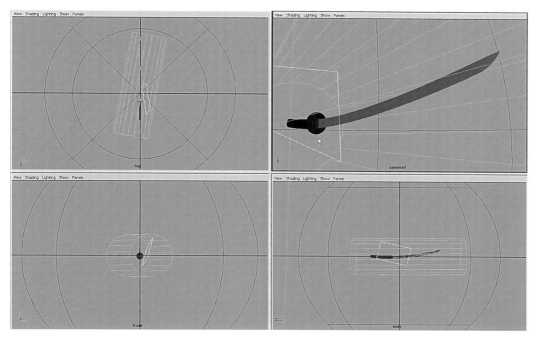

Figure 4.31: The katana fire in the Maya panel

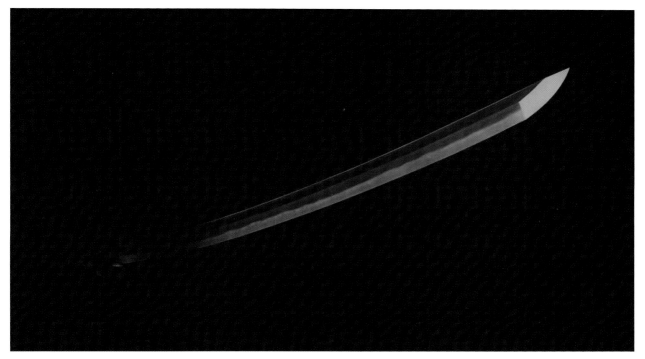

Figure 4.32: The katana fire render

Real-World Application: Research Lab

This exercise concentrates on using mental ray's IBL with Final Gathering to create realistic CGI elements for integration into a live-action plate for an independent short film.

Since this tutorial focuses on IBL and rendering solutions, we won't discuss the other aspects of the scene except as they relate to lighting and texturing nodes specific to IBL and Final Gathering.

Right, then, off we go.

The first step in approaching any lighting problem is to decide specifically on the desired final effect. We should analyze the existing assets and make sure that we can achieve all our objectives with the tools at hand.

For instance, in this shot, we want to ensure that our props and character integrate into the scene properly. We need to do the following:

- Maintain the mostly monochromatic color palette established by the art director.
- Create visual separation between our "featured" elements and the background. This is accomplished through lighting, fogging, depth of field, backlighting, and so on. In general, elements that are lighter, sharper, and/or more saturated tend to stand out from darker, softer, and/or more subdued backgrounds. Visual separation can also be supplemented by a strong backlight, a popular technique in film and television lighting.
- Generate the proper render passes to tweak the final look in the composite.

Art directors often intentionally design costumes and props that are used by the main characters to stand out from the background. The end result ranges from subtle to extreme—depending on the needs of the scene. It is helpful to keep these design decisions in mind when creating your CGI elements. Work as closely as possible with the art director to determine whether an individual element is meant to blend with or stand out from the rest of the scene.

We want to start with CGI elements that match the way the real-life set was decorated. When we add additional lighting cues, everything should blend nicely.

Always remember when working on commercial and special-effects projects that the lighting you are matching was specifically designed for the needs of the shot and that it is often not "realistic" in the strictest sense of the word. For instance, a person sitting next to a small table lamp that is visible in the shot appears to be lit by that lamp. In all likelihood, however, the lighting on the actor's face is probably coming from a separate spotlight just out of view that has the brightness necessary to properly expose the actor's face, while still appearing to originate from the practical lighting fixture.

HDR versus LDR

HDRI would definitely help in this case as it could represent all the light sources in the scene if the HDRI had been generated on the set under the same lighting conditions of the shot.

However, in this example, since there were no HDR images generated on the set, we will be using LDR imagery pulled straight from the background plate to provide overall ambient lighting. We will supplement the ambient lighting with a NURBS plane to match the bright overhead light source. In these cases especially, it's best to have a good indication of the lighting conditions on the set. To this end, it's a great idea to take a lighting pass when you shoot your scene using a gray sphere and ideally a second chrome sphere using the same camera as was used to shoot the scene.

For example, if you shoot a simple digital video scene with an off-the-shelf digital video camera, after the scene is shot and the director is happy with the take, shoot a few seconds of a gray sphere and then a chrome sphere in the scene to show you later, once the footage is digitized, what the lighting looked like on the set. You can gauge easily the primary lighting locations and even, with the chrome ball, specify the exact light locations behind the camera.

An HDR image can prove critical to the success of a car shot or a product shot, as it preserves the relative intensity of bright light sources so they reflect properly on the subject. However, our scene contains few reflective elements. Therefore, the LDR image, pulled directly from the filmed footage, is adequate for our needs. In many or most motion picture settings, shiny and reflective elements are carefully avoided or treated with dulling spray as they tend to be difficult to control. You can see this by analyzing just about any still frame from a major motion picture. Obvious exceptions are specific items, such as a mirror or a shiny murder weapon, that would be crucial to the storytelling. These items are usually filmed under specialized lighting schemes to carefully control their appearance on screen.

We will assume that additional shadows and final color correction will occur in the compositing phase, which is beyond the scope of this chapter.

Lighting CGI Props

The lighting setup will consist of three lighting nodes:

- A spotlight, with its intensity turned down to 0, to prevent Maya from using a default light. In many cases, you want to use Maya lights to replicate specific lights within the environment; these can often produce sharper shadows than provided by the IBL solution alone. A raytraced distant light is often used for direct sunlight in exterior daylight scenes.
- A mental ray IBL node. This creates the subtle ambient-colored lighting with soft shadows that tie our element into the live-action plate.
- A NURBS plane with a Surface Shader to illuminate the scene via Final Gathering.

To start the scene off right, follow these steps:

1. Starting with a fresh new scene (choose **File** → **New Scene**), enable the mental ray render settings outlined earlier.
2. Import the file Scenes\Props\TurboProp_TXTR.mb from the CD (choose **File** → **Import**). This scene contains the CGI prop (a simple turboprop bypass valve) that we want to integrate into the scene, a camera, and an image plane with the background from the shot into which we want to merge the prop. The camera angle has already been matched to the background plate. We will be concentrating only on the lighting.

It is important to include the background plate as we do our test renders, so that we can get an idea of how our lighting is progressing. When we get ready to do our final render, we will turn off the image plane so that we can get a clean matte to use in our composite.

3. Open the Render Global Settings window, and click the Mental Ray tab. In the Image-based Lighting section, click Create to create a mentalrayIBLShape node (see Figure 4.33).

IBL Settings

Next, we will need to set up the IBL parameters for our scene. Follow these steps:

1. Open the Attributes panel for the IBL Shape node if it isn't open already. (With IBL Shape selected, press Ctrl+A.)

2. Click the folder icon to the right of the Image Name field. Load `Textures\LDR\int-Shop_Angular.bmp`. This can be either an HDR or an LDR image. In this case, it is an LDR image that has been edited in Photoshop to fabricate an approximation of a panorama of the set. We then processed it in HDRShop to create an Image Probe or angular image. This is the type of image that can be most readily obtained by shooting a highly reflective sphere—the simplest way to create an HDR image. (See the HDRShop sidebar earlier in the chapter.)

3. In the Attribute Editor for the IBL node, change the **Mapping** to Angular as shown in Figure 4.34. Angular is for using the Light Probe image layout, popular for its ease of use and compact size. This image layout takes a panoramic shot and condenses it into an image that looks as if the contents of the picture are reflected in a chrome sphere. HDRShop readily converts among the most popular panoramic layouts.

4. If you have Hardware Texturing and Smooth Shading on, you should now be able to see the IBL shape in the viewport. Verify that the newly imported image is correctly oriented.

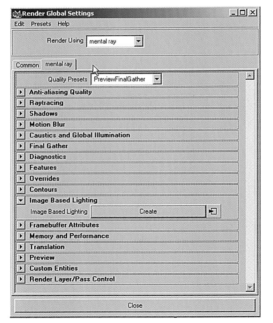

Figure 4.33: Creating IBL

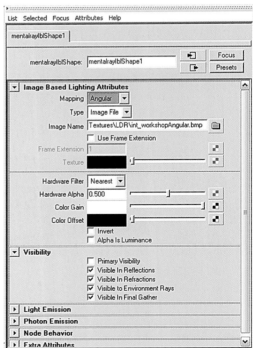

Figure 4.34: IBL attributes

5. In the Visibility section in the IBL Attributes dialog box, turn off Primary Visibility, but leave the other options checked. This will ensure that the IBL shape itself doesn't appear in the final render, but contributes to reflections and Final Gathering rendering.

6. Render! There will be two passes during the rendering—one to calculate the Final Gathering solution, and a second to complete the render. The screen may go blank, but the render should finish in a minute or two.

The camera need not be inside the sphere in this case, as the sphere we've created for IBL has its Primary Visibility turned off.

The render will most likely be a bit dark like Figure 4.35, so we will have to tweak our settings to find the right balance.

7. In the Image-based Lighting Attributes section, click the color swatch next to **Color Gain**, as shown in Figure 4.34. You can now enter values for the colors.

8. Change the **V** attribute to 4 similar to Figure 4.36. You can crank this value up high if necessary—don't be stifled when the sliders only go to 1. Figure 4.36.

Cranking the brightness (**V**) of the color well above the default maximum of 1.0 is a key concept in all forms of GI. This kind of adjustment is possible for many attributes that were previously limited to a finite range of 0 to1 or sometimes –1 to 1.

Figure 4.35: This render is too dark.

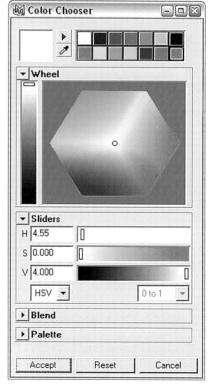

Figure 4.36: The Color Chooser

Floating-Point Images

To simulate the wide range of values in the real world, mental ray processes all scene elements internally as floating-point values. Material attributes, light attributes, camera attributes, and volumetrics can all take advantage of this extended range. At the last stage of rendering each frame, mental ray intelligently maps the floating-point values to the 8-bit range viewable on our monitors. We can choose to save to a floating-point format before the remapping occurs, however, which can provide additional flexibility later in the compositing phase.

In the early days, most 3D rendering engines were limited to processing information as a maximum of 8 bits per RGB channel. This always presented a big challenge in creating photo-realistic graphics. It is only in the past several years that the industry has begun to break out of that cage. As technical and artistic progression surges forward, fueled by the rapid exchange of information via the Internet, we are introduced to new techniques, solutions, and workarounds that move the art form forward at a mind-numbing pace. Thankfully, the software gurus have been right there in the thick of it, providing ever greater artistic and technical tools, while all the time making them easier to use.

The additional computing power offered by today's personal computers is also bringing us closer to the ability to simulate real-world photographic attributes in our renders. This is exciting because it presents a unique opportunity to learn from real-world photographers and cinematographers. We can now begin to speak a common language concerning key-to-fill ratios, true specularity, depth of field, shadow density, and shadow edge transfer. Developments such as Final Gathering gives us easy-to-use tools for simulating real-world setups, such as large studio softboxes and nature's ultimate softbox—earth's atmosphere

By far, the key component in all this innovation is the ability to generate high-contrast ranges that can more accurately simulate the conditions on location and in the studio.

9. Render!

10. Better. We can see how Final Gathering is using the information from the image to color and light our object—without any standard Maya lights. But it's still a little bland—too evenly lit. We need more drama, more variation.

Adding More Lighting

Instead of relying completely on IBL, we're going to let the IBL handle our ambient/fill light, but use another Final Gathering trick to bring some hotter, more directional lighting into play.

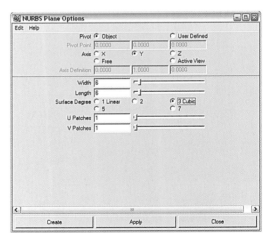

1. Create a NURBS plane, with width 6 and length ratio 6 as in Figure 4.37. Rename it overheadLight_NURBS. In the Attribute Editor in the Render Stats section, uncheck Primary Visibility, as shown in Figure 4.38.

2. Move the plane several units above and slightly to the left of the prop. This is where instinct comes into play. To

Figure 4.37: A NURBS plane for additional Final Gathering lighting

match the light to where it would likely have been on the set, use the image sequence and your knowledge of the set to determine.

3. Rotate the plane to point more or less at the prop. You can tweak the rotation as you experiment further.

4. Create a new Surface Shader material and apply it to the NURBS plane. Set Out Color to White. But wait! Before you leave the Color Chooser, crank the V value up to 20.

5. Temporarily turn off the IBL node by opening its Attribute Editor and unchecking Visible in Final Gather in the Visibility section, as shown in Figure 4.38. This is so we can see only the lighting from the ceiling light in the render while we adjust it.

6. Render! Pretty good but really bright, as you can see in Figure 4.39. A lot of the surfaces facing the light are completely white and have lost all shading and texture detail.

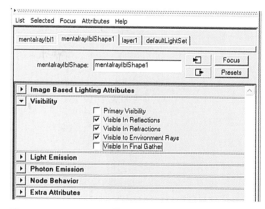

Figure 4.38: Turn off Primary Visibility

Figure 4.39: This render is too bright.

Virtual Softbox

Using a plane with a bright texture applied to it is a great example of how to create a virtual softbox, mentioned several times throughout this chapter. In real life, the softbox is a rigid or flexible box attached to a light fixture, with special diffusion fabric stretched over the opening. The box blocks any light from spilling out, while the diffusion material scatters the light so it creates much softer shadows than a typical Fresnel spotlight, as well a larger more intense reflection on the surface of the subject being photographed.

Final Gathering takes into account the direction the plane is pointing to throw light into the scene. The most easily accessible way to control the intensity is by adjusting the color gain of the Surface Shader material. (Other material types can be used as necessary. The **Incandescence** or **Ambience** attributes are the most likely to contribute significantly to the Final Gathering solution.)

Maya's area lights can achieve similar shadows without Final Gathering, but the really cool thing here is that the NURBS plane will show up in reflections, thereby duplicating the true specular reflection of a real-life light source and also contributing to the scene lighting!

7. Select ceiling light's surface shader again, click the Out Color swatch again, and lower the **V** value to 12.

8. Reselect the mentalrayIBLshape node, recheck the Visible in Final Gather attribute, and click the Color Gain swatch. Change the **V** value to 1, just enough to provide some nice colored fill light for our scene.

9. Render. We should be getting a lot closer to the final look, shown in Figure 4.40.

From this point on, the trick is to reach a lighting balance that provides the most flexibility for compositing into your background plate. This generally takes a bit of trial and error and is going to be subjective. Typically, further blending, blurring, and color adjustment in the compositing stage provide that extra touch to really make the prop feel integrated.

A great way to gain more flexibility is to render to a floating-point format such as Maya .iff, .hdr, or OpenEXR. This type of render preserves the maximum amount of information possible from mental ray's internal buffers so that you can make creative adjustments in the compositing phase to get the final look you want. The specific format you choose depends entirely on the compositing package you use; certain compositors are limited to a select few image formats. In order to send the right information to the file, you must go into the Render Globals' mental ray tab and change the **Framebuffer Attributes** to a floating-point setting (for example, RGBA (Float) 4 x 32 Bit) to send the proper information to the final rendered image file.

All things considered, ILM's OpenEXR image file format probably has the most promising future as the de facto standard, but is not yet supported in all applications. See www. openexr.org for details and supported applications.

Figure 4.40: The final render

Additional Things to Try

Here are some other things to try to add more flexibility to the process.

- Instead of using the standard **Image Name** attribute, connect an image (or other texture) via the Color input of the IBL node so that you can adjust the image using standard Maya utility nodes such as Gamma and Curves. (You'll find the IBL node in the Lights tab in the Hypershade section.)
- HDR textures can be mapped to other geometry as well for more control over the shape of Final Gathering light sources. Instead of the IBL node, apply a Surface Shader to the geometry, with an HDR file texture applied to the Out Color of the Surface Shader.
- Create a shelf with a Front Projection texture (camera projection?) to add additional color and shadows to the element.
- Bake GI lighting into texture maps for items that don't move in the scene. If you bake the diffuse solution, but no shadows, other objects can still cast useable shadows onto the baked object.
- Bake ambient occlusion for additional control over density and color of shadow areas.

Essential Techniques

The following list of techniques highlight the essential elements of a good workflow for lighting your scene using images. The more you experiment with how best you work with this lighting method, the easier it will become to balance the right techniques together for a great result.

- Overcrank values—lights and surfaces. Set high values for both colors and other channels like specularity, reflectivity, and emission to get wider ranges of lighting effect. Use HDR imagery for surfaces to get the same advantage.
- Know your image formats, both RGB and HDR.
- Gamma correct your footage and HDRs.
- Add very bright light sources as necessary.
- Add a little mixed color to everything. Nothing ever shows up as a pure color or white on film.
- Match shadow and light colors. (This is where Final Gathering shows its true strength.)
- Create and adjust materials in a neutral lighting environment first, before trying to create special lighting effects. That way, your assets will work in many types of environments.
- Use HSV to adjust brightness. You can overcrank this; it is not limited by values from 0 to 1.
- You can also overcrank a surface by specifying values greater than 1 for diffuse or reflection or the V component of any HSV value.
- Match reflection values. In real-world reflections, only very bright elements are plainly visible in the reflection. The sky usually contributes the most in exterior car shots. Lighting mimics this in the studio where the look can be carefully controlled. Massive light boxes are used to create bright, reflective light sources.
- Use the Fresnel Effect, which is very important for realistic effects.
- Always work in real-world units if at all possible. High-end rendering algorithms are coded that way, and out-of-scale scenes can make it difficult to control your settings.
- Study as much about real-world photography and cinematography as you kind. This is usually the kind of carefully designed and controlled lighting we attempt to re-create. Many think realism is about mimicking the real world as we see it every day. But for CGI production, we are much more interested in the subjective artistic decisions that are intended to enhance the meaning and emotional impact of a scene. Pay close attention to these techniques, and gather as much information as possible to help in re-creating the setups.
- Real-world specularity is the reflection of an actual light source. This is one of the first things to be learned in comparing photography and computer-rendering techniques. Phong and Gouraud specularity are fake; they substitute perfectly round light sources with various controls to assimilate the way light interacts in the real world. Although this is fine for some applications, when rendering for photo-realistic results, turn off standard specularity channels and use the reflection channel to get appropriate specular highlights, either from HDR imagery or stand-in geometry mapped with a Surface Shader or other material with incandescence. This technique is often effective even without using GI or Final Gathering. Mental ray still renders the reflections of the overly bright items.

Always Learning

HDR imagery and GI are extremely valuable for creating realistic, shiny reflective objects. But you can also use the new mental ray Image-based Lighting node to great benefit for quickly matching lighting, even from a low dynamic range background plate, especially when supplemented with overcranked brightness values and stand-in objects that also contribute to the Final Gathering lighting solution.

The addition of several important enhancements in Maya make GI and IBL easier and much more practical to use in hectic production environments. The techniques are more powerful than ever, and you can adjust them for productions in which access to the set and time for capturing proper HDR imagery is not an option. Proper preparation makes for a greater level of accuracy and flexibility, speeding up the CGI production process immensely.

Resources

The following is a list of resources to further your education of Image Based Lighting. We've only just scratched the surface, and there is quite a bit more out there to help you find your own stride.

www.learning-maya.com/ Great tutorial resources for beginners and experts alike.

www.highend3d.com/ More Maya resources, a bit more technical in nature.

www.debevec.org/HDRShop/ The godfather of IBL.

www.cgtechniques.com/ Excellent general HDR information and tutorials.

http://hdri.3dweave.com/ Probably one of the largest repositories of free HDR imagery on the Web.

www.alias.com/ Check out the community section for more resources and training materials.

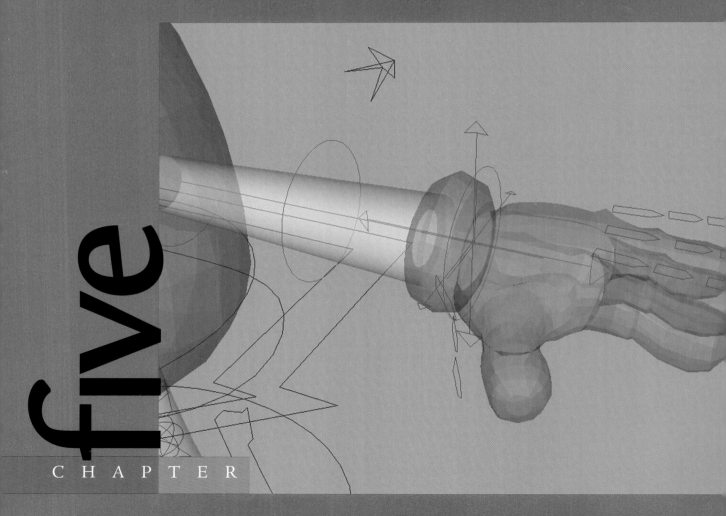

five

The Character Pipeline

Stephen K. Mann

A character pipeline *is really just the process of getting your character through its stages of evolution, from concept to modeling to rigging to animation, and then passed on to lighting. Three main data transfers take place: one between modeling and rigging, one from rigging to animation, and one from animation to lighting. But the pipeline might have any number of transfers. In this chapter, pipeline simply refers to the processes that make that transfer happen. Of primary importance is how that movement helps in the overall process and creates a situation in which modelers, riggers, animators, and lighters can all work simultaneously in safety.*

The purpose of a creating a pipeline is not only to make the data transfer work, but to make that transfer easier for everyone involved. Separating the technical issues from the artistic issues lets you can spend more time being creative.

The Structure of Things

Creating a structured pipeline can ease the normal headaches that come from this process, especially when more and more people get involved, and several iterations take place during the life of the production. A strong pipeline makes managing all the data that gets moved around and where to find it seamless.

Ninety percent of a good pipeline involves creating and maintaining an organized structure for all your project files. Any member of the team should be able to find the latest final geometry, rig, or animation without having to call you at 6:00 A.M. Through character

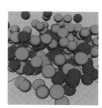

definitions, careful file management, and simple routines, the process of moving and updating along the pipeline can be streamlined, which lets teams work simultaneously and efficiently. Keeping Maya's scene files clean and organized can stabilize the hurdles most often found in a production pipeline.

Building on the organizational foundation, you can simplify updateable rigs, animation, and geometry and automate them using MEL. Keeping the pipeline and the pipeline tools simple, flexible, and easy to understand is of utmost importance. Ideally you want to control the flow of the pipeline with one or two simple tools.

Pipeline Flow Control

The two main types of character pipelines are unmanaged and managed. An *unmanaged pipeline* is the linear approach to creating your characters. In an unmanaged pipeline, the character is modeled, once the model is approved, the rigger imports the file into a new file and begins rigging. When rigging is completed, the animators can import the final rig and start their work. An unmanaged pipeline is primarily an organization of files and folder structures. Barring a lot of animation hand-transfer and rebinding of geometry, the linear approach involves little or no overlap between teams. Each team must wait for the work of the previous team. If a project has only one creator, this can sometimes be a blessing in disguise, keeping you from doing any major reconstructive surgery on your models and rigs once you're in the animation phase. In larger productions, this approach can bring the project to a halt. Updating characters by hand is no fun. Even though they say the second time around you can make it better, that might not happen when the deadline is looming and it's your fifth time rebinding a character. Once animation has begun, fixing characters that are already animated can mean completely replacing a character to just fix a bad IK handle, all of which must be done scene by scene. Ideally, you can manage all this using MEL, but not always.

In a *managed pipeline* the movement of data is set up so that it is automated and so that progressive updates are possible. The overlap time is increased, making it possible for animators to start blocking much earlier and rigs to be updated at any point in the production process. Although this may take a little more effort on the front end, it can result in great benefits on the back end. Being able to fix rigs at any moment and update them seamlessly shortens your days and gives you more time to build the cool rigs you've always wanted without missing your deadlines. This can ensure that all the rigs in all the animation files are exactly the same. It's bad enough fixing 20 identical files, much less troubleshooting 20 different files that were supposed to be the same. It's amazing how Maya scene files can have a life of their own, especially in larger productions.

At the core of all pipelines is the process of transferring animation and or geometry from one update or resolution of a character to another. How you decide to do that depends not only on your style and choice, but on the requirements of the overall production. I have separated this process into three types of managed pipelines:

- Import
- Reference
- Assembly

All three types share similar setups and requirements, access to character components, attention to folder structure, and clean scene files. The best way to start is to keep things simple and build on the basic structure that you create. With MEL and hard work, you can find solutions to almost any problem, but you can definitely make things easier on yourself by planning ahead.

The Import Pipeline

In this type of pipeline, each member of the team imports the file into their current scene to rig, animate, or light the scene. This style is similar to an unmanaged pipeline, but the processes necessary for updating can be MEL-coded to ease transfer. You must follow certain routines to make this process possible without creating too much garbage in the scenes. You must set up models, rigs, and animated characters in such a way that automating the import process is possible. For example, you need to automate the process of updating and importing characters in animation scenes rather than doing so by hand. You need to create a process for disconnecting the animation, deleting the character from the scene, importing a new or different resolution rig, and reconnecting the animation to the new rig. With an organized setup, you can automate most of this can be automated rather easily.

When using an import-based pipeline, you must create routines to prevent names from changing as they travel down the pipeline, or you must employ other methods of accessing nodes that aren't name reliant. Since anything can be changed in an import-based pipeline, you risk breaking the pipe simply by renaming nodes. One way to allow names to be changed down the pipeline is to add hidden string attributes to important nodes so they can be accessed later. You can also use the MEL command `lockNode` to make it impossible to change the names and connections of objects and attributes, without first unlocking them.

```
// to lock a node
lockNode -lock 1 MyObject;
// to unlock a node
lockNode -lock 0 MyObject;
```

The Reference Pipeline

This type of pipeline uses Maya's internal referencing to move data. Referencing is like importing, except that any changes made to the referenced file are automatically updated in the referencing scene when you open the referencing file. Anyone who has dabbled in Maya referencing might feel that this is a nightmare, but with the same routines needed for other pipelines, this option can be viable. You must be careful not to break the references. Keeping files clean and avoiding duplicate names is of utmost importance, but this is true of all pipelines. By creating specific controls for the animators to use, the rigger can change everything except the names and channels of those objects, allowing everything else to be changed. This means that you can change an entire character as long as you leave the control objects intact. References have the benefit of fast update as well as protection against accidental deletion of important nodes. Referenced nodes are automatically locked against deletion, renaming, and disconnection. Updating is as simple as reopening a scene

The Assembly Pipeline

This type of pipeline relies on creating new files based completely on parts of existing files or combining entire files. In an assembly pipeline, animators export their curves rather than the character. The lighter imports a high-resolution character rig and the animation curves and then applies the animation to the character. This type of pipeline might be necessary when final rigs are too slow for the animators, when large numbers of characters need to be created, or to speed up certain parts of the process that only certain teams need to deal with. For example, muscle- and cloth-dependent rigs can be heavy, and animators can have difficulty working with them. An assembly pipeline gives each team a lot of freedom. Animators can design their own rigs or use customized rigs for specific shots. You can export animation from the control objects of the rigs or from baked rotation animation from the joints, as with motion capture. Because rig updates can be more involved than reference pipelines, you must use similar methods so that animation can transfer. Assembly pipelines are susceptible to name changes, so like an import pipeline, the `lockNode` command can be used. Another benefit to assembly pipelines is that files tend to be cleaner. Only the required data required is transferred; any excess data is discarded. This allows individuals to work with whatever tools they want.

The Importance of Naming

Careful naming in scenes is important not only for your peace of mind and personal debugging, but for others who have to interpret your scenes and for keeping Maya in good working order. Since everything in Maya is name based, naming is critical for making an efficient pipeline. That goes for any scripts or automatic rigging tools you create too. As a rule, I try to match my naming conventions to Maya's default naming when possible. I also try to keep names as simple as possible.

Generally, it is best to create and maintain a guideline to keep names consistent. In most facilities, a guide outlines the names of almost every possible object and situation in a scene with descriptive suffixes and prefixes, or *descriptors*. This guideline basically outlines how to name objects in your scene, from controllers to utility nodes to deformation nodes. Using descriptive prefixes and suffixes for relations in space to each other, such as top left, right bottom, and so on, should be commonplace, but adding node types to certain items can be equally important. I generally name blend shape nodes with either BS or blendShape as the suffix. That way I can use a simple `select` command to select all the blend shape nodes in a scene.

Names should be simple and short. You want to be able to read the name in the Channel box, as well as not give yourself carpal tunnel when naming everything. Changing left to LF and right to RT is just the tip of iceberg. Using Bck, Frnt, Mid, Up, Dwn, Hi, Lo, GRP, and Cntrl are all great ways to define your node. In reality, there is no standard to these names, so it's best to choose the names that make most sense for your characters and scripts and then stick with it. It is a good idea to also pass this list around to your co-workers to get their opinions before laying down the law. Using the Maya default standard naming convention tends to be a good plan. Using uppercase letters, rather than spaces or underscores, is also a good idea. Underscores tend to only make names longer, so I try to limit their use. Using armUpLfCntrl rather than upper_arm_left_control results in something simpler, smaller, and more readable. See the sample in Figure 5.1.

I generally name all animation control objects with the suffix Cntrl so that a search for *Cntrl finds all the controlling objects in the scene. This consistency ensures that animators never have any doubt as to which objects they are allowed to animate. Descriptors also make it possible to create simple MEL scripts that can use these naming conventions. Whichever naming conventions you choose, the most important thing to do is to abide by them.

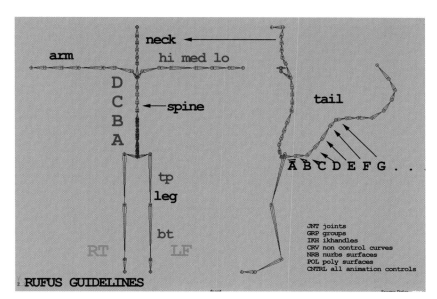

Figure 5.1: A naming guideline

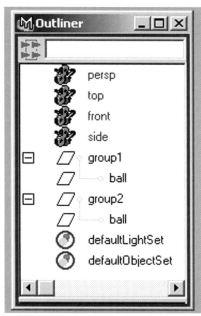

Figure 5.2:
Duplicate names
in the Outliner

Avoiding duplicate names in a scene is critical. Maya is really just a collection of nodes connected to one another, and those connections are created through MEL, which, as a text-based language, relies heavily on naming. Duplicate names can wreak havoc on your pipeline, not to mention scripts and files.

If you give two objects the same name, Maya adds a number to the end of the name when they are on the same parent level. Thus, in world space parent level, there can only be one object named ball. Every object named ball after that gets a number added to the end of it. In parented groups, however, Maya lets you have duplicate names of children, as long as they have different parents. So group1|ball and group2|ball can exist in the same scene (see Figure 5.2).

If you try to select the object named ball using the MEL command:

```
select ball;
```

Maya returns an error stating:

```
// Error: More than one object matches name: ball //
```

Unfortunately Maya does not always check with the parents before making a connection with the child node. If we tell Maya to connect the translateX channel of control to the translateX channel of ball using

```
connectAttr -f control.translateX ball.translateX;
```

Maya will not know which ball to connect to.

Maya connects to the first object named ball it finds in the scene. This can be dangerous, of course. A referenced scene that contains similar names has the potential to connect to the wrong objects when you open a scene. Since our control can connect to either of the two

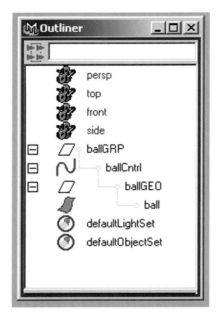

Figure 5.3: The hierarchy of an object
in the Outliner

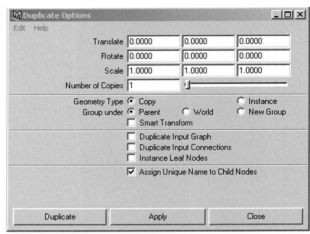

Figure 5.4: The Duplicate Options dialog box

Figure 5.5: The Numeric Input field

objects named ball, it is extremely important to avoid duplicate names. When making connections, Maya plugs in the name of the object you request. For example, if someone says to you, "Please give this dollar to John Smith," you would have to ask, "Which John Smith?" Maya does have the ability to use long names. Long names are based on the entire object's hierarchy (see Figure 5.3). To show the difference from parent to child, Maya inserts a pipe (|). Therefore, a NURBS sphere named ball with a parent of ballGEO with a parent named ballCNTRL with a parent of ballGRP is written as follows:

    ballGRP|ballCntrl|ballGEO|ball

Unfortunately, not all commands and procedures are written to use long names. I recommend using them in your own pipeline scripts when possible. The flag that most commands use for this is -ln, but check the documentation to make sure.

You can protect you scene file from duplicate names in several ways. One is to open the Duplicate Options dialog box and turn on Assign Unique Name to Child Nodes, as shown in Figure 5.4. This renames the children of a duplicated group. If you duplicate group1|ball, the resulting objects are named group2|ball1.

Another way to protect against duplicate names depends on your own personal working habits. Renaming objects using the Channel box or Outliner can easily result in duplicate child names because the rename command of the Channel box and the Outliner do not check for duplicate names. The Numeric Input field on the Status line, however, checks for duplicate names (see Figure 5.5).

The numeric input automatically adds a number to the end of an object name. This is why you can rename multiple objects using the Numeric Input field and why you can't with the Channel box The only problem with the Numeric Input field is that trying to rename objects that already have the same name returns the following error:

```
// Error: More than one object matches name //
```

just as when you were using `select ball;`.

In this case, it is usually best to rely on the help of a good renaming script. Several that are floating around on the Web can be quite handy. One of my favorites is `cometRename.mel` by Michael Comet. (You can find it at www.comet-cartoons.com/.) You can also rename the objects using your own renaming loop for a quick-and-dirty solution. The `rename` command by itself does not check for duplicate names; you have to add the additional numbers within the loop.

I'm in the habit of renaming only with the Numeric Input field, and I use the following script or a similar one to give the objects with duplicate names a generic name and then use the Numeric Input field to rename to something more appropriate.

```
global proc renameSel (string $newName)
{
 int $i = 1;
string $sel[] = `ls -sl -l`;
for ($each in $sel)
{
rename $each ($newName + $i);
$i++;
}
}
```

I recommend making a hot key to take your focus to the numericInputField and command line. In Maya 6, pressing the tilde key (~) changes smoothing on polygons. In version 5 and earlier, that hot key was Alt+~. Now in Maya 6, Alt + ~ changes polygons to subdivision surfaces. I recommend changing this back to the Maya 5 default of setting focus to numericInputField. The input field does not need to be visible for this to work.

Using Spaces and Underscores in Object Names

As mentioned earlier, I never use spaces or underscores in naming control objects or anything that will be animated. I've found that all underscores do is make names longer and more difficult to parse with MEL. If you stick to the rule of no underscores in object and attribute names, you can leverage Maya's internal naming that uses underscores. By default, Maya uses underscores for prefixes, animationCurve node naming, constraint naming, and other connection type nodes that it creates. Use this feature to your advantage. It is more difficult to parse with MEL because of the possible number of underscores that can be added to a name. Not all objects need a side modifier, and so they will have fewer underscores than those that do. This will force you to make more matching MEL scripts to find names, rather than just using the `tokenize` MEL command and counting the number of underscores.

Maya bases the names of animationCurve nodes on the object and attribute animated. When you key the translateX channel of an object named ball, Maya creates a new animation-Curve node named after the object name and channel name, resulting in a new node named ball_translateX. In a normal Maya session, this wouldn't really matter, but in a rigging pipeline, this can become important. We can use that naming style to get the animation of objects, as well as reattach animation. This is also why duplicate names can be a problem. You only want one animation curve with that name. Using a simple MEL script with the tokenize command, we can find the name of the object and its animated channel from the naming of the animation curve node. For example, an object named armUpRtCntrl that has its ringLat animated will have an animation curve named armUpRtCntrl_ringLat. Notice where the underscore is—simple. On the contrary, an object named elmers_Arm_Cntrl with the channel named ring_finger_lateral animated results in an animationCurve named elmer_Arm_Cntrl_ ring_finger_lateral. Not only is that a mouthful, but it is difficult to parse with a MEL script. Just eliminating the underscores can relieve this problem. We can use the tokenize or match command to find the last element separated by an underscore, as in the following script:

```
//
string $name = "elmer_Arm_Cntrl_ringFingerLat";

string $tokenBuffer[];
int $tokenSize = `tokenize $name "_" $tokenBuffer`;
print ("the animated channel is " + $tokenBuffer[$tokenSize -1] + "\n");
//
```

We can also get the prefix name if one exists by the items in the array we ask for, as in the following:

```
//
print ("the prefix name is " + $tokenBuffer[0] + "\n");
//
```

Getting the rest of the name would certainly be easier if all those underscores weren't in there. It can be done; it's just more work, as you can see here:

```
//
int $n = 1;
string $theObject = "";
for ($n = 1;$n <= ($tokenSize -2); $n++)
{
$theObject += $tokenBuffer[$n];
// dont forget to add the "_" back in
if ($n != ($tokenSize -2))
    $theObject += "_";
}
print $theObject;
//
```

OK, so this doesn't look like much, but I'm also not accounting for all the other possibilities such as more underscores or different numbers of underscores. If all objects have the same number of underscores in their names, we can always find what we want. However, the chances of that are slim, especially since not all the objects need the same number of descriptors. Just saying no to underscores eliminates that issue. Besides, if you're not putting underscores in the attribute names, why not avoid them in the object names too and avoid the headache? Trust me on this one!

The Golden Rules of a Successful Pipeline

Keeping a few rules in mind can make creating pipelines easier. Consistency, ease of use, flexibility, and cleanliness are the four major rules to keep things running smoothly.

Consistency

Consistency is imperative. By creating guidelines and methods to follow you can create routines for every rig you make, as well as specify how things are done for the pipeline. If all characters are brought in the exact same way, all tools that are based on that pipeline should work the same. You want everyone to know that no matter what kind of rig they open, from a cyber-octopus to a flying logo, the controls do the same thing—how the character is brought into the scene, where to find controls and what they look like, how to switch from HiRes to LoRes, and how to get the answers the rest of the pipeline needs. Consistency minimizes error and makes the pipeline as a whole more efficient.

Using a naming guide is a good way to keep channels and functions the same from character to character and will be less confusing for the animators. Once they use the flex channel on an arm, they'll remember what it did and how to best use it to their advantage when they see the **Flex** attribute on a new character. I try to use the same terminology for all channels. All IK/FK blend channels are named ikBlend, all constraint switches are named switch, all eye controls are named eyeCntr, and so on. Beyond naming, the way things work should be the same as well. If 0 is IK off, and 1 IK on, you don't want to switch that between characters; 0 should always be IK off. Similarly, all min max values should match, for example, 0 to 1 or –10 to 10. To make this easy on myself, I create simple for loop MEL scripts to create attributes:

```
// add finger attrs to selected objects
// get the selected nodes
string $sel[] = `ls -sl`;
//loop through each of them
for ($each in $sel)
    {
// add an attribute with min of -1 and max 1 that is keyable
addAttr -keyable 1 -min -1 -max 1 -ln "indexCurl" $each;
addAttr -keyable 1 -min -1 -max 1 -ln "midCurl" $each;
addAttr -keyable 1 -min -1 -max 1 -ln "ringCurl" $each;
addAttr -keyable 1 -min -1 -max 1 -ln "pinkyCurl" $each;
addAttr -keyable 1 -min -1 -max 1 -ln "thumbCurl" $each;    }
//
```

Notice that I leave the side descriptor off the attribute name. This is so you can select multiple controls that have the same named attributes and change all of them simultaneously.

To keep things consistent, I use curves to control everything that will have animation applied to it. I create the same curves for the same kinds of controls. Even before an animator selects the object or checks its name, they have a good idea what that curve does. I use curves because they don't render and take up little memory to display. This allows the animator to quickly hide all the controlling objects for a playblast or review using the panel view menu and turning off curves. Animators can also turn off everything but curves in the selection mask, so they won't accidentally select anything but animation controls. Using geometry without shaders disconnected is a good idea, but it makes it harder to hide them quickly and reveal them again, as well as discern selection. I use MEL to create these shapes for me, to make life easier and less repetitive.

To create a simple curve control and attach it to a DAG (Directed Acyclic Graph) node, follow these steps:

1. Using the CV or EP Curve tool, create your curve or curves as you normally would.
2. Show the curves' CVs, and click the Snap to Point button to make a new curve, snapping to its points.
3. On finishing the curve, Maya show the MEL script for creating that curve in the Script Editor. Copy and paste that one line into an editor.

   ```
   curve -d 3 -p -0.779152 0 -2.30167 -p 3.87703 ... ;
   ```

4. Add the -name flag to the MEL script to get the following:

   ```
   curve -name "CNTRL" -d 3 -p 0 3.2 2 ...;
   ```

Either use that as a sourceable entity on your shelf, or make it into a global proc.

To attach the curve to a controlling group, follow these steps:

1. Snap the curve to your group
2. Freeze its transformations.
3. Select the curves' shape nodes by pick walking down once or by showing and selecting Shape Nodes in the Outliner.
4. Shift+select the group, and use the following MEL to parent the shapes under the transform:

   ```
   //
   parent -r -shape;
   //
   ```

With this, you can create one transform node with any number of shape nodes, but when you select using object mode, the DAG or transformation node is automatically selected, not the curve shape or component level node. You can parent multiple shapes under one transform to make elaborate control curves, but keeping it simple is always a good idea. Too many shape nodes can slow down the Outliner tremendously when show shapes is turned on (see Figure 5.6).

Employ the same consistency for hierarchies. The upper groups of a character should always match. This can often become redundant for some characters, but it is better to have it there for consistency. Groups take up little memory and add options for control, so the more the merrier. I generally make a top group named ALL and then parent under that two groups COG and PARTS. The COG will generally have its pivot at the root or hip of the character and be the top control for moving all the character. PARTS will contain all the parts that cannot be

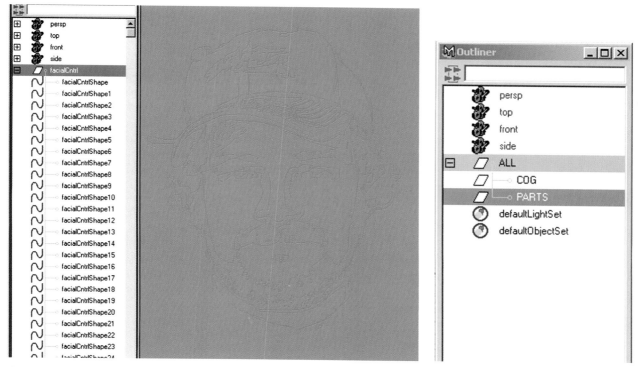

Figure 5.6: Control shape   Figure 5.7: A clean hierarchy

moved or will cause double transformations, such as bound geometry. For the PARTS group, I turn off the inherit transforms so the group doesn't follow the parent. This keeps the character condensed into one main group and keeps the Outliner and Hypergraph clean (see Figure 5.7).

Also be consistent in all pipeline scripts, plug-ins, and their storage areas. Keep all scripts in a centrally located folder that everyone can access. They should all work similarly. Mainly I use the same naming conventions for scripts, as most people do. I also use the same name for the name of the script and the global procedure that must get called. For example, a MEL script named fixBarneyArmRt.mel would be run by calling fixBarnyArmRt in Maya. I also tend to suffix MEL scripts that have a user interface or window with either UI or Win. The user automatically knows to expect a window to pop up when they run such a script.

Ease of Use

Making a pipeline easy to use is extremely important. The job of a rigger is to create an easy way to control the character. In doing so, it should be readily apparent what each control does and how to use the character. Don't expect the animator to have read the same "how to rig a character" book that you did, and to know that the spiral curve mover behind the character's back is to control breathing. Name and place controls where they make sense. Again keeping it simple is important. If there is better place to put a control or a better order for channels in the Channel box, move them. You're creating a new program or a new interface for the character, so be sure it makes sense. The same should hold true for all the pipeline scripts. The closer you can get to a one-button approach, the happier everyone will be.

Using the one-button approach means that the user need press or click only one shiny button to run your script.

Flexibility

Flexibility is a one of the hardest things to achieve with a character pipeline. You want to create a pipeline that can handle many possibilities. Luckily, since you're creating the pipeline and guidelines to follow, you can ensure certain things—most important where to keep and name scene files for geometry, rigs, animation files, and so on. You can take all the known factors and hard-code them into your rules and scripts. Keeping things generic is also a good general rule of thumb. Your import and animation transfer tools shouldn't rely heavily on naming and certain nodes, but rather on objects and animation, so they can work on any type of rig. When creating scripts for automatically rigging characters, or autoRigs, I tend to keep them as simple as possible and use them more like building blocks, rather than complete rigs. For example, create an arm rig, a spine rig, and a foot rig that can be implemented separately, rather than a "human" rig that has everything already put together and is harder to repurpose for other characters. Just as it is hard to create any one rig that can do it all, it is better not to limit yourself to an autoRig that cannot be interchangeable.

Cleanliness

Cleanliness is just a matter of keeping things organized. The cleaner, the easier. Delete unnecessary geometry and history. For geometry, my main rule of thumb is to delete all history and freeze transformations. Brush nodes can be created by certain procedures that don't necessarily create Paint Effects, and they are not always automatically deleted from the scene. These nodes can build up in the scene and make it heavy. Polygon tweaks can easily become a mass of nodes that are unnecessary to the character rig, but can impede and corrupt several deformers down the road; so clean 'em up! Turn off the Show DAG Objects Only in the Outliner, and turn off show shape, hidden, and underworld nodes in the Hypergraph to help you see offending nodes and clean your scenes. Check connections on unknown nodes before deleting, and name the ones you want to keep. Watch for shape nodes, those that are created and hidden when a deformer is applied. These are known as Orig nodes and aren't necessarily deleted when history is deleted (see Figure 5.8). In most cases, you can just delete them.

When experimenting with a new technique or rig, use a disposable file, and once you have the process nailed, reopen an old scene and implement the changes there. Using Undo doesn't always get rid of everything you created or the hidden nodes Maya creates for you. Always prefix anything imported or referenced into a

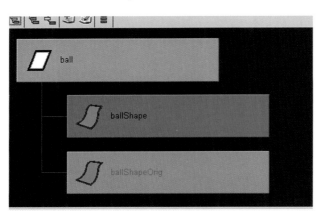

Figure 5.8: Orig nodes

scene. I use dummy prefixes when importing rig and geometry components into a scene so that I can find the extra nodes brought in, such as shaders and sceneConfigurationsScript nodes. That way I can find them using `select dummy_*` and then check if they are necessary. Beware using `optimize scene`. This can delete empty sets that might be needed for your rigs and script and delete unconnected shape nodes that might be needed down the pipeline. It's better to look for them by hand or to write your own clean-up scripts if you can.

The Rigging Curtain

To keep the technical side of things away from the creative, I employ what I call the "rigging curtain"—basically all the things that go on behind the scenes that the creative side doesn't need to see. The rigging curtain is purposely hidden from the animators. If you find that the animators are digging into the rigs and trying to find objects to move and ways to control things that you didn't intend them to animate, you might want to rethink they way your rig works. Most animators will open a new rig and immediately use the Show All menu. Generally, I try to make everything that the animator doesn't need completely inaccessible, by hiding anything that is unnecessary. This includes IKhandles, lattices, clusters, joints, and almost all deformers. To control the display of these items I generally put in a rig-specific control that controls their display. Keep this control out of the keyable set so it doesn't get animated. If it is animated by accident, the animation on it should be discarded and not moved down the pipeline.

Hide all rig specific geometry, such as wraps and blend targets. Hide and lock all unnecessary channels so they are not accidentally changed. Use import scripts to bring characters into a scene and correctly name and place nodes. If necessary use `lockNode` on objects you think might get changed. No one should need to dig around in the folder structure either; that's behind the curtain too.

Defining a Character for the Pipeline

Let's begin by talking a little about bringing a character into a scene. To avoid name clashing and Maya's automatic changing of names, I strongly suggest you always use Resolve All Nodes when importing and or referencing with Use NameSpaces turned off. First, this configuration makes it easier to find all the parts of a character. By using (`"select -r "barney_*""`), you can select all the nodes that came in with your imported/referenced character. Name spaces make things slightly more difficult, in that some MEL scripts treat the colon (:) as a special character so it can't be used as easily as an underscore. Second and more important, prefixes ensure that no names in the scene clash, causing problems down the line. When referencing multiple characters of the same name, rather than letting Maya add suffix numbers to objects that clash, add a suffix to the prefix. For example, the name barney, when referenced again, will have a prefix of barney1_. To help me do this automatically, I created a window that automatically checks for characters in the scene with the current prefix and, if they exist, adds a number to the prefix (see Figure 5.9).

To gain access to the relevant parts of your character once they are in a scene, it's best to develop an organization for them. A character template

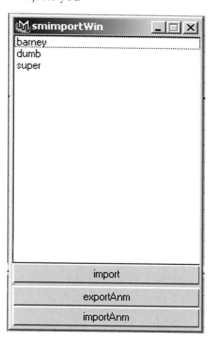

Figure 5.9: A simple character window

or map that defines all the relevant parts of your character makes it possible to manage them. You'll want to access the high-resolution geometry, low-resolution geometry, animation controls, and rigging components. This makes it possible to select, delete, and get animation from a character quickly and easily in any scene. This is especially important when importing rather than referencing. In a referencing scene, all objects that are referenced can be easily selected within Maya's Reference Editor. When importing into a new scene, there is no automatic way to keep track of those imported objects. The most common ways to organize a character are with Maya's character sets, layers, and selection sets (seen in Figure 5.10). Personally I prefer to work with selection sets.

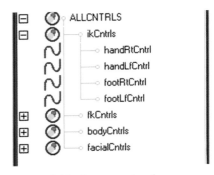

Figure 5.10: An example of selection sets

Character sets, although great to use with clips and Trax, tend to be intrusive and can produce more overhead than needed. Numerous connections can slow things down quite a bit, and since you can delete, cut, break, and in many other ways disconnect a channel from its character, the danger of a broken pipeline is high. Re-creating the character tends not to be a viable option once these connections are broken. Even though you can tell your animators not to delete animation through Break Connections in the Channel box, it can still happen easily.

Layers have similar issues to Maya's character sets, in that they are easily accessible and can be quickly changed at any time, breaking your pipeline. Another issue with layers is that when an object is hidden by a layer, its visibility is overridden, but not displayed as such in the Outliner or Hypergraph, making it difficult for the other teams to find all the geometry that needs to be visible. A bigger problem with layers is that they are exclusive, meaning objects can be a part of one and only one layer, making it easy to accidentally remove objects from layers if someone decides to create new layers with the same objects and again breaking the pipeline. A character definition without layers frees up the layers for people to use without fear of breaking the pipeline. My rule on layers in general is, don't use them, and if you do, delete them before sending your scene file down the pipeline.

I find selection sets the fastest, most flexible, and least intrusive option for character organization. When using sets, you can hide individual objects or the entire set, and the layer isn't overriding the object visibility channel but changing it, so objects retain the color coding that most Maya users are used to. You can temporarily hide objects and then easily display them by showing the set. Unlike layers, objects can be in multiple sets. This makes it possible to have lots of sets that contain the same objects, without intruding on normal work flow or overriding any objects. Objects aren't as easily removed and added to sets as layers. Even if they are using sets, animators can create a new set without affecting the "pipeline" sets.

Last, sets can contain other sets. You can, therefore, make a hierarchy of organization. I can break up all my character controls into separate sets, such as ARMRTset, ARMLFset, and so on and then put those sets underneath one main set called ALLCNTRLSset. For keying purposes, I can select just the arm controls or all the animation controls.

I name these sets with either all capital letters or in some way that delineates them from the naming conventions for the rest of the sets. As mentioned, I generally make one set called something like ALLCNTRLSset, make subsets for the arms, legs, and various other parts of the character, and then make those sets part of the ALLCNTRLSset set (see Figure 5.11).

To make it easier for riggers to deal with sets I added some tools to the Outliner for creating, adding to, and removing objects from sets:

```
// create set
 CreateQuickSelectSet;
```

Normally to create a quickSelectSet, you choose **Create → Sets → Quick Select Set**, which isn't such a bad thing, but by directly accessing the command, you can speed up the process. To add and remove objects and/or sets to sets, choose **Window → Relationship Editors → Sets**. To speed that up, I wrote addToSet and removeFromSet scripts. You can drag these to the shelf or make them into procedures and use them as MEL scripts.

```
// select the object and then the set to add to
//AddToSet
string $sel[] = `ls -sl`;
for ($each in $sel)
{
sets -in $each $sel[0] ;
}
//
```

```
// select the object and then the set to remove from
//removeFromSet
string $sel[] = `ls -sl`;
for ($ech in $sel)
{
sets -rem $each $sel[0] ;
}
//
```

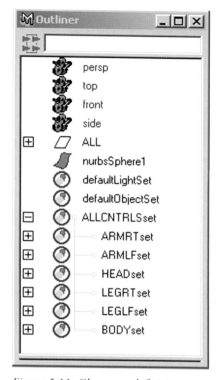

Figure 5.11: Character definition sets

These tools will work with both objects and sets; simply select the object and then the set. Generally, I make a MEL script to create these sets for me automatically. That way I don't have to do it by hand every time, and it ensures consistency.

To control the visibility of animation controls, I use an empty group and add attributes to it that are connected to parts of the character. I generally create Boolean attributes for the left and right sides of the arms and legs, as well as their IK and FK controls, controls for the face, controls for the fingers, and anything that might not always need to be visible in the scene (see Figure 5.12). I connect ikArmsLF to all the IK arm controllers for the left side of the character

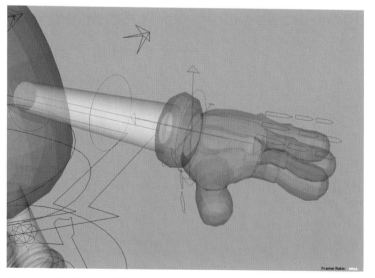

Figure 5.12: IK and FK arm controls

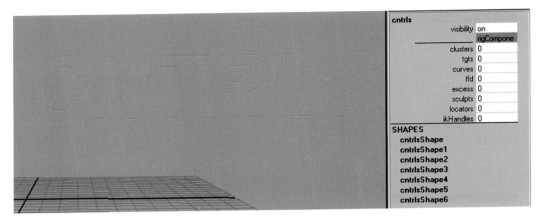

Figure 5.13: Visibility control

and so on. These need to be connected to the actual controls themselves and shouldn't hide any geometry of the character. Although shape nodes don't show it in the Channel box, their visibility channel can be connected. If need be, you can connect to the visibility channel of the actual shapes that show the control groups. You can do this with the Channel box or with a MEL command. Remember, you can create a MEL command for any repetitive task; this is one of those tasks.

I create a second empty group and use it to control all the deformers and rig components in the same way. For example, I create **ffd, clusters, ikHandles,** or any types into channels to control the nodes I don't want animators to see, but that I can still access easily for myself and others (see Figure 5.13).

To create this control, I used the text command to create curves and then parented all the curves under one group called **cntrls,** using the process described earlier. I also have a channel that is named and locked. This is purely for organization and readability. This is an enum channel named _____ that I changed to rigCompone. I use blank attributes like this all the time to make reading the Channel box easier.

As far as naming attributes, simple is the name of the game. Using the guides described earlier, name channels with few characters, no spaces or underscores, and no redundancy. There is no sense in naming a channel **rightFingerBend** when it's on the **handRTCntrl.** This approach is limiting in that you can't combine the channels with other controls. If both the **handRTCntrl** and the **handLFCntrl** the **fingerBend** channel, you can bend both fingers at the same time, merely by selecting both controls and using the virtual slider from the Channel box (select and MMB drag).

Also, you need not name character parts with the name of the character. Naming a control **barneyHandRtCntrl** is going to be redundant once the character is brought into a new scene. As discussed earlier, when importing or referencing a character into a new scene, a prefix of the character name is added to all nodes. The name **barneyHandRtCntrl** becomes **barney_barneyHandRtCntrl.** Just keep it simple and generic.

Because of the sets and the naming on import, it is easy to tell whether a character already exists in the scene. By searching for `"*_ALLCNTRLS"`, you can find all the characters in the scene (`ls -name "_ALLCNTRLS"`).

```
ls -name "*_ALLCNTRLS"
```

From the selected objects, it's just a matter of a simple loop statement using `tokenize` or `match` to get the prefix and therefore the character's name in the scene.

```
//
  string $chars[] = `ls -name "*_ALLCNTRLS"`;
for ($each in $chars)
    {
    string $buffer[];
    tokenize $each "_" $buffer;
    print ("The characters name is " + $buffer[0] + "\n");
    }
//
```

Creating a Ref Window

As I mentioned earlier, whether I am referencing or importing, I always turn off Resolve All Nodes and Use NameSpaces. I prefer to keep Use NameSpacesoff because all the scripts I've written are based on prefixes that contain underscores. Prefixing all nodes makes it possible to grab all the parts of your character. In an import or reference pipeline, you can always use a basic `select` command to find all the relevant nodes. I use a reference window to ensure that correct names are always used for the prefix, as well as to keep track if multiples of a character are brought into the scene. Generally, I name the rig the name of the character, but add a rig suffix. For example, the filename for barney is `barneyRig.ma`. By using `match` or `tokenize` I can get the base name of the file.

```
    //
    string $name = "barneyRig.mb";
    // search for the name prior to "R"
  string $charName =  `match"[^R]*" $name`;
  print $charName;
  //
```

Once you have the name of the character, you can use that as your prefix. The command for referencing, importing, and general filing of scenes is `file`.

```
    //
    file -reference -type "mayaBinary" -rpr $charName $file ;
  //
```

But, of course, before we get that far we should get the relevant files. We can use any folder, so for this example I'll use scenes. In the following code I'm getting the files in the scenes folder that are named without the suffix `Rig.mb`.

```
// get the current project and scenes directory
  string $currentProject = `workspace -q -fn`;
  // concatenate the current project with the scene dir
  string $charFolder = ($currentProject  + "/scenes/");
  string $characters[] = `getFileList -fld $charFolder -fs "*Rig.mb"`;
//
```

Once you get the list, you can add it to your window. This, of course, depends on your window. Let's build a down-and-dirty GUI using `columnLayout` and `textScrollList`.

```
//
global proc smimportWin ()
{
if (`window -exists smimportWin`)deleteUI smimportWin;
 string $window = `window -w 200 -h 250 -title "smimportWin" -mxb 0
     smimportWin`;
 columnLayout;
        string $scrollList = `textScrollList -h 250 -w 200 -
allowMultiSelection
     false`;
        button -l "import" -w 200 -c "smimportChar";
        setParent ..;
   showWindow $window;


 }
 //
```

Now we need to create a procedure to fill the `textScrollList`. Later we can embed this into the window script.

```
//
    // fill scroll list
      string $currentProject = `workspace -q -fn`;
      string $charFolder = ($currentProject  + "/scenes/");
   string $characters[] = `getFileList -fld $charFolder -fs "*Rig.mb"`;
        for ($eachChar in $characters)
            {
            // search for the name prior to "R"
              string $charName =  `match"[^R]*" $eachChar`;
              print $charName;
            textScrollList -e -append  $charName $scrollList;
            }
//
```

Now we need to create the procedure that will actually import the character.

```
//
//
global proc smimportChar ()
{
string $char[] = `textScrollList -q -si smimportWinScrollList`;
string $file = ($char[0] + "Rig.mb");
// select all obects with _allCNTRLS
string $chars[] = `ls -ap "*_ALLCNTRLS"`;
string $prefix;
int $v;
int $i;
```

```
if (`size $chars` >=1)
    {
        for ($each in $chars)
        {
        // use tokenize to get the base name
        string $buffer[];
        tokenize $each "_" $buffer;

        // use match to get the basename without a number
    string $name = `match "[^0-9]*" $buffer[0];
    if ($name == $char[0])
                {
                $v++;
                }
        }
  $prefix = ($char[0] + "_" + $v);
    }
else
$prefix = $char[0];

file -reference -type mayaBinary -rpr $prefix $file;
}
//Done
```

When you call the window, the script the script automatically fills the window with the available characters. By selecting a character and clicking the Import button, you can import the character into the current scene with the proper naming and prefixes. New characters with the same name will be prefixed with a number. I use tokenize here to split the name of the available characters based on the underscore. To use tokenize, first create a string array variable $buffer[]. Then run the tokenize procedure using that variable to store the resulting information. The tokenize procedure takes the first argument, in this case the name of the character, and then searches and splits that string using the second argument "_". It stores what's before and after each of the split strings into the third argument, in this case buffer[]. The tokenize procedure returns only the integer number of items split. For example, name_is_steve results in 3, putting name into buffer[0], is into $buffer[1], and steve into $buffer[2]. To get the results of the first part of the string, or the character prefix, you want $buffer[0]. I take the results of that and use match to strip off any numbers at the end of the string. This code actually looks for all the characters that occur before any numbers. Therefore, super or super58 both result in super.

In an import pipeline, you can update characters by saving the animation, deleting the character from the scene, reimporting the character, and then reattaching the animation. To do this, you need a way to get that animation and transfer it. Obviously, you can move that animation in a lot of ways. For this example and script, I'll be using character sets and clips. To create the character set, I simply select the *_ALLCNTRLS set and then create the character set. Since we're using MEL and the set to create the character set, it will be created in the same order every time, limiting the possibilities for nonmatching character sets. Once we create the character set, it's a simple matter to create a clip and export it to a scene file.

To import the animation back in, create a character set again from the ALLCNTRLS set, import the clip, and assign it. I then delete the character set and the clips, keeping the scene clean but leveraging the power of clips and character sets. I've included two scripts for automatically doing that. They are fairly simple, and you can easily change them to match your own production pipeline: smExportCharacterAnimation.mel and smImportCharacterAnimation.mel. To use them, simply write the procedure in the Script Editor and add the name of the character.

```
SmExportCharacterAnimation barney;
SmImportCharacterAnimation barney;
```

Instead of typing the script, you can add a button to smImportWin and use the selected character instead, just as in this script.

Expressions and Utility Nodes in Rigs

Using utility nodes in rigs can produce two major benefits, speed and reliability. Unlike expressions, utility nodes don't need the frame to change to update, don't need to be parsed, and each node as code serves one purpose. Consequently, a string of utility nodes calculates much faster and without a change in time. Since a utility node is already binary code, Maya doesn't need to read it first and then parse it; it can be used immediately. Replacing all expressions with utility nodes might not be practical or possible, but use them whenever you can, and save expressions for mathematical equations that are too long or difficult to create with nodes. Keeping the expression count low boosts the interactivity rate.

Since direct connections and not names connect utility nodes, you can change the names of the connected nodes without fear of destroying their communication. Thus, they are useful in import and reference pipelines. As discussed earlier, prefix all characters brought into a new scene. However, renaming nodes when referencing or importing them into a scene can cause any expressions that use MEL to fail. Basically, Maya renames nodes based on the prefix selected inside an expression, but Maya won't change names embedded within MEL code that is inside the expression statement. For example, the following fails on reference.

```
$ballTx = `getAttr ball.tx`;
ball.ty = $ballTx * 5;
```

The only name to be changed will be ball.ty that starts the second line. I try to convert simple expressions such as these to utility nodes. In this example, I would connect ball.tx to a multiplyDivide node's input1X. Set the multiplyDivide node's input2X to 0.5. Then connect the multiplyDivide node's output1D back to the ball.ty (see Figure 5.14). It may seem simple, but it can make a difference.

The basic math nodes in the Create Render Rode window are plusMinusAverage, multiplyDivide, clamp, and setRange. Several other nodes that perform similar functions such as addDoubleLinear and multDoubleLinear, do not appear in this window. As the names state, these nodes add double linears, which refers to the type of channels used to connect. A double linear is a float channel—any number including decimals. Double linears are limited to connecting only two float values, but they are hidden by default in the Hypershade window. Therefore, they can't be accidentally deleted or used by your lighting department. They are safer than renderNodes. Choosing **Edit → Delete Unused Nodes** will not affect

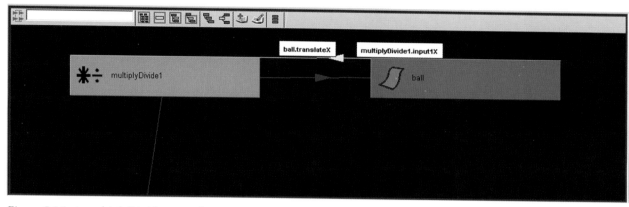

Figure 5.14: A multiplyDivide example

these nodes, as they are not considered render nodes. To create these nodes, you use the MEL `createNode` command.

```
//
createNode addDoubleLinear;
createNode multDoubleLinear;
//
```

You can use several other nodes for varying conditions; blendTwoAttr and pairBlend are just two examples. You might have noticed some of the nodes Maya creates for you when making connections, such as the unitConversion node. For a list of all the nodes in Maya, you can check Maya Help, "Nodes and Attributes."

Now let's take a look at some examples using utility nodes. I created most of these connections using the Connection Editor, but you can also do so using MEL. I'm in the habit of creating these connections with small MEL procedures that I keep as simple connection tools on my shelf.

When creating animated constraints by animating or connecting the "weights" of a constraint, I use a reverse node (see Figure 5.15) to make the link between the two weights. Add an attribute named **blend** to your control with Min and Max set to 0 to 1. Connect blend to the w[0] of the constraint node, and then connect the w[0] to the input of a reverse node. Connect the output of the reverse node to the w[1] of the constraint node. I find this much easier, cleaner, and faster than creating a set driven key or an expression. In this instance, you can't use a multiplyDivide node with its input2X set to –1; the math would be incorrect.

Rather than writing an `if/then` statement, you can use conditions or even `clamp` depending on your desired result. For this example, we'll use `clamp` to make a square that can tip up on its edges depending on the rotation of the control. Create a cube, and group it to itself twice. In the front view, place the pivot of one group on the right corner of the square, and name it rightGRP. Place the pivot of the other group on the left corner of the square and name it leftGRP. Create a clamp node.

```
createNode clamp;
```

And finally create a curve for the control and name it cntrl.

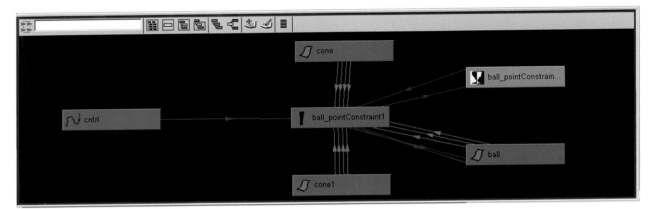

Figure 5.15: Using the reverse utility node

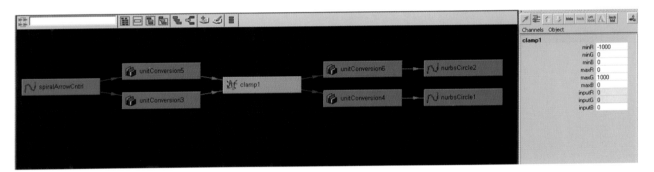

Figure 5.16: Using the clamp utility node

Connect the rotateZ of a cntrl to the clamp nodes inputR and inputG. We'll use the R channel as the right side connection and the G channel as the left side connection. Connect the outputR to the rotateZ of the left group, and connect outputG to the rotateZ of the right group. Set the clamp node's minR to –1000 or more, and set maxG to 1000 or more. Now when you rotate the cntrl in positive Z, the left group should rotate in Z, rotating the box off that corner. That is, any number greater than 0 rotates the left group with the same number as the cntrl. Now rotate the cntrl in negative Z. The leftGRP should now rotate the same amount, lifting the box of its left corner. Even though the clamp has three channels (RGB) to use we are only using two, and with different numbers. You'll find that different nodes use input RGB, input XYZ, and in some cases input2D[0] [2] [3] (see Figure 5.16). The best way to check these inputs and outputs is by putting them in the Connection Editor and looking at the possible connections.

Now let's create a simple animation control for offset and speed using a single animation node, two multiplyDivide nodes, and one plusMinusAverage node. Follow these steps:

1. Create a NURBS sphere and name it ball.
2. Keyframe the ball at frames 0 and 10 with a translateY value of 0 and a keyFrame at frame 5 a value of 1.
3. Turn off pre- and post-cycle for the animation.

4. Add some attributes to ball named **timeOffset, speed,** and **heightOffset.**
5. Create the utility nodes—two multiplyDivide nodes and one plusMinusAverage node.
6. Graph the up and downstream connections for the ball in the Hypergraph.
7. To create the height offset control, connect the animation node, which should be called ball_translateY to one of the multiplyDivide node's input1X.
8. Connect the ball.heightOffset to the multiplyDivide's input2X. Now this will multiply the animation node's output by whatever you choose. A value of 1 is the default. Anything below or above that value causes the ball to bounce higher or lower.

To create the time and speed connections, connect the ball.timeOffset to the plus-MinusAverage node's input1D[0]. The input 1D is an array, so you need to use brackets to delineate which object in the array you are connecting to. For the first connection, the Connection Editor will allow you to do this, but for the consecutive connections, it is easiest to do it with MEL. Now it's time to connect the plusMinusAverage node's input1D[1].

```
{
connectAttr time1.outTime plusMinusAverage1.input1D[1];
}
```

Time is directly connected to the Timeline. You can have only one time node, and it has no connectable inputs. Now connect the plusMinusAverage's output1D to the other multiplyDivide's input1X. Connect ball.speed to the multiplyDivide's input2X. Finally, connect the outputX of the multiplyDivide to the animation node's input (see Figure 5.17).

```
{
connectAttr multiplyDivide1.outputX  ball_translate.input;
}
```

Now you can change the ball bounce speed and offset the timing of it by changing the ball.speed and the ball.timeOffset channels.

To make this exercise practical, duplicate the ball with Duplicate Input Graph on. This not only duplicates the ball object, but the animation node and the utility nodes connecting them. Time is connected to all since it cannot be duplicated. Now, by adjusting each ball's speed, heightOffset, and timeOffset channels, they can each have a different animation but still be based on the same simple animation cycle.

You can then create a large number of bouncing balls just by duplicating the original ball and randomizing each of their attributes. Of course, the easiest way to do this is with a MEL script. I've included on the CD the MEL script dupeball as an example. It duplicates

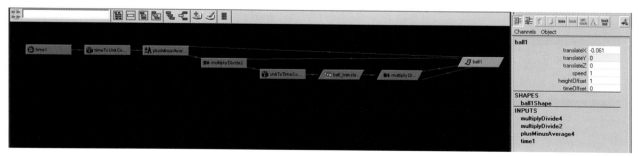

Figure 5.17: The offsetAnimation utility nodes

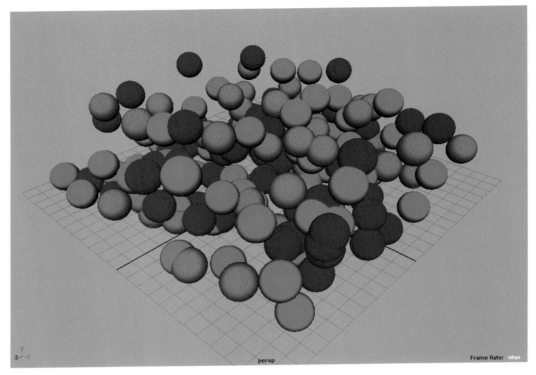

Figure 5.18: Multiple animated objects

the object with upstream on and randomizes the attributes on each, creating a random grid of bouncing balls. Now, when you watch the animation, it appears as if all the balls have different animation and timings (see Figure 5.18).

Simple Tools You Should Be Using

Now let's look at some scripts I wrote that make things simple when dealing with characters and character setup.

You can use `smattrUp.mel` and `smattrDwn.mel` to move user-created channels in the Channel box. Ordinarily, you would have to open the Maya file in ASCII format and reorder these attributes by hand or re-create them in the correct order. Using these scripts, all you need do is select the attribute in the Channel box, and then run either `smattrUp` or `smattrDwn`. The attribute moves up or down in the list of channels. It won't move the translate rotate scale and visibility channels, as they are not permitted to move.

The script `HideLockChannel.mel` basically hides and locks the selected channels in the Channel box. When you hide a channel in the Channel box, you make it unkeyable. Unkeyable attributes are not displayed in the Channel box.

By definition a channel is a keyable attribute.

The scripts ShowTranslate, showRotate, and showScale work on the selected objects. As their names suggest they display or make keyable the translate, rotate, or scale of the currently selected objects.

I either put these scripts on my shelf or add them to my Channel box pop-up menu. To do that, locate the generateChannelMenu.mel script, and copy it to your local scripts folder. You never want to overwrite an original Maya script; if you do, you might have to reinstall to rebuild it. By copying the script to your scripts folder, it will get sourced last, and the procedure for that Maya session will be overwritten, rather than the MEL script itself. In your copied script, simply find the generateChannelMenu procedure. Within that procedure, you some lines similar to the following:

```
//
menuItem -l "Key Selected" -c "channelBoxCommand -key" keyItem;
menuItem -d true;
//
```

The menu -d true is the divider you see in your Channel menu. You can add your own scripts simply by adding a new menu item and calling the script you want.

```
//
    menuItem -divider true;
    menuItem -l "upAttr" -c smattrUp;
    menuItem -l "downAttr" -c smattrDown;
    menuItem -l "hideLockAttr" -c hideLockChannel;
//
```

You can just as easily add to your Outliner menu the set scripts that were discussed by editing OutlinerEdMenu.mel.

In this chapter's section on the CD, I am including MEL versions of the scripts discussed earlier in this chapter, although I recommend you learn how to write them on your own. I hope that what I showed will at least put you on the right track.

Always Learning

I hope that this chapter has been helpful in the creation of your own pipelines and pipeline tools, or at the very least give you some building blocks to start with. You can expand on this information in a million ways. Nothing is set in stone, and you can accomplish any task in many ways. Building a successful pipeline doesn't happen overnight, and most likely your pipelines will evolve with each successive production.

six

Hair Systems

Petre Gheorghian and Dariush Derakhshani

Hair systems *use a collection of dynamic NURBS curves generated from hair follicles to simulate natural movement of long hair, hair blowing in the wind, hair motion when a character is swimming underwater, and various hair styles (including braids and updos).*

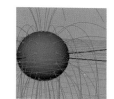

Although we're talking about a sub-module of the Dynamics module called Hair, *you can put Hair dynamics to myriad uses beyond just hair. In this chapter, we will jump into Hair dynamics with a few examples to take a look at how to use them to create animations for scenes.*

Each hair follicle contains one NURBS curve, but it can also contain a number of hairs that make up a clump. The follicle has various attributes for modifying the simulation as well as the appearance and style of the hair, including a **Braid** *attribute. The new Paint Hair tool allows for creating and removing follicles as well as painting hair attributes (including* **Clump Width Scale**, **Stiffness**, *and* **Braid***).*

But since Hair uses a generic dynamic curve simulation engine, you can also use the curves to control IK chains, deformers, surfaces, and so on. And we will continue to focus on that in the following examples. But first, we'll explain how Hair works.

Hair at a Quick Glance

Getting to know a few things about Hair will help build your foundation for the examples in this chapter, as well as prepare you for some other dynamics exercises in Chapter 7.

You can create Hair on both NURBS and polygonal surfaces. But for polygons, UVs should be nonoverlapping and fit between 0 and 1. Automatic mapping is a quick way to achieve this, however. Before you create the Hair system, decide which renderer you will be using because this affects the type of output you select.

You can create Hair in the form of NURBS curves (you use this option if you want to use the Hair system for nonHair dynamic simulations), Paint Effects strokes, or both curves and strokes. For example, you use Paint Effects strokes to create renderable hair for you character, or you create NURBS curves to help you create animations for your scene.

Curve Types

There are three sets of curves for a given Hair system:

Start Position Curves This is the position of the hair at the start frame of a hair simulation. At creation time, these curves stick out straight from the follicles on the surface and show you the origin of your simulation.

Rest Position Curves This is the position of the hair when no forces are affecting it. You can edit the shape of these curves to influence the look of the hair. You essentially set these curves to give the hair curves a goal, if you will.

Current Position Curves These curves show you how the hair behaves when you play the simulation.

To display any of these curves while you set up your simulation, choose **Hair** → **Display**. This is useful in showing how the hair is reacting to forces. Figure 6.1 shows you the Start Position Curves as well as the Current Position Curves as they fall due to gravity.

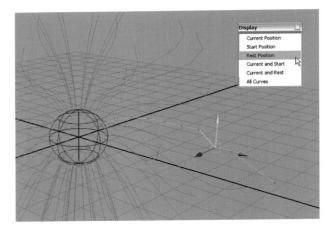

You can easily edit the Start and Rest Position curves by editing their points in Component Mode as you would any other CV or EP curve. This way you can set your simulation as you like it, to create, for example, a simulation in which you hair stands up when you grab onto a power cable. Just don't mess with the Current Position Curves; you want to let Maya run those for you.

Do not edit the Current Position Curves. Doing so yields unpredictable results.

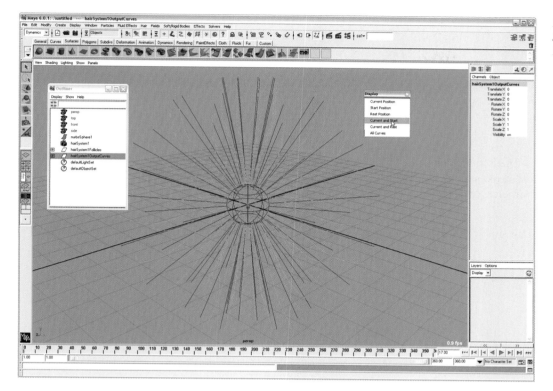

Figure 6.1: The Start and Current Position Curves

Passive Hair Curves

Passive curves interpolate the dynamic behavior of active curves, but are less expensive than simulating every curve. In the Create Hair options window, you can specify a ratio of passive curves (Passive Fill) to active curves to fill in hair without incurring a huge simulation cost. Dynamic forces or collisions are not computed on passive hairs, per se. Instead, they interpolate the motion of the active hairs in their own hair-System node. Figure 6.2 shows passive curves in green and active curves in blue.

The **Simulation Method** attribute on the follicle-Shape node for a Hair system determines whether the hair curve is dynamic, passive, or static, allowing you to change the curve to suit your simulation. Static hairs simply keep their start position and do not animate. That's not fun.

Interacting with the Hair Simulation

What's fun about hair if you can't play with it? In the following steps, you will learn how to interactively

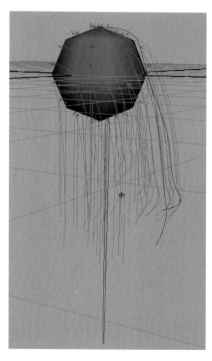

Figure 6.2: Passive and Active curves

move, scale, or rotate the surface with hair while the simulation is playing and see the hair update due to the dynamic forces applied to it.

Choose **Hair** → **Display** → **Current Position** to change the hair curves display to the current dynamic curves, which are those that update when you play the simulation. This is usually the default display so as not to cause confusion. To interact with your Maya object while the simulation runs, follow these steps:

1. Of course, you'll need a surface with hair. Create a NURBS sphere. While it is still selected, choose **Hair** → **Create Hair**.
2. Select the surface with your hair. In the Dynamics menu set, choose **Solvers** → **Interactive Playback** to play the hair simulation and allow you to interact with it at the same time.
3. Select the Move tool, and move the surface with hair while the simulation is running to see how the hair reacts to the dynamic forces.
4. Now select the Scale or Rotate tool and act upon the surface with hair to see how the hair reacts to the dynamic forces.

To tweak the hair simulation, adjust the **Stiffness**, **Iterations**, and even **Gravity** attributes in the Dynamics section of the hairSystemShape node.

Hair Constraints

Choose **Hair** → **Create Constraint**, and then choose from a variety of options that are designed to enhance specific hair looks. When you create a constraint, the constraint is set to affect the selected hair curves. For example, three hair curves in Figure 6.3 have been given a Rubber Band constraint. When you run the simulation, they are affected by the constraint's locator and its position and movement.

In component mode you select the curve components where you want to apply the constraining effect; you do not select the entire curve, unless you fear nothing.

Figure 6.3: Three hairs are constrained by a Rubber Band constraint.

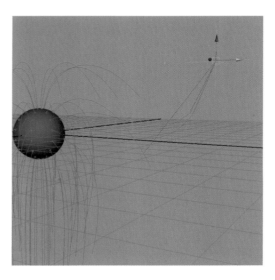

To apply a constraint, first select the hair curves and then apply the constraint type you want. The Attribute Editor for the hairConstraintShape node contains the attributes that affect the way the constraint interacts with the hair. For example, **Glue Strength** rules the strength of the constraint, and **Stiffness** lets you control the elasticity of the constraint. If you want an effect in which you are grabbing the ends of a few hairs forcefully, **Glue Strength** is as high as **Stiffness**. But if you are going for an effect in which the static charge of a balloon rubbed on some rabbit fur gently tugs on the ends of the hair, both **Glue Strength** and **Stiffness** are low.

Using Hair Curves as Deformers

Now that you've seen a little bit of Maya Hair's workings, let's look at a few examples of how Hair dynamics can help run your animation. In this example, we are creating the motion of an octopus's tentacles with hair.

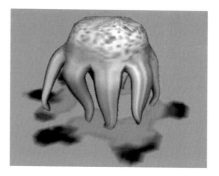

The Hair system curves will be made into wire deformers and will drive the animation/deformation of the octopus. Upon contact with the ground, the tentacles will emit into a 2D fluid container positioned at ground level to create a look of dust getting kicked up. To begin, follow along with these steps:

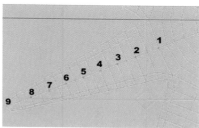

1. Open the file `Octopus_start.mb`. You should see something like Figure 6.4.
2. Go to the top view. From the Create menu, select the EP Curve tool.
3. Holding down the V key (for snap to point), start clicking the tentacle's axis following the order shown at right.
4. Press Enter at the end of the tentacle (after the ninth click) to create the curve. Smashing, isn't it?

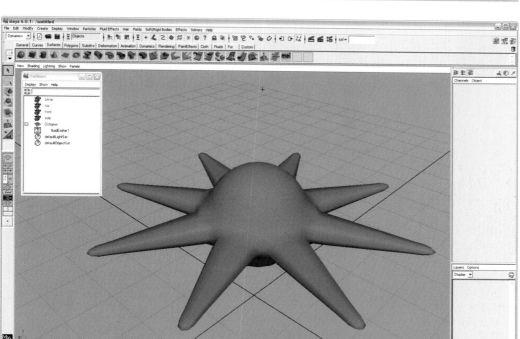

Figure 6.4: Fancy octopus

5. Change the scale on the Y axis to 0 for the curve you created to flatten it.

6. Go to the side view. Holding down the X key, move the curve up until it is in the center of the tentacle. It needs to be positioned here to properly deform the surface.

If you go to the side view when you move with the curve snapping to the grid, it helps because the octopus is 2 units above the ground and the curve will snap in the middle.

---

7. Choose **Edit** → **Duplicate** ❏. Set the Rotate Y value to 45, set the number of copies to 7, and click Duplicate. The next time you duplicate, be sure to reestablish these settings unless you want eight more copies. The curves should be in the center of the tentacle.

8. Open the Outliner, select the eight curves, and then choose **Hair** → **Make Selected Curves Dynamic** to turn the curve into a dynamic curve.

9. In the Outliner, click the plus sign beside hairSystem1Follicles to expand the view. Shift+select all the hair follicles (from follicle1 to follicle8). You need to select the follicle nodes themselves, instead of just selecting the group node.

10. In the Channel box, click inside the Point Lock field and choose Base from the drop-down menu to lock down the now-dynamic curves at their base, which is at the start of the curve.

11. In the Hair menu, choose **Display** → **Current Position** to ensure that you're seeing the curves as they move—not that we don't trust you or anything.

12. In the Animation menu set, choose Deform and then select the Wire tool. This lets you assign the curves as wire deformers.

13. Select the octopus geometry and press Enter to select the affected geometry. Now you can select the deforming curves to be used.

14. In the Outliner, click the plus sign beside hairSystem1Output-putCurves to expand its view as shown in Figure 6.5.

15. Shift+select all the output curves (from 9 to 16) and press Enter. This creates wire deformers for these curves to drive the deformation of the octopus. Again, it's important to select the output curves and not just the top node.

16. Select the octopus geometry, and then select hairSystem1Follicles in the Outliner. In the Constrain menu, choose **Parent**. This ensures that the follicles move with the octopus's body.

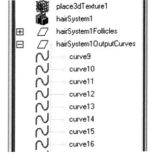

17. Expand hairSystem1OutputCurves in the Outliner. Select the octopus geometry, Ctrl+select curve9BaseWire, and choose **Parent** from the Constrain menu. Repeat this step for all the other BaseWire curves found in hairSystem1Out-putCurves. This step is important since it ensures that the base of the deformers moves with the octopus geometry.

Figure 6.5: Expand the Outliner view to select the curves themselves.

18. Set your playback end to 10000. This is to let you see the simulation run a good long course. Plus big numbers are cool.

Now let's see how the octopus body deforms while you move the geometry around in the Perspective view. Select the octopus geometry, and in the Dynamics menu set, choose **Solvers** → **Interactive Playback**. This plays the hair simulation while allowing you to interact

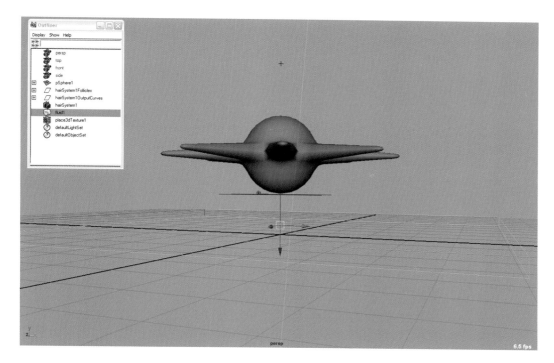

Figure 6.6: Position the fluid container to kick up dust from the octopus's movement.

with the octopus. Using the Move tool, select the octopus and move it while the simulation is playing interactively.

Let's add some collisions to the simulation and add some fluid emission for the fun of it, so that the octopus kicks up a little dust:

1. In the Outliner, select HairSystem1, and in the Attribute Editor, open the Collisions section. Turn on Self Collide and Collide Ground to prevent the tentacles from going through the ground plane or crossing each other.
2. From the Fluid Effects menu, choose **Create 2D Container** to add a 2D fluid container to the simulation.
3. In the Channel box, set the Rotate X of the 2D fluid container to 90 and then move it 0.25 units on the Y axis to place it just above the ground plane, as shown in Figure 6.6.
4. Open the Attribute Editor for the fluid container. In the Contents Method section, set Density to Static Grid, and set Velocity, Temperature, and Fuel to Off.
5. Open the Shading section of the Attribute Editor for the fluid container, and set the color to dark gray for dust.
6. Open the Display section of the Attribute Editor for the fluid container, and set Boundary Draw to None. This will just turn off the bounding box view of the fluid container to clean up our view.
7. In the Outliner, select the fluid container, and then Ctrl+select the octopus geometry. From the Fluid Effects menu, choose **Add/Edit Contents → Emit from Object**. This will make the octopus emit inside the fluid container.

Now when you play back the simulation, dust will be emitted at the contact points when the tentacles touch the ground, as you can see in Figure 6.7.

Figure 6.7: Crazy like Footloose!

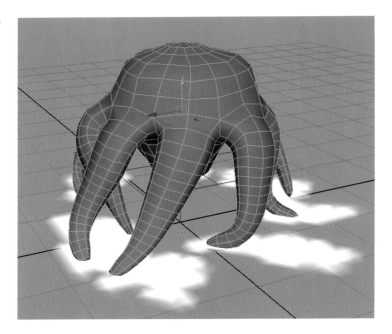

Open up the Octopus_finished.mb file to take a look into the finished simulation. You can use this sort of setup to animate a mop or broom, for example, though you would have more strings and bristles than tentacles to play with.

The Breaking Rope Effect

In this exercise, we will use constraints to create an effect of a rope breaking. It sounds fairly simple, though it's a complicated procedure that is made easier with Maya's Hair tools. You can use this type of animation on something like a rope bridge snapping just when the hero jumps to safety and the villain falls to his all-too-deserved death.

You can open the Rope_Finished.mb file to take a quick peek at the effect, shown in Figure 6.8. But essentially we'll just attach two ends of two dynamic curves together using a constraint and then break the influence of the constraint to get the rope to break apart.

To create a breaking rope, follow the beat of this drum:

1. Go to the top view. From the Create menu, select the EP Curve tool. We'll draw the curves to use for the rope.

2. Start creating a curve by holding down X (for snap to grid) and first clicking 12 units to the left of the origin on the X axis. Continue clicking at 8 units to the left and then 4 units to the left, and finally click the origin and press Y to complete the creation of the curve and keep the EP Curve tool as the current tool. (See Figure 6.9.)

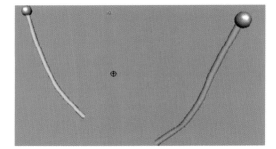

Figure 6.8: The desired effect

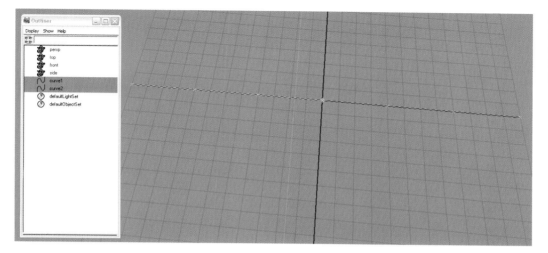

Figure 6.9: Drawing the two curves to be used for the halves of the rope

3. Start creating the second curve by clicking first at the origin (while holding X), then at 4 units to the right, 8 units, and then finally at 12 units. Now press Enter to complete the second curve.

4. Select the second curve, and in the Edit Curves menu, choose **Reverse Curve Direction** to orient the curve properly when we lock down the ends of the dynamic curves.

5. In the Outliner, select the two curves you just created and choose **Hair** → **Make Selected Curves Dynamic**. This will make the two curves dynamic. But since you had both selected when you ran the operation, you'll make them dynamic using a single Hair system. This way you can edit the dynamic attributes for both curves easily with one hair system node.

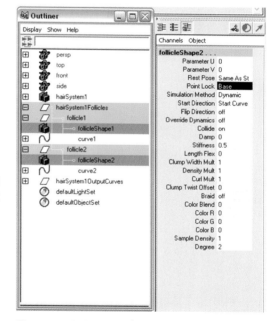

6. In the Outliner, expand hairSystem1Follicles by clicking the plus sign. Select the first follicle, and open the Attribute Editor for follicleShape1. Set the **Point Lock** attribute to Base. You can also access this attribute in the Channel box, as shown in Figure 6.10.

7. Repeat the previous step for the second follicle.

8. Play back the simulation by clicking the Playback button in the animation controls. Stop after 60 frames. You should see something like Figure 6.11.

9. In the Hair menu, choose **Display** → **Current Position**.

Figure 6.10: Setting a base point lock for the two curves

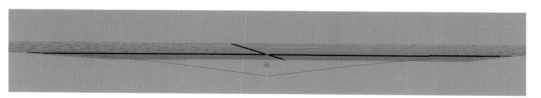

Figure 6.11: Play back the first 60 frames.

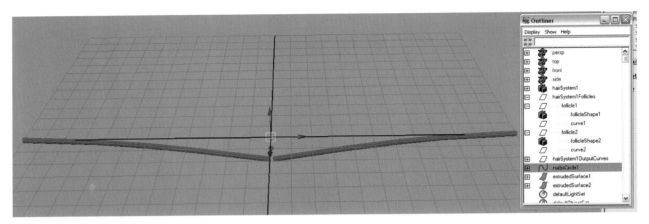

Figure 6.12: The two rope halves

Now that we have the dynamic curves in order, let's give the rope a bit of thickness. For this, a simple extrusion will work great. Make sure history is turned on before you proceed since you will use history to animate the rope.

10. From the Create menu, choose **NURBS Primitives** → **Circle.** We'll use this profile curve to extrude the shape of the rope.

11. In the Channel box, scale the circle down to 0.3 on the X and Z axes.

12. In the Perspective view, select the circle first and then Shift+select the first curve. In the Modeling menu set, choose **Surfaces** → **Extrude** → ❏ and set the following attributes: **Style** to Tube, **Result Position** to Path, **Pivot** to Component, **Orientation** to Profile Normal, **Output Geometry** to NURBS. Click Extrude. This will give your rope thickness.

13. Select the circle, and Shift+select the second curve. Extrude again using the settings in the previous steps.

14. Do not delete the circle or the history on any of the curves or objects in the scene, since the history of the extrusion deforms the surfaces. And by keeping the history, you can adjust the thickness of the rope at any time by scaling the circle. Figure 6.12 shows the result of the extrusions.

15. In the Outliner, select hairSystem1, and open the Attribute Editor. In the Dynamics section, change **Stiffness** to 0.003 and, in the Stiffness Scale section, change **Gravity** to 5.

16. Select the two curves, and in Component mode, select the CVs at the origin (from both curves), as shown in Figure 6.13.

    By selecting the CV points, you're telling Maya exactly where you want the constraint to take effect.

    In the Hair menu, choose **Create Constraint** → **Hair to Hair** as shown at right.

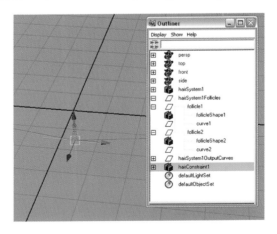

17. Rewind your simulation, and then play back the first 100 frames. The curves will bow down, but stick together to form a single slack rope.

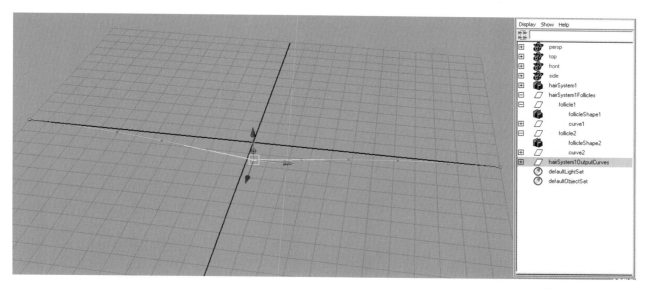

Figure 6.13:
Selecting the CVs
at the end

18. In the Perspective view, select the two curves (in object selection mode), go to the Hair menu, and choose **Set Start Position** → **From Current**. This sets the current position shown here as the beginning position for the dynamic curves.

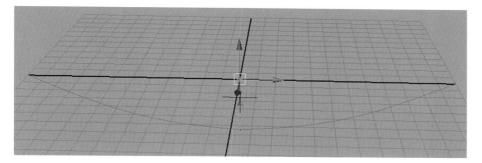

19. Now we will keyframe the **Glue Strength** attribute on hairConstraint1. This will allow us to get the breaking effect since this attribute basically controls the influence of the constraint on the dynamic curves.
20. We'll decide to break the rope at frame 150, so go to frame 149 to set a keyframe for the rope as a single piece. At frame 149, in the Outliner, select hairConstraint1, and set a keyframe in the Channel box for the attribute **Glue Strength** at a value of 1.
21. Go to frame 150, change the value of **Glue Strength** to 0, and set another keyframe. This essentially turns off all influence of the constraint keeping the two rope halves together, effectively breaking them apart like a good argument.
22. Now when you play your animation, the rope should break at frame 150 as we see in Figure 6.14.

You can add some turbulence strength and frequency to the hairSystem node in the Attribute Editor on the Turbulence section to enhance the realism of the simulation. This will

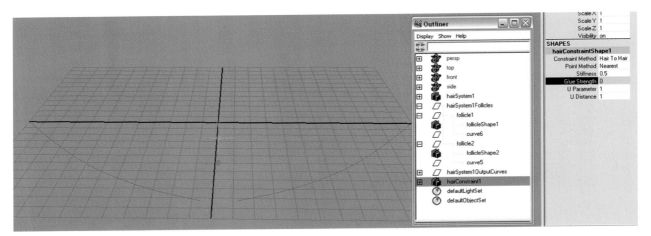

Figure 6.14: Breaking up is hard to do.

make a big difference in your animation as it will give the rope at least a little bit of a sway. Creating believable simulations depends on layers upon layers of animation.

Furthermore, try to animate the settings on the turbulence or other forces to make it seem as if the forces acting on the rope cause it to break. A good exercise is to animate a wind sock using Hair.

Driving a Character's Secondary Motion

With character animation, any professional will tell you that an incredible amount of work goes into making a character move well. Getting Maya to create as much of that animation for you as possible can be a blessing, as long as the simulation is well thought out, and intricately prepared and executed.

In the following tutorial, we will use dynamic hair curves to drive the secondary motion of skeleton joints. We'll be using these joints as influences on flesh on the character. This will help us produce realistic flesh inertia while the character is moving that reacts to the animation given to the body.

The curves will be set up as IK spline handles for the additional deformation joints. After creating the additional joints and the IK spline handles, we will adjust the hair system attributes to achieve the right amount of inertia from the character's movement.

Setting Up the Rig

From the CD, open the file Hair_Walk_Start.mb. A rig of a biped with a simple walk animation is already applied to the rig. Figure 6.15 shows the file loaded in the persp view.

To begin adding secondary movement controls to the rig, follow along:

1. From the Create menu, select the EP Curve tool. We will trace a curve along the thigh bone of the right leg in the next step.
2. Holding down the V key (snap to point), click once on the right_hip joint and once again on the right_knee joint. Press Enter to complete the curve shown as the green line running up the thigh in Figure 6.16.

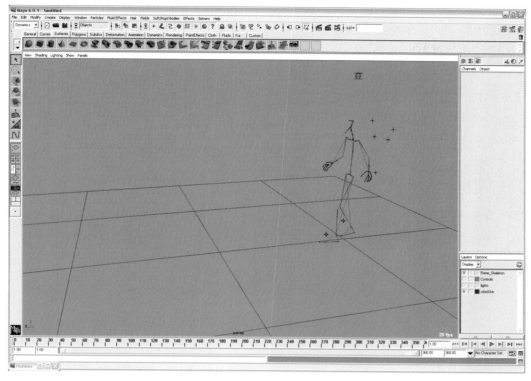

Figure 6.15: The starting rig and walk cycle file loaded and ready to go!

3. With the curve selected, choose **Edit Curves** → **Rebuild Curve** → ❑. Set **Rebuild Type** to Uniform, set **Number of spans** to 4, and click Rebuild as shown below. This ensures that we have a uniform curve with the six CVs that we will need.

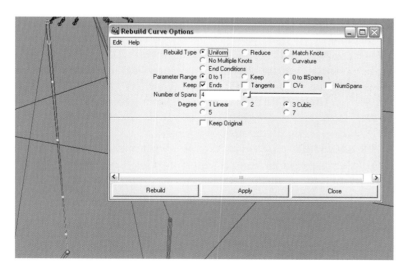

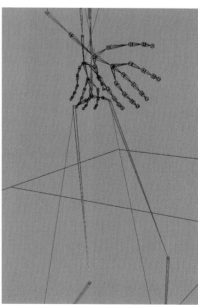

Figure 6.16: The curve runs along the thigh bone, seen in green.

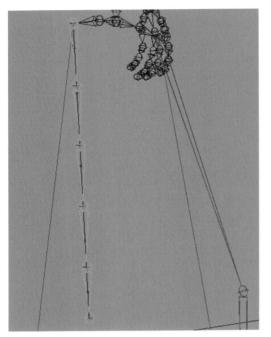

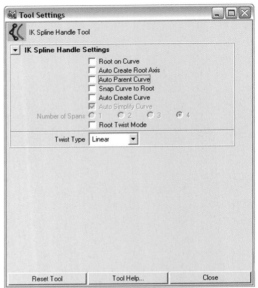

Figure 6.17: Draw six evenly spaced joints along the curve.

Figure 6.18: The IK Spline Handle Tool option box with the right settings

4. Select the right_hip joint, and in the Display menu choose **Hide → Hide Selection** or press the hotkey Ctrl+H. This just gets the joint out of our way. You can always easily unhide it through the Outliner.

5. Select the Joint tool, and, holding down the C key (snap to curve), click six times on the curve, starting from the hip area toward the knee area. The joints should be evenly spaced and look similar to Figure 6.17. You might have to try this a few times until you get the joints fairly evenly placed. Just make sure you keep snapping to the curve.

6. In the Outliner select the curve created earlier, and in the Hair menu choose **Make Selected Curves Dynamic**.

7. Choose **Hair → Display → Current Position**. This just simplifies the view so that we don't have to see the Start Position Curve as well as the Current Position Curve as the default.

8. In the Skeleton menu (found in the Animation menu set), open the IK Spline Handle Tool option window. Set **Root on Curve** to Off, **Auto Create Root Axis** to Off, **Auto Parent Curve** to Off, **Snap Curve to Root** to Off, and **Auto Create Curve** to Off. Figure 6.18 shows the option box with the proper settings.

9. With the IK Spline Handle tool selected, click the starting joint of the new hierarchy created earlier, click the last joint, and finally click the curve. This creates a Spline IK control with the top joint (at the hip) as the root and the knee as the end. It also sets the six-CV curve we created earlier as the driving curve for the Spline IK Handle.

10. Select the starting joint of the new hierarchy created earlier, Shift+select the right_pelvis joint, and press P to parent the new joint hierarchy to the old one as shown in Figure 6.19.

11. In the Display menu, choose **Show → Show Last Hidden**. You can also select that hidden hip joint from step 4 in the Outliner and choose **Show → Show Selected** instead. Figure 6.20 shows the leg.

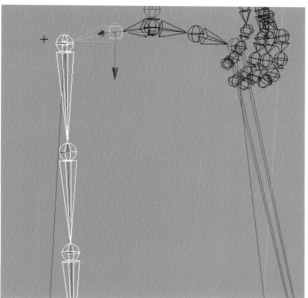

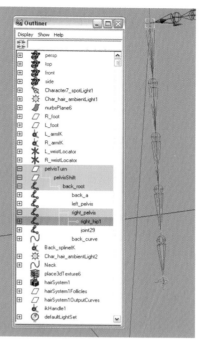

Figure 6.19: Parent the joint hierarchy

Figure 6.20: The joints revealed

12. In the Outliner, select hairSystem1Follicles, and Shift+select the right_hip joint in the Perspective window. Press P to parent the follicles to the right_hip joint. Figure 6.21 shows the Outliner view.

Figure 6.21: Parent the hair system follicle node under the right hip joint.

OK, so much buildup, but this is really cool. Play back the animation. The dynamic curve is driving the six-joint skeleton you made, flopping the chain around in direct reaction to the leg's animation. We have some more work to do figuring out the right settings, but you can see where this is going. For a bit of a nicer look, follow these steps:

1. In the Outliner, select hairSystem1 and open the Attribute Editor.
2. In the Dynamics section, set **Stiffness** to 1.3 and set **Length Flex** to 0.2.
3. Now when you play back the animation, you should get the right amount of motion for the new joint hierarchy. These settings will make the secondary movement of the thigh muscle tighter and more believable.

Of course, if you continue playing, you can begin to judge the best weight for the character's various parts, especially once other parts of the body are set up similarly.

An Old Man on His Horse

As cool as this is, it's really important to keep in mind that you'll never get a great character from setting everything up this way. A character is so definitive of the person who is making it that automating everything ends up hiding a lot of personality and karma of the animator. And any experienced animator will back us up in a nasty bar fight over this.

Personality in animation, of any kind, really has to come from the animator. But it's also a horribly time-consuming and exhaustive process to create any length of fantastic animation. Using tricks like this to quickly and accurately give weight to your animation is important and extremely effective. How do you combine the two? How much of your tool do you forsake for art?

The answer is to create sliders, set driven keys, and editable modifiers that affect the dynamics of the rig. For example, why don't you throw a modifier on to the **Stiffness** attribute for every hair system node you have created? This modifier could be a simple added float attribute that acts as a multiplier in a simple expression to change the elasticity of the thigh (let's say) on the fly according to a slider you animate by hand. The multiplier need not be terribly high; it can be a wickedly short range so as not to affect the **Stiffness** that much, but just enough to give it some essence of the animator. Even if it is just the right thigh.

Don't ever rely on a rig to animate for you.

Secret of the Pros for Those Trying to Step Up

Most experienced professionals in the CG field usually just look for a quick introduction to a solution to a particular problem. What begins to distinguish the good from the poor is their ability to be able to take a kernel of an idea and assess the probability that it will lead to a successful solution system to accomplish any number of complex problems at hand. A lot of the time, you will come across an opportunity to pick up a nugget of information about CG that might seem alien to what you do, but quite quickly you'll find ways to use those thoughts and ideas to your benefit in the search for an animation. Successful pros have built their careers on them, so stay patient with it.

Learning how to do things differently is a diamond mine, but keeping in mind that most solutions never come in direct forms is your shovel. The first step to launching yourself into professional work is to realize that tools only work best in conjunction with one another, as do work flows and methodologies. The best way to pick that up is to stop thinking about how to do things.

Animating a Shark

This example combines motion path animation with Hair dynamics for a nifty effect. We will add secondary motion to a moving character. We will animate a shark along a motion path that will also be used to deform the skeleton of the shark, to give it a sense of swimming through water. But, as you saw with the tutorial of adding secondary animation to a walking character, we'll automate the movement of the fins to give them a little bit of pepper in this animation.

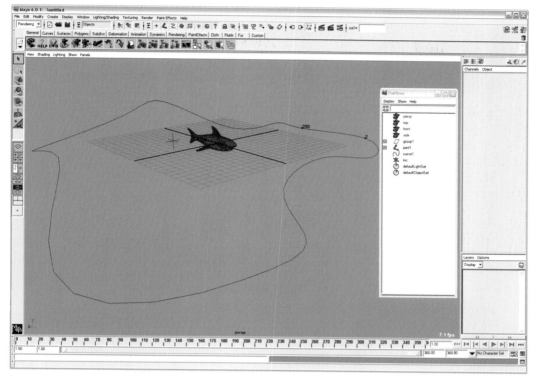

Figure 6.22: The shark scene

You can take a look at the completed file before starting the project, or you can always use it later as reference (see Shark_done_hair.mb). Start by opening the file Shark_start.mb shown in Figure 6.22. Now follow these steps:

1. Select joint1 and curve1, and then in the **Animation** menu set, choose **Animate → Motion Paths → Attach to Motion Path → ❑**. Set the following before attaching: **Time Range** to Start/End, **Start** to 1, **End** to 200, **Follow** to On, **World Up Type** to Object Rotation Up. In the text field, enter the node name **loc**. Set **Bank** to On, and then click Attach, as shown in Figure 6.23.

   You should really reset the Attach to Motion Path tool before you enter these attributes to make sure the other settings for creating a motion path for this object are at the Maya default.

2. Now we will use curve1 as an IK spline for the shark's spine. In the Skeleton menu (found in the Animation menu set), open the IK Spline Handle Tool option window shown in Figure 6.24. Set

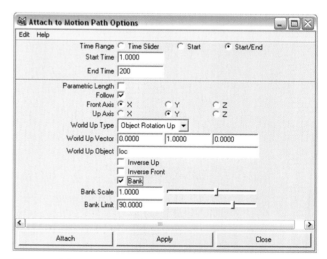

Figure 6.23: Motion path options

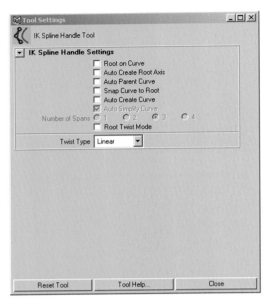

Figure 6.24: IK Spline Handle Tool option window

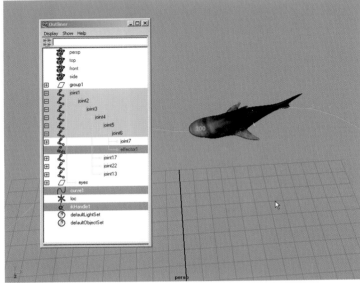

Figure 6.25: Shark on a string

Root on Curve to Off, Auto Create Root Axis to Off, Auto Parent Curve to Off, Snap Curve to Root to Off, and Auto Create Curve to Off. Consider resetting the tool before you enter these values. Doing so will give a motion as if the shark is gliding through the water, bending and curving to match the current.

3. With the IK Spline Handle tool selected, click the starting joint of the new hierarchy created earlier, click joint7, and finally click the curve. This attaches the curve to the IK handle as seen in Figure 6.25.

4. You'll notice that the shark will swim backward a bit. To fix this, select the curve, and in the Channel box in the Output section, select motionPath1. Open the Graph Editor, select U value, and press F to frame the animation curve. Now select the last keyframe (frame 200), and change the value to 0. Select the first keyframe (frame 1), and change the value to 1. This will correct the shark's direction.

5. Click the animation curve in the Graph Editor (see Figure 6.26), choose **Curves** → **Pre Infinity** → **Cycle,** and then choose **Post Infinity** → **Cycle.** This keeps repeating the animation past frame 200. Under View in the Graph Editor, choose **Infinity.** You'll see the cycle extend beyond your last frame.

6. We'll now get some flipping around, not quite the graceful creature we need to animate, so select the IK handle and open the Attribute Editor. In the Advanced Twist Controls section under IK Solver Attributes, check Enable Twist Controls. Change **World Up Type** to **Object Up** and change **Up Axis** to **Positive Z.** In the World Up Object field, enter the node name **loc.** This will correct the flipping (due to the fact that the position of the locator called "loc" will be used to constrain the orientation of the IK, thus eliminating the flipping).

7. Now, using the steps outlined in the earlier tutorial on creating secondary motion on a character, create curves for the fins and the tail of the shark. You will be attaching dynamic curves to the joint structure of the shark as we did for the thigh of the walk

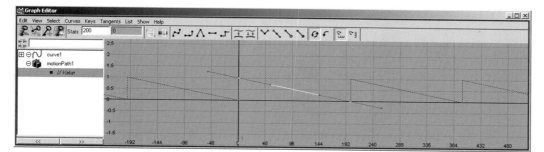

Figure 6.26: The Graph Editor

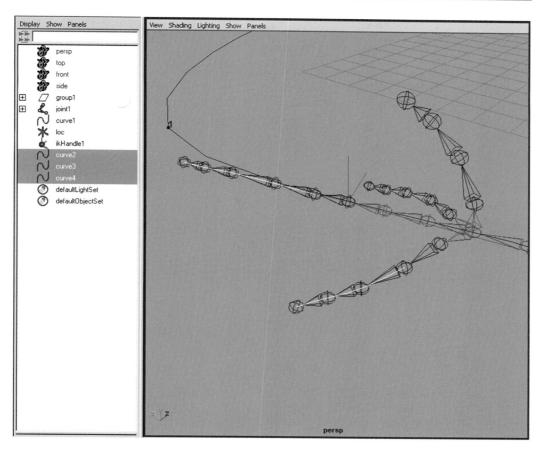

Figure 6.27: We'll affect the last three joints of the fins

cycle rig. This will add secondary motion to the fins to follow along with the swimming pattern of the shark. They will respond to the shark's movement as it swims.

8. You will be using the last three joints for the skeleton belonging to the fins (see Figure 6.27) and four joints for the skeleton belonging to the tail to trace over for your new curve (again, think of the thigh joints we traced over in the earlier tutorial). Create these curves that will be used as IK splines by holding the V key (snap to point) and clicking the joints downward along the length of the body to the extremities, the fins.

9. In the Outliner, select the curves created earlier, and in Hair menu, choose **Make Selected Curves Dynamic.**

10. In the Hair menu, choose **Display** → **Current Position.**
11. Select the appropriate joints, select the respective curve using the IK Spline Handle tool, and then turn the current curves into IK spline handles.
12. In the Outliner, expand the hairSystem1Follicles by clicking the plus sign.
13. Select the first follicle, and open the Attribute Editor for follicleShape1. From the Point Lock menu, choose **Base**. This places the solid portion at the base of the fin at the body. Do the same for the other two follicles.
14. In the Outliner, select hairSystem1 and open the Attribute Editor. In the Dynamics section, set **Stiffness** to 1 and set **Length Flex** to 0.1.
15. In the Outliner, select hairSystem1Follicles, and parent the follicles under their respective joints. Figure 6.28 shows the shark in action.

When you play back the simulation, you will get the nice secondary motion of the fins and tail. Try playing around with the severity of the dynamics on the curve to see how that affects the animation.

A further thought is to make the motion path curve itself dynamic. By combining dynamic motion with the path of the object, we can give the animation a secondary movement particularly useful for adding atmospheric motion to a character or an object.

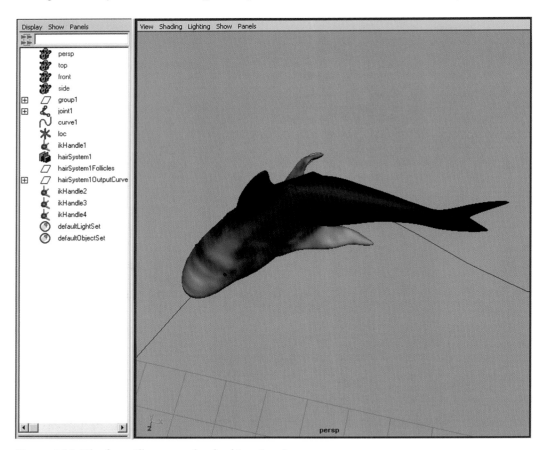

Figure 6.28: The fins will react to the shark's animation

Strong dynamic movement, with a high turbulence set at a high frequency will give a sense of chaos or, better yet, entropy to the animation. A slower paced, yet strong interference will give the sense of a more viscous environment that is in turmoil, such as a fish traveling through choppy waters.

This type of combined animation can be extremely useful for adding secondary movement to parts of a whole that need to react to the overall movement, giving inertia in short. The amount of dynamics you choose to apply to the animation will define the environment. Try creating a dynamic curve that is then used as the animation path for the shark. What kind of settings would you need to make the shark swim through a soft tidal disturbance? What are good dynamic settings to put the shark swimming through a dreadful storm?

And this animation can be easily scaled and changed to give the director a chance to change their mind, as they are often so wont to do. Choices really are what this gives you, and choices are key.

A Dancing MP3 Player

You've perhaps seen the commercials for a popular, fruit-named company's MP3 player in which graphics of brightly colored people dance against a single-colored background to the music playing through their MP3 players. The eye-catching element of these ads is the white headphone cord that hangs down from their ears and connects to the MP3 player in their hands. We'll take a look at how the new hair dynamics can make an animation like this a cakewalk as we animate our own version of this effect using dynamic curves.

We use digital video footage of a person holding an MP3 player and moving about to create dynamic motion in the cord that we will create in CG.

Let's begin by studying the footage available to create this animation. Notice how our dancing fool in Figure 6.29 moves about in frames to start thinking about how best to attack the issue. The ear-bud–style earphones he is wearing have a primary cord that comes from the headphone jack on the top of the MP3 player and go directly to the right-side ear bud, which is snug in his ear. There is also a single cord that stretches from his left ear down and across the back of the base of his neck and attaches to the main cord about 18 inches below the right-side ear bud, looping up and over his left shoulder.

Figure 6.29: The dancing fool is available for parties.

Figure 6.30 shows you a sample of one of these ear-bud headphones. Your animated ones will be white, though, since our dancing fool forgot his white shirt that day. Accordingly, it's important to understand the subject of your animation. If you have a pair of headphones, by all means get them out and try watching how they move when you wear them and walk around; dance for heaven's sake!

Create the Cord

Let's start by creating curves in the layout of the ear-bud cord. You can use an image like the one in Figure 6.30 to outline your curves to mimic the real cord or just create your own. Don't bother attaching the cord from the right-side ear bud (shown in bright blue in Figure 6.31) to the main cord yet, though it will be good to try to place the final CV close to the main cord, but not on it. We will cover attaching it soon, but for now these are two distinct curves. Figure 6.31 shows the cord curves we're using here. Notice they've been modeled as if they were already fitted to the actor in the background.

Now we need to attach the left ear-bud cord to the main cord. Follow these steps:

Figure 6.30: Ear-bud–style headphones that we will animate with hair dynamics

1. Select the new Soft Modification tool from the Tool Box on the left, and click the short ear-bud cord at the end of the curve, preferably on its last CV. This creates a deformer object much like a cluster, except that the Soft Modification Handle (called softMod1Handle) has a falloff area whereas a cluster affects the CVs attached to it directly. This means that if we select the Soft Modification Handle and move it, it will pull along with it the curve parts under its influence, graduating softly along its influence radius.

2. Deselect everything, and then select the Soft Modification Handle. In the Channel box, click the softMod1 node. Change **Falloff Radius** to 1.50. If you move the handle around in the view panels, you'll see how it affects the curve. The greater the falloff radius, the more the curve will move when you tug on the Soft Modification Handle. Figure 6.32 shows the Soft Modification Handle attached to the end of the short ear-bud cord.

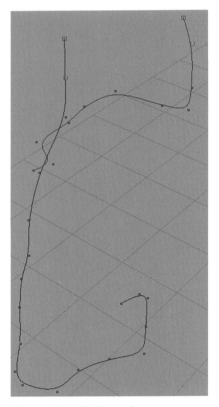

Figure 6.31: We'll use these curves to extrude a profile shape—like a simple circle—to create the cord.

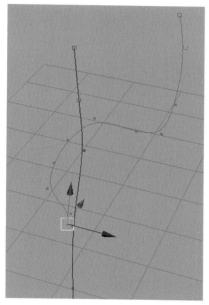

Figure 6.32: The Soft Modification
Handle now controls the end of the
short cord.

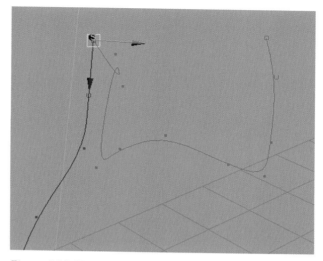

Figure 6.33: Using an animation path to attach the cord
end to the main cord

By creating that Soft Modification Handle, you have positional control for the end of
that short ear-bud cord. You can place the Soft Modification Handle on the main cord, even
snapping it to one of the CVs of the main cord. The problem becomes apparent, though,
when the main cord deforms dynamically when either the actor's head or the MP3 player
moves. If that happens, how do you keep the end of the short ear-bud cord on the main cord
curve?

If you already answered that you can use path animation to keep the end of the short
curve attached to the main cord, you're right! Give yourself a nice cookie and a pat on the
shoulder. Now, continue to follow along for how to attach the cord:

3. Make sure you're not still in the Soft Modification tool (select the Move tool, for
   example, to exit out of making more handles). Then select the Soft Modification Handle
   and the main cord. In the Animation menu set, choose Animate → Motion Paths →
   Attach to Motion Path to place the end of the cord at the top of the main cord, as
   shown in Figure 6.33.
4. With the Soft Modification Handle still selected, click the motionPath node. Highlight
   the **U Value** attribute, as shown in Figure 6.34, RM click, and select Break Connections to disconnect its connections to erase the animation of the motion path. This
   takes out the animation of the motion path, but keeps the Soft Modification Handle
   stuck to the path curve.
5. In a similar fashion in the Channel box, disconnect the **RotateX**, **RotateY**, and **RotateZ**
   attributes to disconnect the rotation animation from the Soft Modification Handle. You
   can then rotate the Soft Modification Handle to position the cord just the way you'd
   like it, as shown in Figure 6.34.

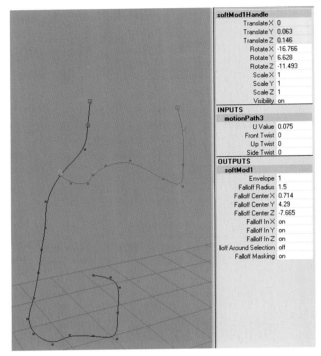

Figure 6.34: Disconnect the animation from the motion path, and orient the handle as you like.

Figure 6.35: The new output curves

6. Back in the Channel box, highlight the **U Value** attribute, and set it to a point where the ear-bud cord matches with about the fourth CV down from the top on the main cord. In this example, it is set to 0.075. Now the end of the cord will stick to this point, even as the main cord moves about dynamically; once we set it up to, that is.

Dynamic Curves and Animation

The intent here is to make the curves dynamic. Both cords will become dynamic, and both will be locked down at both ends. Even the short ear-bud cord will be locked at both ends. This way only the middle parts of the curves will be dynamic, and we will be able to animate the ends to match the footage of the guy dancing around.

To create the dynamic curves, follow these steps:

1. Select both the curves, and choose **Hair** → **Make Selected Curves Dynamic**. The new output curves appear in magenta, as shown in Figure 6.35.
2. Select the newly created follicle nodes in the Outliner individually, and check to make sure that **Point Lock** is set to BothEnds for both nodes.
3. Select the hairSystem1 node, and for the time being, set the **Stiffness** down to 0 to see the maximum flexibility for the cord. If you play back the simulation, you will see the output curves fall and sag as shown in Figure 6.36.

At this point, it's a matter of placing the cord in the shot. Bring in the frames of the video of the dancing fool in the Dynamics folder from the CD, and load it as an image plane as shown in Figure 6.37.

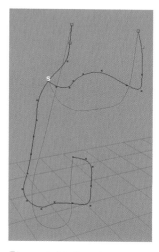

Figure 6.36: Sagging curves!

Figure 6.37: Solid gold!!

Make sure to match your camera to the footage settings so that your renders will composite properly. The footage is 640 × 480. Your Maya camera should have its default 35mm focal length, and **Film Gate** should be set to 35mm TV Projection for the best fit. In the Image Plane attributes, set **Fit** to To Size. In the Render Global Settings dialog box, select the preset resolution of 640 × 480, as shown in Figure 6.38. Since the original footage is in that layout, Maya's settings should match. Now we can proceed with fitting the cord to the ear buds for our dancing maniac.

The only real animating we have to do is to set the ends of the ear buds to match the dancer's ears. A photo like this would more than likely have been shot with ear buds already in the dancer's ears, so all you need to do is replace the cord, that is, match the CG cord to the ends of the real ear buds already in place in the ears. The same goes for the plug end of the cord. In all likelihood, the MP3 player will have a plug already in its earphone port, with perhaps an inch or so of the original cord sticking out of it. In our example, since I'm too cheap to cut my own ear-bud headphones, we'll extend the ends of the ear-bud cords to the ears and extend the plug end directly to the MP3 player.

1. Position the ends of the cord as close as possible to the ears and the MP3 player in the background plate, as shown in Figure 6.39.
2. To place the ends perfectly and animate them to match the movement of the dancing fool, you can animate the CVs (not a great idea), animate clusters at the ends (a viable option), or, better yet, animate Soft Modification Handles so that they tug on the cord a bit when you move them. Clusters will not let you do that and will stretch the cord. So attach Soft Modification Handles to the ear ends and the MP3 end of the cord as in Figure 6.40.

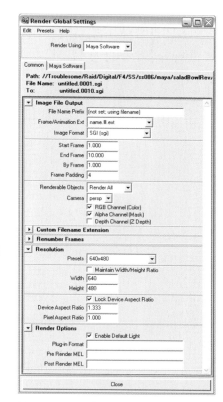

Figure 6.38: The Render Global Settings dialog box

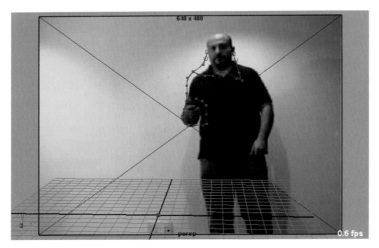

Figure 6.39: Position the headphone wire to fit.

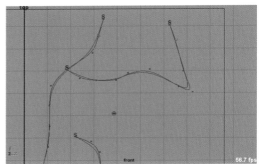

Figure 6.40: Place Soft Modification Handles at the ends of the cord.

Be sure to place the Soft Modification Handles at the ends of the original NURBS curve and not at the resultant hair dynamics output curves. The original curve acts as a goal object of sorts, or at least the ends do, so if we can control the ends of the curves easily with these Soft Modification Handles, we can drive the rest of the dynamic curve to react with the dancing fool's motion.

Track the location of the three Soft Modification Handles to their respective locations (ears and the MP3 player headphone jack) on the dancing fool, and when you play back your animation, the headphone cord will be dynamic. Adjust the **Stiffness** to your liking, though usually a low number is best.

To actually create the cord, just extrude a simple circle along the length of the two output curves, and shade and light it to your satisfaction. Keep in mind, white is a good color here because the fool's shirt is black. We need to extrude the surface to the hair output curves for a simple reason: those are the dynamic curves, and if you extrude with history on, they drive the shape of the extrusion to look like a cord. That's it!

Creating Collisions

Once the animation is complete, you'll notice the cord flailing around almost as much as the dancer, if you can call him that. To add some more realism to the scene, you can create collisions for the hair dynamics so that the curves bounce off the dancing fool's impressive stature. This is simple, though it requires you to match proxy objects, as shown in Figure 6.41, to the dancer's graceful machinations.

Once these proxy objects are in and matching the action, you can enable them to collide with the dynamic curves by selecting the surface and then the hairSystem node (in this case hairsystem1) and choosing **Hair → Make Collide**. You can set the bounciness of the cord as it collides with the proxy dancer body by manipulating the **Resilience** attribute. You can find that in the GeoConnector node that will attach to both the hairsystem node and the colliding geometry's node.

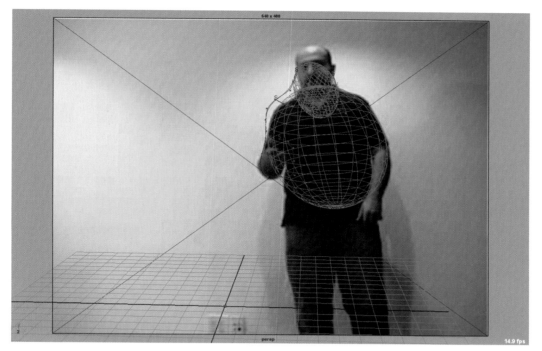

*Figure 6.41:
Matching proxy
objects to the
dancer's move-
ments will let
you create colli-
sions for the
dynamic curves
to add more
realism to the
simulation.*

When you run back your animation, you'll be able to tweak the dynamic attributes to make the cord react as you best like it. This kind of setup was only possible in the past using soft body curves with intricately worked-out rigid body colliders, but hair dynamics has finally made this type of animation a pleasure.

Always Learning

Take what is in here and make your own stuff happen. Tutorials are not a means to a particular end; they are a beginning and exercises to model a mode of thinking. If you study the motion of the shark, should its fins really be reacting to the swimming movement of the body? Perhaps applying these ideas to creating those parasitic fish that latch onto sharks would make better targets for this type of simulation? The point is not to take things for what they are, but to make them what they can be, and you'll see some more of those dynamics in the next chapter.

seven

A Dynamics Collection: Flexible Objects

Dariush Derakhshani

Soft body dynamics *(as well as cloth) in Maya focus on deformable objects and surfaces, such as drapes or a rubber ball. Pliable surfaces deform in reaction to a force or impact. In Maya, you simulate the deformation of soft body dynamics by assigning dynamic particles to the CVs (control vertices) of the model's surface (or to the points of a corresponding lattice deformer). When a field, a collision, or expressions move the particles, they pull their corresponding surface point, deforming the surface.*

The "play" in dynamics is figuring out the precise amount of elasticity to give an object for the proper effect for your shot and the efficient calculation of the scene, and this is the tricky part. Finding an effective way to set up a flexible object or surface within the confines of your resources is the tough part.

Expanding on the Hair and Dynamic Curves we explored in Chapter 6, this chapter focuses on a few production problems, each of which uses secondary motion and ways to automatically generate that secondary motion dynamically. We'll start by studying a car's antenna; then we'll use hair dynamics to generate inertial movement for a simple car suspension; and finally we will end with a soft body solution for a puddle on a rainy day, and kick up some dust with a rolling object.

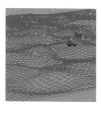

The Antenna: A Three-Pronged Approach

With flexible objects, or semirigid objects as I like to call them, such as a fencing sword (a foil) or car antenna, figuring out the right settings for the dynamic simulation to take into account all the factors of a scene involves precise tweaking on myriad attributes and settings. But it's possible to do so in several ways, some subtly different and others whole new approaches.

This section focuses on a single production problem, tackled in three ways. Creating the same effect in three ways demonstrates the beauty of Maya—that you can create the same effect in multiple ways to suit your own work flow.

We will start with soft body dynamics to create the motion of a car antenna on a moving car. We'll then compare and contrast the new hair dynamics that Maya Unlimited 6 affords us. Finally, we'll try using deformers and expressions to create a similar rig to achieve a simplified version of this effect without the use of dynamics.

Using Soft Bodies

For a car antenna, we need to create a thin object that is flexible and attach it to a car. The simplest way to go if you are running Maya Complete is to use Soft Bodies. However, if you are running Maya Unlimited 6 or later, you can use Maya hair and dynamic curves, which will make this exercise a snap. We'll take a look at dynamic curves and simple expression work to simulate the effect later in the exercise.

Setting Up the Antenna

With soft bodies, you assign surface points to dynamic particles. But the fewer particles you can get away with, the better the simulation will run. Instead of making the antenna surface itself a soft body, we will create a joint system to drive the surface and use a spline IK (Inverse Kinematics) handle to control the spline running the joints. This gives you a much cleaner scene with the same effect, along with cutting down the amount of work you have to do to tweak it just right.

We'll start with a simple car and antenna model, as shown in Figure 7.1. You can use a simple cube for the car if you don't want to expend the energy on the high-class car model I've made here. Just make sure the antenna has enough subdivisions to create vertical sections as shown in Figure 7.2. Otherwise, the antenna will not bend well.

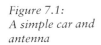

Figure 7.1:
A simple car and
antenna

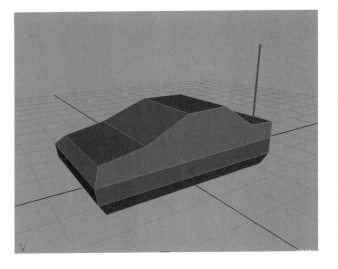

Figure 7.2:
A subdivided
cylinder is used
for the antenna.

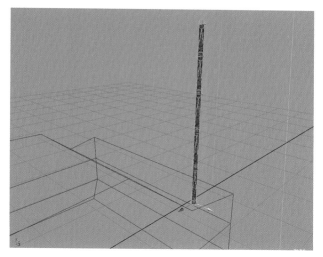

Figure 7.3: Create joints to run up from the base.

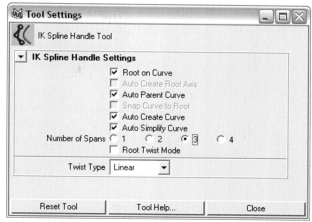

Figure 7.4: Creation options for the IK Spline Handle tool

To create the skeleton system and spline-based IK handle, follow these steps:

Figure 7.5: A six-CV curve will drive the curvature of the skeleton and hence the antenna (shown without the antenna).

1. Create a joint system running *up* from the base of the antenna. You don't need too many joints, so five bones will work fine for us here (see Figure 7.3).
2. Use a Smooth Bind to bind the skeleton to the antenna. You won't need to paint weights or anything, unless you want to tweak the antenna movement. Using a Smooth Bind rather than a Rigid Bind will give you the option to paint weights instead of forcing you to use flexors.
3. Group the car and the root of the joints under a car_grp node. You will be animating the car_grp node exclusively to move the car.

Do not group the antenna; its movement will be driven by the joints solely.

---

4. In the Animation menu, choose **Skeleton → IK Spline Handle Tool ❑**, and return the settings to their default state. Then set Number of Spans to 3, as shown in Figure 7.4. Create the Spline IK Handle from the root of the skeleton to the top joint. The Spline IK Handle tool automatically creates a curve with 6 CVs, as shown in Figure 7.5. The file car_soft_bodies_setup.ma on the CD will bring you up to this point of the exercise.

Creating Soft Bodies

Now we have to create the soft body version of the curve that will drive the dynamic motion of the antenna. When you create a soft body, you have the option of creating a goal of the original object. This goal sets the desired shape of the dynamic curve, which then, according to the goal weights of its particles, assumes the same shape and position of the goal.

You can create the original curve as the goal and make the copy a soft body, or you can make the original soft and make the copy shape the goal. In some cases, it doesn't matter if the duplicate or the original is soft, but in this case, the original curve is driving the animation of our spline-based IK, so we need to create the original as the soft body with the duplicate as the goal. This way, the soft body (according to the weights we set) will try to reform into its original shape. Follow these steps:

1. Select the spline IK curve, and choose **Soft/Rigid Bodies → Create Soft Body → □**. Set Creation Options to Duplicate, Make Original Soft. Click Hide Non-Soft Object to get the copied curve out of the view, and click Make Non-Soft a Goal to create the goal relationship. You can keep Weight set to 1.
2. If you disable curve display for a moment, you will see six particles created where you CVs are positioned (see Figure 7.6).

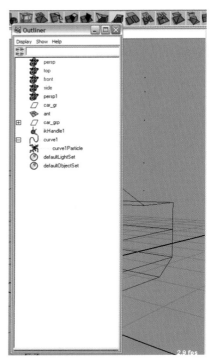

Figure 7.6: A new particle object places a particle at each CV location.

Playing back the scene yields really no results; the antenna is still stiff. This is where you will need to either paint weights or set them manually through the Component Editor. Since there's no surface to paint on, and it's just a matter of six particles, it's much easier to set them manually. You will want to create less weight as you go *up* the antenna, with a full weight of 1 for perhaps the bottom two particles so that the base of the antenna stays put with the car.

Remember, setting a goalweightPP for a particle is a modifier that multiplies whatever the global goal weight is for the object. If you have a goalweightPP of 1, but the particle still does not stay with its goal as it should with a weight of 1, check the goal weight for the object. It is probably set to less than 1.

---

3. In component mode, turn your selection mask to select particles only. (RM click the Points filter to access the Particles filter.) Select the bottom two particles and note their names in the Component Editor (choose Windows → General Editors → Component Editor, and then click the Particles tab). The particles should be called pt(0) and pt(1) respectively.
4. Now select all the particles. They will run down from pt(0) to pt(5), with 5 being the top particle. Carefully decrease the goalweightPP of each particle from pt(2) up to pt(5). Something like the values shown in Figure 7.7 will yield a fairly good result.

You can check your work against the finished file `car_soft_bodies_finished`.ma on the CD. You can use springs with a soft body curve instead of the goal object we used in this example, but the computation for a goal is much better than springs and will give you a

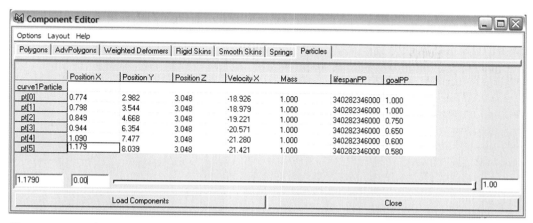

	Position X	Position Y	Position Z	Velocity X	Mass	lifespanPP	goalPP
curve1Particle							
pt[0]	0.774	2.982	3.048	-18.926	1.000	340282346000	1.000
pt[1]	0.798	3.544	3.048	-18.979	1.000	340282346000	1.000
pt[2]	0.849	4.668	3.048	-19.221	1.000	340282346000	0.750
pt[3]	0.944	6.354	3.048	-20.571	1.000	340282346000	0.650
pt[4]	1.090	7.477	3.048	-21.280	1.000	340282346000	0.600
pt[5]	1.179	8.039	3.048	-21.421	1.000	340282346000	0.580

Figure 7.7: Use the Component Editor to define the goalweightPP.

Figure 7.8: Dynamic Curve attributes

better result faster. Later in this chapter in the section "Raining Cats and Dogs," you'll see a soft body example using springs.

Dynamic Curves and the Antenna

Now with Maya Unlimited 6, hair dynamics makes our previous process of using soft bodies to create a flexible object into a virtual push-button procedure. And that is done using the Dynamic Curves introduced in Maya Unlimited's new hair module.

Dynamic curves automate much of this process and make the dynamic animation of something like a car antenna much easier, without the steps needed for soft bodies. It's a welcome addition that will serve the ends of a series of utilities. It's rather straightforward, and I estimate it will be a key part in Maya's future, perhaps making its way down to the Complete level, hopefully sometime in the future. A boy can dream, eh?

Setting Up the Antenna

Flexible curves that are simple to control is a terrific asset, let me demonstrate by showing you the same soft body example as previously, but using dynamic curves.

1. Load an earlier version of your car before you added soft body dynamics to it, or just select the particle system grouped under curve1 and delete it while at frame 1 to get rid of the soft bodies in the scene. Then select the copy of that curve (aptly called copyOfcurve1) we made as the soft body goal (found grouped under car_grp) and delete that as well. You will retain the original curve that drives the ikHandle1 node. You can also load the simple car model from the CD using the file car_model.ma in the Chapter 7 folder.

2. Select curve1, and (while in the Dynamics menu set) and choose **Hair → Make Selected Curves Dynamic**.

3. If you try playing back in the Timeline, nothing will happen. Assuming that you keep the animation on the car from before, your car will go back and forth, but the antenna will stay there. No need to panic; the curve is indeed dynamic. In the Channel box, you will notice a number of new attributes, as shown in Figure 7.8.

4. If you set the **Stiffness** attribute to 0 and turn up **Turbulence Strength** to 1, you'll see the middle of the curve wiggle when you click Play in the Timeline. The ends don't move because the Timeline is currently locked at both ends.

5. Open the Outliner, and select the hairSystem1 node. Notice that nothing really changed in the Channel box. That's because this is the node that contains all the attributes you will need to affect the dynamics of this curve. Well, almost all of them. Notice that when you created the dynamic curve, you also created a node called hairSystem1Follicles with one node under it called follicle1. Select this follicle1 node. Notice the curve (curve1) we created is now grouped under this node (see Figure 7.9). Some Outliner views may simply show the follicle1 node, however.

6. In the follicle1 node you will find the **Point Lock** attribute, which is by default set to BothEnds. Change that value to Base, and now, when you play back the animation, the top of the antenna should flop around (as long as you left the **Turbulence** attribute set to 1 (or higher).

7. Select the hairSystem1 node again, and decrease the stiffness to 0 if it is not already set 0. The antenna will turn into a wet noodle (see Figure 7.10).

8. Notice also that the blue curve that is flopping around now, the curve that is dynamic, is not actually the curve we started out with. Look in the Outliner, and you'll see that curve is curve2, which is grouped under the hairSystem1Output-Curves node. This curve is being driven by the dynamics. This means that our original curve is still driving the ikHandle for the antenna, and since it is not being driven by the hair dynamics, the antenna will not move.

9. You will have to reconnect the new dynamic curve to our existing ikHandle and its driven joint system to get the antenna to move at all.

10. Open the Connection Editor, and make sure that the left column has curveShape2 selected and that the right column is showing ikHandle1.

11. Scroll down the left column and find World-Space. Scroll down to the middle of the right column and find InCurve. Select WorldSpace and then select InCurve to connect them, as shown in Figure 7.11. This way, the original curve drives the spline ikHandle, and we will see the antenna deform as shown in Figure 7.12.

Figure 7.9: The follicle1 node in the Outliner

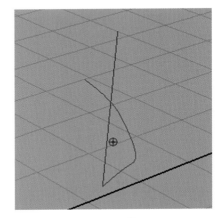

Figure 7.10: Wet noodle

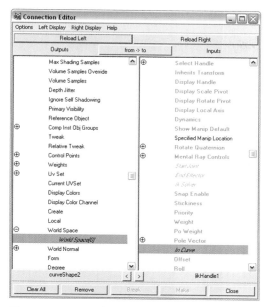

Figure 7.11: *Use the Connection Editor to reconnect the influence of your dynamic curve to the spline that controls the spline ikHandle of the antenna*

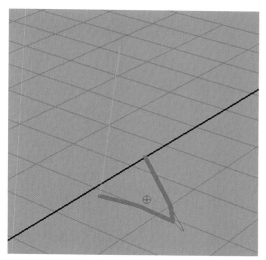

Figure 7.12: *The antenna deforms*

Connecting the Animation

But why deal with the existing IK chain and bones? Can't we set this up easier? You could have just as easily created a new curve for the antenna, made it dynamic, and then extruded a circle shape along its length to create a new antenna. This way, if you have history enabled, the curve will deform to the hair dynamics and will deform the antenna tube directly, with no need of ikHandles and joints. It was just a nice exercise to show you how to connect the influence of one curve's spline ikHandle to another curve. Figure 7.13 shows the connections in the Hypergraph once they've been made. See what you get when you read close enough?

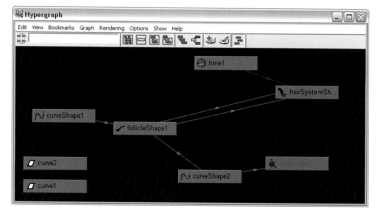

Figure 7.13: *The Hypergraph view of the reconnected spline ikHandle. It is now being driven by our dynamic curve.*

Now it's a matter of finding just the right settings for the hairSystem1 node to make the antenna move right and attach it to the car. Follow these steps to continue:

1. To attach this thing to the car, you will have to group the follicle1 node under the car_grp node to get the dynamic curve (and the rest of the antenna) to follow along with the car. Figure 7.14 shows how the antenna now swings back as we animate the car back and forth. It is attached to the car's group.

Figure 7.14:
The still-floppy
antenna will
swing behind as
the car lurches
forward and
whip around as it
moves back

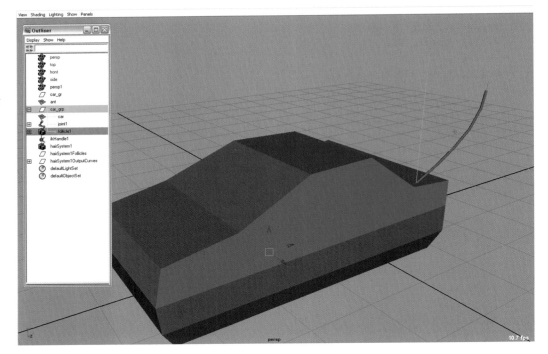

Figure 7.14:
The still-floppy
antenna will
swing behind as
the car lurches
forward and
whip around as it
moves back

2. Let's pretend we want the antenna to whip around like that, like a rope stuck on the trunk. You would want the rope to smack the sides or back of the car and bounce off; now it whips right through the car's geometry. We must enable the collisions for this dynamic curve.

3. Select the hairSystem1 node and then select the car geometry. Choose **Hair → Make Collide** (see Figure 7.15). The antenna will flop over and smack the back of the car as the car goes back and forth. But you probably need to animate the antenna like a normal antenna and not like a ribbon.

4. Now it comes down to getting the right settings worked out to make this a nice-looking antenna. Select the hairSystem1 node, and open the Attribute Editor, as shown in Figure 7.16.

5. You're going to need to move the stiffness value back up to get some rigidity into the antenna. This value doesn't like to creep up past 1 too much, but if you set it to 1.2, you'll find a fairly flexible antenna at your hands that will react as the car moves back and forth. At this point you can turn down the turbulence we set earlier, as well as get rid of the collisions with the car's body.

To delete the antenna collisions with the car, select the car and open the Attribute Editor. Scroll to find the geoConnector1 tab, and select it. At the bottom of the Attribute Editor, click the Select button to select the geoConnector1 node, and in a Maya view panel, press Delete to get rid of the node. This will keep unnecessary nodes out of your scene, which is a good way to keep your scenes.

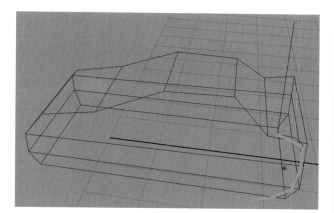

Figure 7.15: The antenna will now collide with the car's body.

Frankly, I think Dynamic Curves have been a long time in coming and are a welcome addition to Maya's tool set. As you can tell from the previous soft body example, animating the flexible antenna can be much more complicated than necessary, for those with Maya Unlimited and access to hair dynamics at least.

With dynamic curves, you can do anything you're used to doing with regular curves—creating surfaces, driving spline IK handles, and so forth. Getting a good bead on how to set the attributes to work in your dynamic scene requires some experimentation and patience.

Using Expressions for Simple Antenna Animation

Sometimes the challenge for a TD (Technical Director) who has to set up this antenna shot is that using dynamics may just not be feasible (without caching constantly after every change). Scrubbing an animation to see timing and whatnot will not play well with dynamics—since dynamics must be played from the beginning of the simulation (again, without the benefit of caching a scene, which can be time-consuming for an animator when you have constant changes and several iterations). Plus sometimes, you need a simple fix, and shooting a fly with a shotgun is a little much.

For example, starting with the model of the car with its antenna, you can attach a bend deformer to the antenna, and once everything is grouped properly, you simply animate the car and then animate the deformer to bend the antenna as you see fit; there's no need for extensive dynamics. It's quite easy to see where this is going. By merely grouping the bend deformer with the antenna and animating the top node of the car, antenna, and deformer to move around, you can keyframe the deformer to bend the antenna appropriately. When the car accelerates, the antenna bends farther in the opposite direction of the car. Then the car slows down and stops, the antenna springs back upright. You can easily animate all this with keyframes, and it's hardly a professional secret.

To automate the process a bit without dynamics and get our hands dirty with some advanced concepts, we can add a few expressions to direct the deformer to bend the antenna as the animator keyframes the car around. We will set up this antenna with a few expressions that detect the acceleration of the car and drive the bend of the antenna via the deformer. For simplicity's sake here, we'll limit the motion of the car to the X axis only.

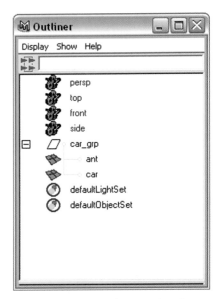

Figure 7.17: Properly grouping the antenna with the car

1. We will start with our simple model of an antenna (a subdivided polygonal cylinder to give it vertical sections) attached to a simple car model. (See Figure 7.1 earlier in this chapter.) The antenna is grouped with the car under car_grp, as shown in Figure 7.17. Position the car_grp so that the bottom of the car touches the ground plane as shown. Place the pivot of the car_grp at the origin and freeze transforms to reset the attributes of the car back to zero.

2. To create the deformations in the antenna, we will use a nonlinear deformer, bend. Group the deformer under car_grp so it moves along with the car. Set **Low Bound** to 0, and place the deformer so it bends from the bottom of the antenna upwards, as shown in Figure 7.18.

3. Keyframe the car_grp at frame 1 where it is. Go to frame 40, move the car in X, and set a keyframe. You can settle the car in that position for a few frames and then animate it to somewhere near the origin to back up the car. You can play with your translateX curve to smooth out the animation if you wish (see Figure 7.19).

We are using this simple animation in X as a way to create deformation in the antenna using expressions. In theory, you will determine if the car is in motion, the direction in X of

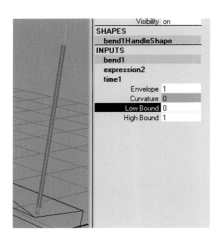

Figure 7.18: Position the deformer to bend the antenna from the bottom up.

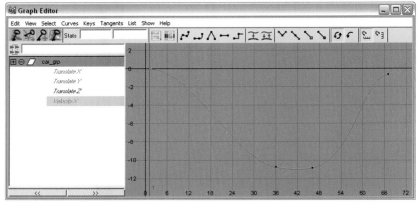

Figure 7.19: The car's animation curves shown in the Graph Editor

travel, and the acceleration of the car to drive the bend in the antenna. So first you must create an attribute for the car_grp to attach such a value.

4. Select the car_grp and create a float attribute called **accelX**.
5. RM click the **accelX** attribute and choose **Expressions** from the context menu to open the Expression Editor.

Here we will query Maya to find out the position of the car group node at the current time and compare it with its X position a few frames ago. This will give us an acceleration value that tells us how much and which way the car is accelerating in X.

6. In the Expression Editor, type the following expression:

```
$f = `currentTime -q`;
$posX = `getAttr -t $f car_grp.translateX`;
$lastposX = `getAttr -t ($f -1) car_grp.translateX`;
car_grp.accelX = $posX - $lastposX;
```

The first line queries the current time in Maya (that is, where your Time Slider is sitting) and assigns it to the variable *f*. The next line finds out what the position of the car group node is in X and assigns it to a new variable called *posX*. The third line does exactly the same thing as the second line, but for the previous frame to find out where the car was in the last frame. Finally, the last line assigns our new attribute **accelX** to the difference of this frame's position in X and the last frame's position in X. This difference in position is the acceleration of the car in X.

We will use this new value to drive the amount of bend the deformer will give the antenna object by applying a new expression to the deformer object.

7. Select the deformer, and in the bend1 node RM click the **Curvature** attribute and choose **Expressions** from the context menu.
8. Type the following expression and click Create:

```
bend1.curvature = (car_grp.accelX)
```

Simply put, this expression sets the curvature of the bend deformer to the value of the acceleration attribute we created for the car_grp node. If you play back your animation, you will see the antenna bending back and forth as the car moves, as in Figure 7.20. (If you scrub in the Timeline window, the expression will update in real time.) Keep in mind that the antenna will bend only when keyframes are set on the car; it cannot evaluate as you move the car itself.

You may notice that the antenna bends in the direction of the car's motion in X, as opposed to bending away as it's supposed to. In this case, you can either orient the deformer 180 degrees to fix it or set the value of the bend to be the opposite of the car's **accelX** value as shown here:

```
bend1.curvature = -(car_grp.accelX)
```

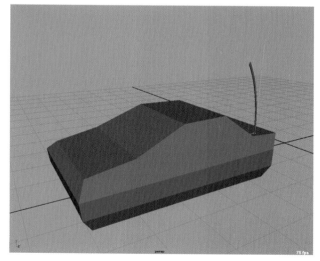

Figure 7.20: The deformer bends the antenna in the wrong direction and may bend too much.

You might feel as if the bend in the antenna is too severe. You can easily adjust the amount of bend in the antenna (that is, its rigidity) by adding a multiplier value to the expression like so:

```
bend1.curvature = -(car_grp.accelX) * 0.25
```

This sets the amount of curvature to a quarter of the acceleration value from the car's movement in X. You might adjust that number as you see fit, or you can create a new attribute (called **Multiplier**, for example) on the bend deformer node for easy access and editing, as shown here:

```
bend1.curvature = -(car_grp.accelX) * bend1.multiplier
```

This way you can easily change or even animate this number to tweak the rigidity of the antenna by merely selecting the deformer and adjusting this value, as opposed to opening and editing the expression every time.

Also, you will notice that the antenna does not move smoothly; it bends just when the car moves and sits back upright as soon as the car stops. To create a smoother animation, select the car_grp node again and adjust the expression as follows:

```
$f = `currentTime -q`;
$posX = `getAttr -t $f car_grp.translateX`;
$lastposX = `getAttr -t ($f -12) car_grp.translateX`;
car_grp.accelX = $posX - $lastposX;
```

Here we are evaluating the difference between the car's current position in X to its position from 12 frames ago. This will give you a much smoother bend in the antenna. As we did for the bend deformer's multiplier, you can easily add your own multiplier (called **Smooth**, for example) attribute to the car_grp node. You can then insert this value into the expression to easily control the smoothness of the bending:

```
$lastposX = `getAttr -t ($f -car_grp.smooth) car_grp.translateX`;
```

It's the start to a rather nifty trick, but making it work to perfection is the tough part. In any event, it's easy to see how this type of expression work can help drive your scene in creating secondary motion without resorting to what could be a costly or complicated dynamic setup. Remember, animation is the illusion of motion, so really anything goes. And as my bosses always say, "Just make it look good." If it looks right, it is right. And if animating it by keyframes works better, that's the way to go. Keep your options open, and you'll find yourself saving your butt time and time again.

Car Suspension Using Hair Dynamics

You can create some nice setups using the follicle node that will automate some animations, using the dynamics from Hair to drive the simulation. I had the opportunity to pick the brain of Alias's Principle Scientist Duncan Brinsmead a little bit. He had some interesting ideas about using hair dynamics, in particular attaching the dynamics from a follicle to drive the secondary animation on a car's suspension. After a couple conversations with Duncan, I realized this sounds a lot tougher than it actually is. But yet it opens a slew of possibilities, allowing us to think beyond what we see with dynamic curves and hair with a few tricks.

Setting Up the Car

Let's begin with a rudimentary setup to illustrate the dynamics of what you'll need. Figure 7.21 shows two basic polygonal shapes representing the top and bottom parts of our "car." Our intent is to use hair follicles to create the secondary animation for the top of the car as we animate the bottom to move around. The top will jerk back and forward as the car moves. To continue the setup, follow these steps:

1. Select the bottom portion of the car (bottom) and create hair by choosing **Hair** → **Create Hair** ❏. Figure 7.22 shows the options for creating hair. Set **U Count** and **V Count** to 1 each, and set **Points Per Hair** to 2. Set **Output** to Paint Effects, move **Length** down to 0.5, and click **Create Hairs**.

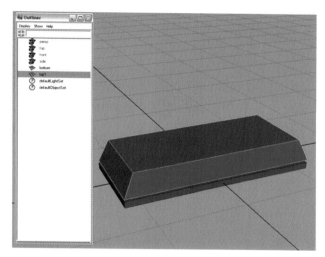

Figure 7.21: Two shapes to use for the basic "car suspension" setup

A new hair node called hairSystem1 is created along with a follicle node (in this example, it is grouped under the hairSystem1Follicles node and is called bottomFollicle5050) and a pfxHair1 node (see Figure 7.23).

2. Select the hairSystem1 node and turn **Hairs per Clump** down to 1 from the default of 10.

3. You then need to reposition the follicle to the top side of the bottom car piece. Select the bottomFollicle5050 node and adjust the **Parameter U** and **Parameter V** values to place the follicle in the center of the top side of the bottom car piece, as shown in Figure 7.24. In this case, the U remains at 0.5, but the V goes to between 1.5 and 1.8.

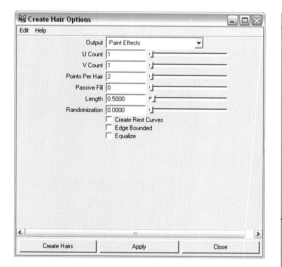

Figure 7.22: The options for creating hair

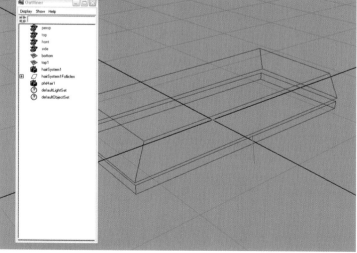

Figure 7.23: A new hairSystem node and Follicle node are created, attached to the side of the bottom part of the car.

Figure 7.24:
Placing the
follicle

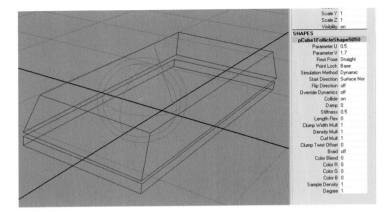

Figure 7.25:
The hair will
swing back and
forth as the
bottom of the
car is played
back with
animation.

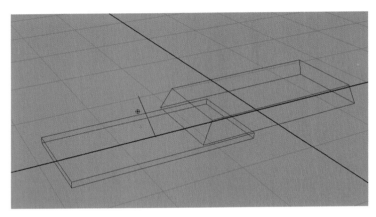

4. Now if you add animation to the bottom of the car, you should see the short hair swing back and forth when you play back the bottom moving around, as in Figure 7.25. Our intent next is to attach the top of the car to this motion.

5. We'll have to attach the top of the car to the hair. Now, the best way to attach the top end of the car to the bottom is to create a new follicle and attach it to the current hair on the bottom. To that end, convert the Paint Effects hair node to polygons by selecting the pfxHair1 node and choosing **Modify** → **Convert** → **Paint Effects to Polygons**. This creates a polygonal strip on which we can attach the next follicle that will drive the top of the car.

6. With the new mesh group selected, create a new hair object by choosing **Hair** → **Create Hair**. The hair is attached to the polygonal strip that is driven by the first hair system we created.

7. Select all the new nodes except for the follicle by selecting the hairSystem2 and pfxHair2 nodes and pressing Delete. We're only interested in using the new follicle.

8. Select the follicle node. You can use the **Parameter U** and **Parameter V** values to place the new follicle at the base or the top of the polygon strip, or you can just leave it in the middle. There should be no difference where the second follicle lies on the first hair strip.

9. If you play back the animation, you'll see how the new follicle sways back and forth with the animation. In this example, I've placed the second follicle at the base of the poly hair strip.

Connecting the Car Top to the Animation

You can now simply group the top of the car to this second follicle to create instant secondary motion for the car's suspension system. Follow these steps:

1. Select the top of the car, and group it under the new follicle (hairSystem2Follicles node), as shown in Figure 7.26.
2. If you play back the animation, you'll see the top of the car rear back when you start up (see Figure 7.27) and swing around as the animation on the bottom plays. You can play with translation as well as rotation; the top of the car will spring around as it reacts to the motion of the car, as you can see in Figure 7.28.

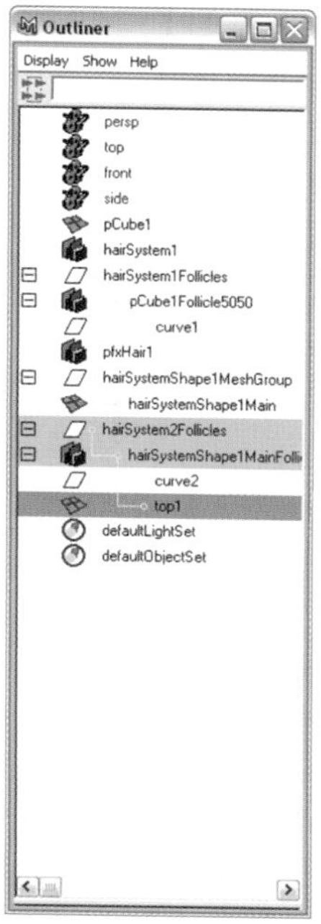

Suspension of Disbelief

You will need to play with some of the **Hair Dynamics** attributes to make the top of the car behave as you'd like. For example, if you want to tone down the amount of spring the top has, increase the **Stiffness** value on the hairSystem1 node. The items in the following short list explain how some of the attributes in the hairSystem1 node will affect your simulation.

Damp This value controls how quickly the top of the car comes to a rest after it has been set into motion in reaction to the car. The lower the value (like 0), the springier the top looks as it jerks around.

Drag The higher this value, the smoother the springiness reacts to the motion of the car.

Stiffness As you've already seen, this value controls how stiff the hair's dynamics will be. The higher this value, the less the top of the car will react. At a value of 0, the top of the car will more than likely just flip over as soon as the car is set into motion.

We can use this type of rig to create secondary motion for a variety of objects, such as the head of a bobble-head doll. The motion of the base of the rig forces the hair dynamics attached to it to react to inertial forces, and once you attach the rest of your geometry to this dynamic movement, you will have an easier way to create secondary motion.

Figure 7.26: The top of the car is now grouped under the second follicle to inherit its motion.

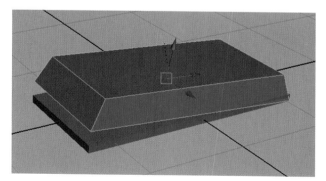

Figure 7.27: The top of the car rears up as the car starts in the animation.

Figure 7.28: The top of the car will react to the bottom's rotation as well as translation.

Deleting Hair

You may have noticed that creating hair and dynamic curves creates quite a few nodes that are dependent on each other for the simulation to work properly. When you need to completely remove a hair system from your scene, you could delete the nodes individually, or much better yet, you can choose **Hair → Delete Entire Hair System** instead as shown here. This ensures that the entire set of nodes is removed from the scene.

Raining Cats and Dogs

In this example, we will revisit our earlier work with soft body dynamics and create surface deformations to approximate a puddle being pelted by rain. We'll use soft body dynamics and springs to create the water's surface, and we'll use particles and fields to create the ripples in the water. We'll also try adding splashes to the water drops as they hit the water's surface, using collision detection to round out the scene.

Let's start by creating the water's surface with a highly subdivided NURBS plane. The plane shown in Figure 7.29 has U and V

Figure 7.29: A highly subdivided NURBS plane will serve as the water's surface.

subdivisions of 100 each. You'll need such a highly subdivided surface for the subtle deformations we'll get from the water drops and subsequent ripples.

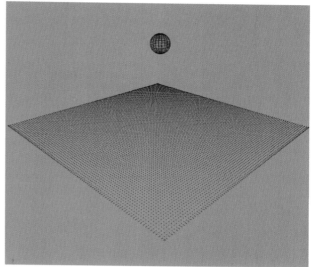

Figure 7.30: The grid of particles for the soft body plane   *Figure 7.31: Place the ball as shown.*

The next steps take us through creating the dynamics for this surface:

1. Select the plane, and (in the Dynamics menu set) choose **Soft/Rigid Bodies** → **Create Soft Body** ❏.

2. In the option box, set **Creation Options** to Duplicate, Make Copy Soft, check **Hide Non-Soft Object,** and turn on **Make Non-Soft a Goal**. Click Create to make the soft body surface.

3. Maya will create a grid of particles that correspond to the location of the CVs on that plane. Figure 7.30 shows the particles with the plane turned off. As a matter of fact, go into the persp panel's menu (choose **Show** → **NURBS Surfaces**) to toggle its display off; we'll just deal with the grid of particles for right now. The file `rain_puddle_soft_body_start.ma` on the CD contains the plane turned into the proper soft body object and will bring you up to this point in the exercise.

Now, we'll make a quick collision object to see how the particles move.

4. Create a polygonal sphere, and place it above the particle grid, as shown in Figure 7.31.

5. Select the sphere and turn it into an active rigid body with a gravity field on it by choosing **Soft/Rigid Bodies** → **Create Active Rigid Body**, and then, with the sphere still selected, choose **Fields** → **Gravity**.

Of course, you can do this a bit quicker by just selecting the sphere and creating the gravity field. Maya automatically turns the sphere into an active rigid body and connects the gravity to it.

---

6. If you play back the animation, the sphere falls and passes through the particles below it. To make the sphere collide with the particles, select the particles, select the sphere, and choose **Particles** → **Make Collide**.

7. Now if you play back the animation, you'll more than likely see the particles not react in the slightest as the sphere passes through them again. This is because the particles still have their goal weight set to 1. Now we don't need to set per particle goal weights on the water surface, so select the particles and in the Attribute Editor, in the Goal Weights and Objects section, turn the nurbsPlaneShape1 weight down to 0.5 for now.

Figure 7.32: *The yellow particles shown here are being pushed through by the colliding sphere.*

8. If you play back the animation, you'll see the particles getting pushed through the grid and bounce back up and down until they settle back into the grid. You may have to increase your playback range to see all this, though. Figure 7.32 shows the particles (colored yellow here) that are being pushed through the grid by the sphere.

Using Springs to Create Ripples

The goal object of the plane makes the particles bounce back into place, but there are no ripples in the surface. This is simply because the movement of one particle does not affect the movement of the others. The goal object merely pulls the out-of-place particles back to their original location at their respective CV. Creating ripples calls for the use of springs.

Soft Body dynamic springs connect individual particles of the same particle object together in a few ways. Follow these steps to add springs to the water surface:

1. Select the particle object, and choose **Soft/Rigid Bodies** → **Create Springs** ❑.

2. In the option box, give the springs a name if you want. Then change Creation Method to Wireframe. This creation method will make springs that attach from particle to particle. Leave Wire Walk Length at 1 (or change it if yours is different). Wire Walk Length specifies how many particles over in all directions to the current particle the spring will be created. With a length of 1, only the immediately adjacent particles will be connected with springs.

Springs can be taxing on a computer when you run the simulation, so use the least number of springs you can get away with for the simulation to work properly.

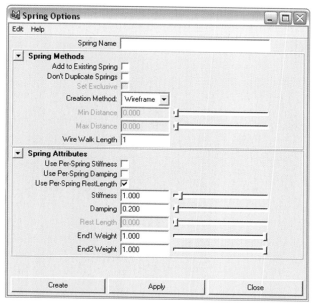

Figure 7.33: The options for creating springs

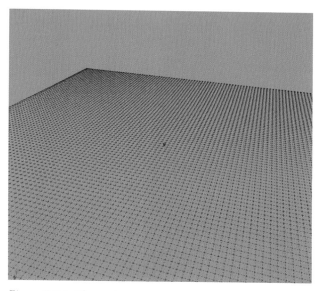

Figure 7.34: The springs

3. Figure 7.33 shows all the creation options for the springs we want to create. Once you match these settings, click Create to make the springs. You should now see dashed lines (the springs) connecting the individual particles, as shown in Figure 7.34.

4. If you play back the animation, you'll see a small amount of ripple go through as the sphere pushes through the grid. We'll need more of a ripple, though, since the ripple doesn't really go far from the impact. Select the springs we just made, and change **Stiffness** to a high number such as 64. This will help pull the adjacent particles into the fray.

5. Also, you can decrease the goal weight for the particles to about 0.3 instead of your current 0.5. Select the particle object, open the Attribute Editor, and decrease the nurbsPlaneShape1 weight to 0.3. This should give you a nice ripple, as shown in Figure 7.35.

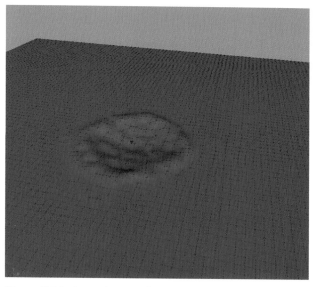

Figure 7.35: A ripple cascades in the softbody surface.

If you find your computer is sluggish during this exercise, you can by all means use a less subdivided NURBS plane instead of our 100-by-100 subdivided plane. This will decrease the computing power you'll need.

This simulation is useful for making a rock hit the surface of a pond, but now let's make rain drops. We may find that with the number of raindrops that fall, we may have to go back in and adjust our spring and goal weight settings so that that puddle's surface does not go too crazy with deformation.

Making Rain

It would not be prudent to create hundreds of little active body spheres that fall onto the pond. Instead, we will use particles to rain down on our water surface. To create the particles, follow these steps:

1. Delete the sphere from the scene as well as its gravity field. Create a volume emitter in the shape of a cube, and size/place it above the surface, as shown in Figure 7.36. To create the emitter, choose **Particles** → **Create Emitter** ❐. In the option box, set **Emitter Type** to Volume, set **Rate** at 50, and make sure **Volume Shape** is set to Cube. In the Volume Speed Attributes section, set **Away From Center** to 0, set **Along Axis** to –1, and set all the other options to 0, as shown in Figure 7.37.

2. If you run the simulation, you'll see particles slowly trickling out of the emitter. Select this new particle object, and add gravity to it by choosing **Fields** → **Gravity**. Select the gravity, and change **Magnitude** to 20. This will help pull the particles down. Figure 7.38 shows the particle rain.

Now the task becomes getting the particles to collide with the water surface. But this is more complicated than selecting the water surface plane and the particles and choosing **Particles** → **Make Collide** as we did with the falling sphere and the particles. Doing that will just make the particle rain bounce off the top of the surface. We need to make the rain particles collide with and move the surface's particles to get the surface to deform. But here's the caveat: particles cannot collide with other particles. The best solution is to create fields that will move the surface particles instead of a collision. To do that, follow these steps.

3. Select the surface particles, and choose **Fields** → **Radial** to connect a radial field to the deforming particles.

Figure 7.36: Place a cube volume emitter above the grid to make the rain.

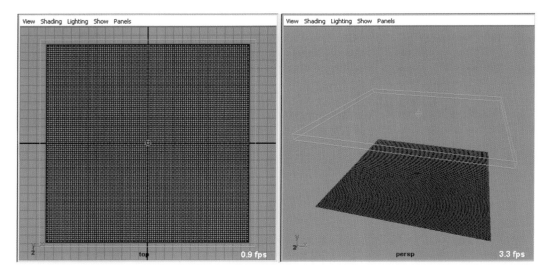

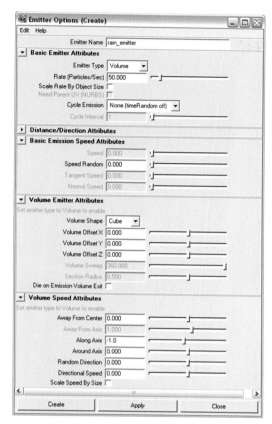

Figure 7.37: The Emitter Options (Create) dialog box

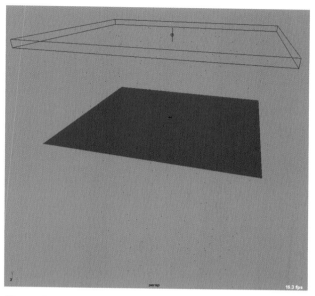

Figure 7.38: It's raining pixels!

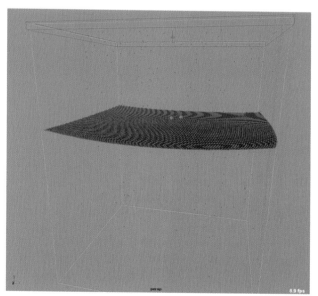

Figure 7.39: The rain particles are acting as a whole to deform the entire soft body surface.

4. We need the rain particles to be the source of the radial field. Select the radial, and then select the rain particles. Choose **Fields** → **Use Selected As Source of Field**. If you play back the simulation now, the rain will begin pushing the entire surface down and warp it, as opposed to creating indentations for each of the rain particles as they pass through the water surface (see Figure 7.39).

5. Select the radial field, which is now grouped under the rain particle node, and in the Channel box, change **Apply per Vertex** to On. You'll now see the particles really warping the surface, as in Figure 7.40.

6. Select the radial field and decrease **Max Distance** to a lower number such as 2. This will make the radial field ineffectual until the individual particles are within 2 units

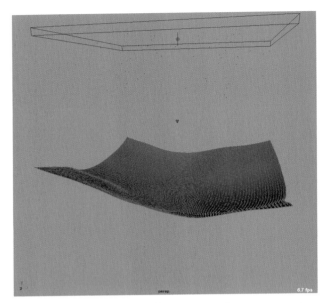

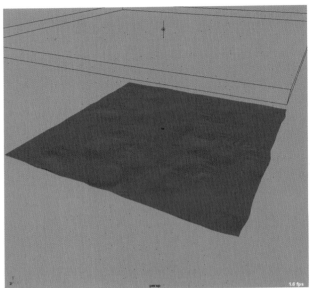

Figure 7.40: The rain particles are more than ever warping the entire surface.

Figure 7.41: The puddle is pelted by rain.

from the surface particles. You can then play with the magnitude of the radial field to dial in the amount of surface disruption you want from the drops. Figure 7.41 shows the radial field's effect with **Max Distance** set to 2 and **Magnitude** set to 10.

Adding Splashes

The next task is adding splashes to each of the rain particles as they hit the puddle's surface. This fairly simple process involves particle collisions. Follow these steps:

1. Create a new NURBS plane, and scale it up to fit the current puddle surface area. Place it just below the puddle surface. This will be the collision surface to generate the new splash particles.

2. Select the rain particles, and then select the new plane. Choose **Particles → Make Collide**. Select the new plane and template it so that it does not render and is out of the way. The intent here is that the rain fall through the puddle surface, cause ripples, and then immediately hit the essentially invisible plane right underneath, creating a collision. If you play back the simulation now, you'll just see the particles bouncing up, as in Figure 7.42.

3. With the rain particles selected, choose **Particles → Particle Collision Events**. In the window, make sure the right particle system (particle1) is selected in the Objects window. For **Type**, check Split, and change **Num particles** to 10. Click Create Event.

4. A new particle system node is created (particle2). Select it in the Outliner, and open the Dynamic Relationships window (choose **Window → Relationship Editors → Dynamic Relationships**. With particle2 selected in the left column, select the gravity field we have on the rain particles (gravityField2).

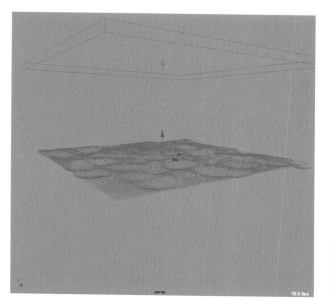

Figure 7.42: *The rain particles will now bounce back up off the collision plane right under the water's surface plane as it ripples.*

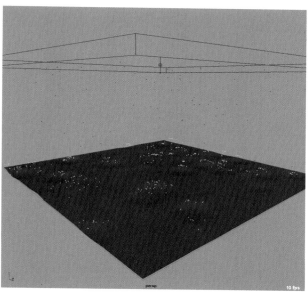

Figure 7.43: *The splashes shown in white are created when the blue rain particles hit the collision surface below the water surface.*

5. Open the Attribute Editor for the new splash particles, set their **Lifespan Mode** to Random Range, set **Lifespan** to 2.5, and set **Lifespan Random** to 0.5. Play back the simulation to see something like Figure 7.43.

The Ring

Now we'll take a quick look at how to kick up dust for a rolling object such as an inner tube. Following in the same vein as the previous exercise on creating rain splashes in a pond, we'll use collisions to create new particles from our ground plane. An effect such as this is tremendously useful for creating a sense of impact when an object travels (rolls, slides, bounces, and so on) along a path such as a dirt road, snow, or the like.

In theory, the exercise is fairly straightforward; we'll use an object (the inner tube) to interact with the ground to generate a particle dust. The setup begins with making the geometry and turning the geometry into dynamic objects. You then give the scene dynamic forces to create motion and to define collisions between bodies and particles. To accentuate the effect, the collisions generate a new particle system to make the dust flare up and out from the impact.

To set up the scene, follow these steps:

1. Create a ground plane for the collision detection and for our inner tube to roll on. Increase the subdivisions to gain a well-tessellated plane.

2. Create a polygonal torus for the inner tube, increase its subdivision axis to 30, and set its shape and location as shown in Figure 7.44. Notice it is placed a few units above the ground plane to give it an initial bouncing.

Figure 7.44:
Place the inner
tube above the
ground plane.

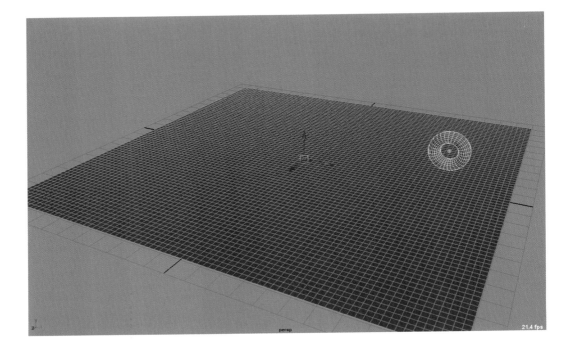

3. Now, we should create collisions for the tube and ground. Select the plane, and make it into a passive rigid body by choosing **Soft/Rigid Bodies** → **Create Passive Rigid Body** → □. In the option box, reestablish the settings before you invoke the action.
4. Select the tube, and choose **Soft/Rigid Bodies** → **Create Active Rigid Body** → □. In the option box, reestablish the settings (just in case something is different from the defaults) and create the Active Rigid Body.
5. Select the tube, and add a gravity field to it by choosing **Fields** → **Gravity**.

If you play back the simulation, you'll notice the tube falls, bounces on the ground, and may fall over on its side. As we would with a bike, we'll have to give the tube some spin to get it rolling on the ground. While we're at it, let's add some momentum to it as well. To do so, follow these steps:

1. Select the active rigid body torus, and in the Channel box, change **Initial Spin Y** to 400. This gives the torus a bit of a spin, but only at the beginning of simulation. When you play back the scene, you'll notice the tube has some momentum to roll forward when it hits the ground.
2. Add a bit more momentum to the tube by selecting the torus and changing the **Initial Velocity X** attribute to –3. If you play back the simulation, you'll see the tube lurch into motion a bit more, bounce a few times on the ground, and slowly roll off the far edge of the plane. Figure 7.45 shows the tube making its first bounce. Depending on how your scene is oriented, you may need to use **Initial Velocity Z** or **Y** instead of **X** to get it moving in the right direction.

The setup for making dust kick up with particles is similar to the earlier puddle setup. Particles on the surface of the ground (like the soft body particles of the pond surface) will

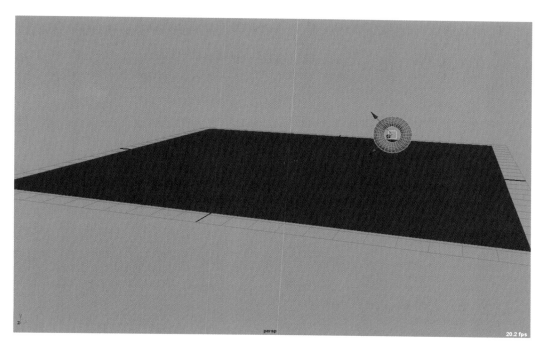

detect collisions with the torus surface and spawn new particles that will create a dust hit every time the tube touches the ground.

Consequently, we have to create a field of particles on the ground plane for the torus to bounce on and roll through. We can do so in a few ways. For example, we can use the Particle tool to create a grid of particles and simply place it on the plane or just above it. This is perhaps the easiest way. We will emit particles from the plane to get a more random arrangement than we would with a grid of particles from the Particle tool.

To set up the dust hits, follow these steps:

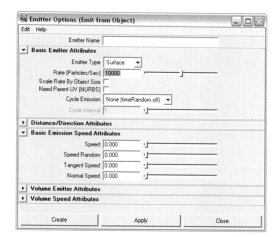

Figure 7.46: The proper options for creating the ground particles

1. Select the plane and choose **Particles →
   Emit from Object → ❑**. In the option
   box, set **Emitter Type** to Surface and set **Rate** to 10000. Set all the **Speed** attributes to zero and click Create. Figure 7.46 shows the option box. Setting all **Speed** attributes to 0 makes the particles appear on the surface, and they will not travel. The high rate will come in handy in the next step.
2. Play back the animation, and watch the plane fill with particles. Stop the playback at about frame 50 or until the plane looks like the one in Figure 7.47.

Figure 7.47: The particles cover the ground plane.

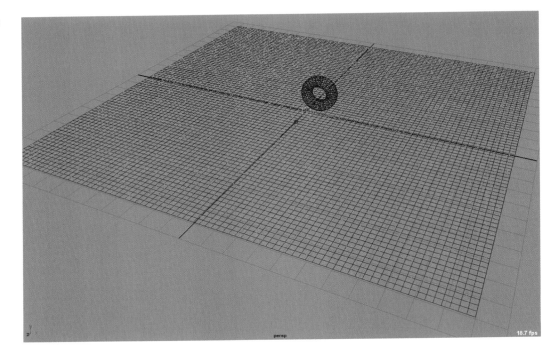

3. With the particle object selected, choose Solvers → **Initial State** → **Set for Selected.** This will display the particles in this state from the beginning. Select the emitter (grouped under the ground plane) and set **Rate** back to 0 as in Figure 7.48. This prevents the plane from producing any more particles; we have plenty now.

Setting Up the Collision Detection

Now we need to create the collision detection that will eventually spawn the dust hits for us as the

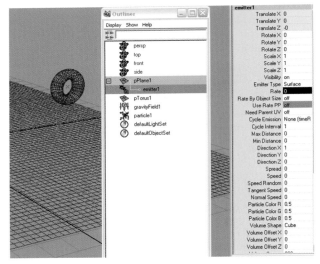

Figure 7.48: Turn off the emission of the particles after you set the initial state.

tube touches down and rolls across the ground. Follow along to create the collisions:

1. Select the particle object and the tube, and choose **Particles** → **Make Collide** → ❑. In the option box, set **Resilience** to 0.3. This will keep the particles from flying away when they get hit by the tube.

2. If you play back the simulation, you'll notice nothing really happens; the tube bounces along, and nothing happens to the particles even if they collide with the tube. This is because the particles need to rest a bit higher in the scene, just above the ground plane that emitted them. So select the particle object node, and raise it just a tiny bit above the ground plane, as in Figure 7.49.

3. If you play back the scene, you'll see some of the particles being hit and flying away, as shown in Figure 7.50. (The particles get pushed down.)

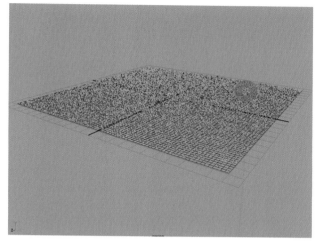

4. Now we'll need to kill some of those particles to prevent them from bouncing around all over the scene, and we'll need them to spawn more particles to give us the dust effect hit. Choose **Particles → Particle Collision Events** to open the Particle Collision Events window as shown in Figure 7.51.

5. Set **Event Type** to Emit, set **Num particles** to 50, and set **Spread** to 0.5. Also check the All Collisions box, and check the Original Particle Dies box. Set **Target Particle** to particle2, which creates a new particle object for the scene.

6. If you play back your scene, you'll see new particles being spawned from the collisions with the grid of particles on the ground plane, as shown in Figure 7.52.

Figure 7.49: The particle grid placed right above the plane.

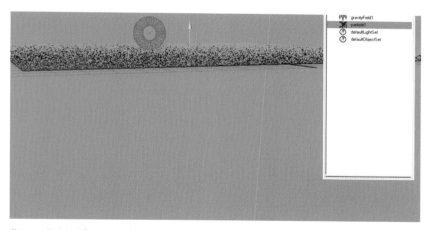

Figure 7.50: The particles are being hit by the tube and flying away.

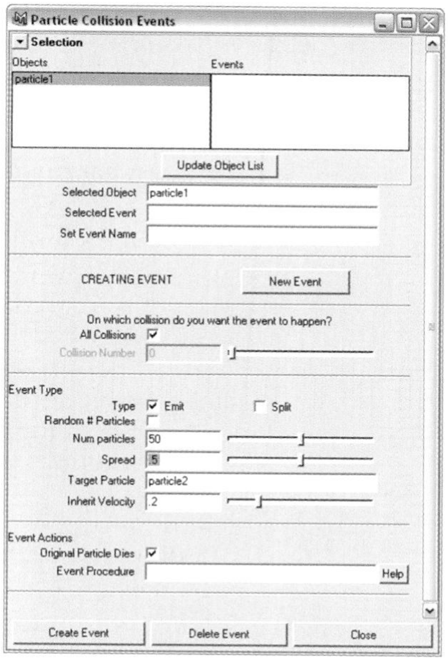

Figure 7.51: The Particle Collision Events window

Figure 7.52:
New particles
are being created
from the colli-
sions with the
grid of particles
on the ground.

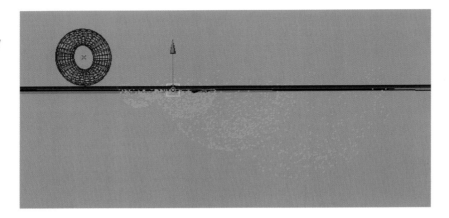

Creating Better Dust Hits

The particles are all going down and away and not making convincing hits. We need them to bounce up and not through the bottom of the ground plane. Easy enough. We'll make the new particles collide with the ground plane.

1. Select the new particles (particle2 in the Outliner) and the ground plane, and choose **Particles** → **Make Collide** → ❐. Set **Resilience** to 0.6 to get a nice bounce as in Figure 7.53.

2. To settle the dust hits, select them and add gravity by choosing **Fields** → **Gravity**. The particles will now fall to the ground plane and act a bit more like dust. Set **Gravity** to 0.2 or so to get the dust to kick up a bit better. You already have it set up to collide on the ground

3. You can control how much the new particles slide across the floor (set into motion from the collision emission) by increasing the friction attribute of the proper geoconnector attribute on the ground plane. There is also an entire chain of events that leads up to a convincing look to the dust as well as plenty of work getting a good movement

Check out `ring_dust.ma` on the CD for this scene. You can play around with its current settings to get a better feel for how the dynamic attributes affect the animation of the scene.

You will begin to see how useful this sort of simulation can be as you work your way through your Maya lifeline. It's actually more the method you use than the procedures you follow. If you take a good long hard look at the animation you've just created, it is actually quite a bit off the mark for a dust hit effect. As a matter of fact, there is quite a bit more to do to get this dust to look like dust as well as act like dust.

So in a sense, you've just been had.

Why You've Been Had

When it comes down to it, it's the guys and gals who can find the ever-so-thin edge of balance between all these settings and can create from it an interpretation of the physical laws that move us all. Getting to the end of a tutorial is really the easy part. The best way to collect ability for CGI is to wander through it slowly. Where this tutorial really begins, and the education earns its merit, is at the end when you've set up your scene. Adjusting the settings

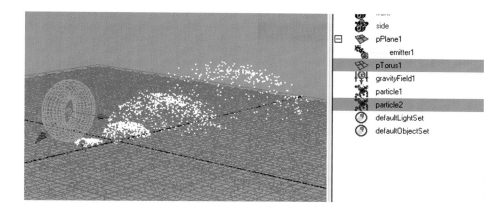

Figure 7.53:
Kicking up the
dust particles

and finding better balances after the scene is set up by the end of the lesson, to find an elo-quent evolution to a nice animation that convinces but also instructs. Imbuing the animation with your own personality is art in any animation.

A primary issue with students (and even some professionals) is their reluctance to stop their "learning" before they really jump into a solid task and come up with a well-considered solution that not only smacks of solution but glows with finesse. A lot of people equate the quantity of facts and techniques gained in a tutorial or class proportional to gaining a better education.

I find too often people jump to learning how to do something new that they hardly ever linger around enough to learn how to do it well. The interest zone has been left behind and the next neat trick needs be assimilated as if picking up cheap plastic screwdrivers from a mass retail bin. One tutorial can well be worth a 10-week course in effects and should be treated as such.

It's really important to remember to exhaust yourself on finding personality in motion and learn how to animate.

Always Learning

Dynamics are a good means to an end. They can help you create automated secondary animation to add to characters or props in your scene that would otherwise take more time from your busy animators. Although there are a lot of straightforward uses for dynamics, such as the antenna, it's always wise to consider as many options as possible to accomplish the task at hand. This keeps your options open, since some solutions work better in some instances than others. Dynamics can also be, in sometimes strange ways, like using hair dynamic follicles to drive secondary motion for a car setup.

In any event, it is wise to consider dynamics as a tool to begin solving a problem. More often than not, dynamic solutions are frequently used as just a jumping-off point to animate a scene. For example, dynamic solutions can be converted to keyframes for easy editing and manipulation. But the power they can offer in creating automation and effects is indeed sweet.

The Art of (Maya) Noise

By Kenneth Ibrahim and John Kundert-Gibbs

One of the amazing aspects *of using Maya for any length of time is uncovering more and more of its amazingly rich feature set, which allows creative people to generate remarkable effects and animation in clever, efficient ways. Maya's built-in Perlin* noise *function is one of those features that people often overlook, but which, in the right hands, can produce an impressive variety of effects. In this chapter, we will introduce you to Maya's* noise *function and show you how to use it to produce animations worthy of big-budget productions. Some of our examples, in fact, are similar to effects created for big-name movies released in the past few years. After reading through this chapter, you may find yourself thinking, "Gee, I know how to do that effect," the next time you pop a hit movie into your DVD player.*

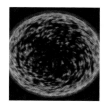

First, a Little Theory

Nearly all programmers and savvy Maya users are familiar with the venerable random (or rand) function, which has been used in everything from war planning, to computer games, to MP3 song shuffling to produce "random" numbers, events, or actions. Using a seed number (a float or integer value), a rand function produces results that appear to have no correlation to one another over a value interval—typically this interval is 0 to 1, –1 to 1 (as float values) or –32767 to 32767 (as integer values). To expand the range of values, you can multiply, divide, add to, or subtract from the raw value returned by the function call. Although the rand function has some great uses, it is not ideal for every situation in which varying values are required. For one thing, the rand function produces numbers that are completely dissociated from one another, which can produce a "popping" effect during animation. For

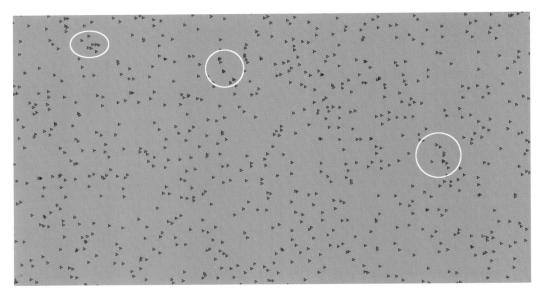

Figure 8.1: High-frequency "clumping" produced by Maya's rand *function. (Note the areas circled in the image.)*

another, the rand function can produce high-frequency "clumping" if many results lie close to one another—a result that can frustrate attempts to produce effective stochastic simulation (see Figure 8.1).

> The random function built into many computer programs is actually any one of a collection of mathematical functions that produce quasirandom rather than truly random numbers. A pseudorandom sequence of numbers appears random when you look at a small sample of the numbers (say, 100 or 10,000 return values); the numbers, however, are completely determined by the starting value—or seed number—and eventually repeat if enough "random" values are extracted from the sequence. Although mathematical formulas do a good job of pretending to be random, no one has yet devised one that produces truly random numbers. Thus, flipping a real coin always produces more random results than writing a "coin flip" program using a pseudorandom number generator.

Fortunately, Maya's noise function can produce elegant results even when the basic rand function fails. There are two important differences between rand and noise. First, although seemingly random over the long-term, the noise function is a continuous function "connected" over short intervals. In other words, moving from one returned value to the next is usually a short distance; whereas with the rand function, values can range from the maximum possible value to the minimum possible with two consecutive outputs. The second difference is that the noise function takes a continuously varying value (often time) as its input, rather than a single seed number. The noise function with a constant input (the number 1, for example) returns a single value when called, rather than a series of values. Figure 8.2 shows the Graph Editor curves for an object animated by the rand function versus an object animated by the noise function. In addition, since the value noise returns is

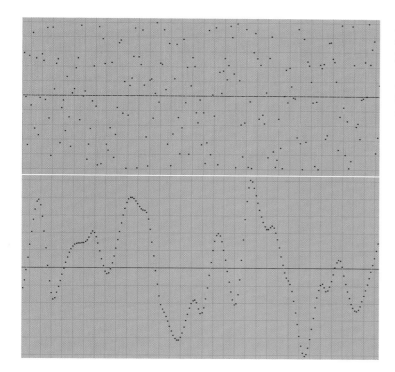

Figure 8.2: An animation curve produced by the rand *function (top) and the* noise *function (bottom)*

determined by the input value, you can safely render repeatable sequences using the noise function across multiple machines provided they have the same operating system, which is useful when you need to batch render.

> Maya's noise function is an implementation of the Perlin noise function, which produces self-similar randomness over a range of scales by taking the results of a series of random numbers and smoothly interpolating over them. In essence, Perlin noise is a way to generate fractal results: results in which the "image" appears the same on a multitude of scales.

Noise depends on the rate of change of the input value. If you use the *frame* variable rather than the *time* variable (with frames increasing 24 times more rapidly than time if Maya is set to film units), the resultant motion looks much more random because the noise function varies far more rapidly over time. This is because we're sampling the continuous noise field at greater intervals, thus returning fewer related values at each step.

As a continuous-but-random sequence, the results of using the noise function can help create any number of effects. Creating a realistically varied fountain of water, our first example, is straightforward to implement using the noise function to vary the velocity, spread, and rate of a particle emitter. In addition to using the MEL script command noise, Maya implements noise in a variety of other areas, including in procedural texture mapping (the fractal texture, and the noise feature on several other textures) and in fluid effects to produce effects such as clouds and smoke. For an artist using Maya, the trick is to "see" noise in patterns and movement around you. Once you see noise in natural phenomena, you're just a few steps from implementing it in Maya. For example, the next time you drink from a water fountain, notice the motion of the water and all those slight variations of pressure and arc in the water. Using a method similar to our first example, you can re-create these phenomena in Maya.

Now that you have a basic understanding of the noise function, let's see how to use it to create a number of compelling effects in Maya.

Building a Variable-Speed Fountain of Water

To start, let's use noise to help generate a volume of water rising from a fountain—an effect that could be used to make the background in a scene more interesting and lively, for example. Although noise is simple to add to the fountain we create, its addition adds subtle realism and interest to the animation, making it more interesting than an unmodified particle emitter.

1. Open a new scene in Maya, create a "water" plane on the ground, and scale it out large. (This plane has nothing to do with the effect. It just helps locate the pool of water.)
2. Create a particle emitter, using the following settings. (Feel free to alter them to suit your taste.)

> **Emitter Type:** Volume
> **Volume Shape:** Cone
> **Rate:** 2000
> **Particle Color R, G, and B:** Around 0.5
> **Away from Center:** 0
> **Around Axis:** 0
> **Away from Axis:** 1
> **Along Axis:** 20

3. Scale the cone volume shape to something similar to that in Figure 8.3. (In the figure, the cone was scaled to 0.8, 1.2, and 0.7 in X, Y, and Z. Scaling the cone a bit shapes the way the particles are emitted from the volume shape. The **Away from Axis** setting controls particle speed horizontally (away from the cone's primary axis), and **Along Axis** controls the speed vertically (up the cone's axis).
4. Play the animation forward some frames, and select the particles. With particles selected, choose **Fields** → **Gravity** (using default settings). The particles should now rise into the air and then fall back through the plane. To reduce the number of particles Maya has to keep up with, select the particles again and set **Lifespan** to 4 (seconds). You can make this lifespan random too if you like, but as the particles will lie under the plane before dying, this step is not really necessary.

Figure 8.3: The volume emitter cone and ground plane

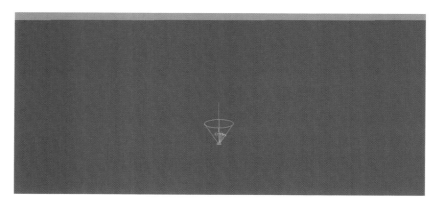

Now we want to use the `noise` function to vary the emitter's **Away from Axis** and **Along Axis** settings to create a varying flow rate for the fountain.

5. With the emitter selected, right-click the **Away from Axis** text, and choose **Expressions**. In the Expression Editor, type the following expression:

```
emitter1.awayFromAxis = 2.0 * noise (time * 4.0);
```

6. Right-click the **Along Axis** text, choose **Expressions**, and type the following equation:

```
emitter1.alongAxis = 3.0 * (noise (time * 3.0)) + 20.0;
```

These two simple expressions control the speed of particles in both the horizontal and vertical directions for the emitter. For the first expression, the `noise` function uses 4 times the value of time (which increments ¼₄th of a second for each frame, assuming film settings are used) to produce an output value between –1 and 1. This number is then multiplied by 2, generating a final number that lies between –2 and 2 for each frame.

The second expression is only slightly more complex. Here 3 times `time` is used as the input for `noise`. (This makes the `noise` function fluctuate a bit less rapidly than in the previous algorithm.) The output of this is multiplied by 3—producing a value between –3 and 3—and this value is added to 20 (the starting speed), thus producing a number between 17 and 23 as the speed along the cone's axis. The results of these two expressions, shown in Figure 8.4, produce a constantly varying rate of speed in particle emission, as well as a fluctuation in how widely the particles are dispersed. If you want, you can vary the rate as well using a similar expression to control the emitter's **rate** attribute.

With this animation as a base, you can do a bit of tweaking to get fairly nice looking results in a minimum of time. By switching the particles to a blobby surface render type, putting a nearly transparent anisotropic shader on them, and sticking an ocean shader on the ground plane beneath, the particle fountain can end up looking like Figure 8.5. Because the `noise` function is time-based here, we included an animation of this fountain on the CD (`noisyFountain.mov`); the scene file that created this movie is also on the CD (`noisyFountain.ma`).

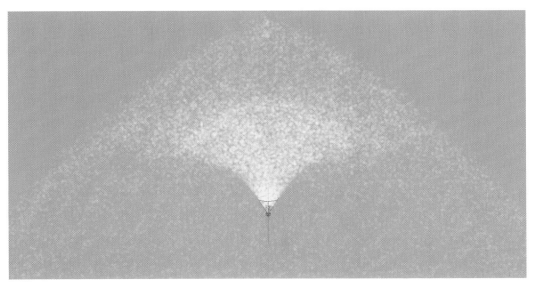

Figure 8.4:
Particles emitted
with varying
speed

Figure 8.5: The particle fountain with some texture mapping applied to it

Creating an Energy Vortex

Our second example creates an "energy ring vortex" that might be used to good effect in a science fiction movie. Here, we will use noise to "punch holes" in particles emitted from a ring, creating an effect that might look like a band of energy being emitted by a circular gate in space.

1. Open a new scene in Maya and create a NURBS torus. Rotate the torus upright (90 degrees in X), scale it out to about 10 units in each direction, and set the makeNurbTorus1 sections to 16 and heightRatio to 0.03. (This makes the torus very thin rather than fat.) You should end up with something similar to Figure 8.6.

2. Now choose **Particles → Emit from Object □**. In the option window, set the emitter type to Surface, **Rate** to about 2000, and all speed attributes to 0.

3. Select the particles you created (it's probably easiest to do this in the Outliner), and then choose **Fields → Radial □**. In the option window, reset settings, set **Magnitude** to –0.1, and set **Attenuation** to 0. On playing back your animation, you should see something similar to Figure 8.7, in which the particles are drawn into the center of the ring.

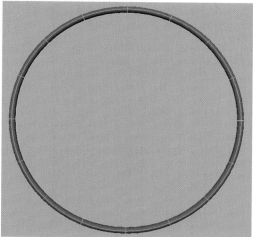

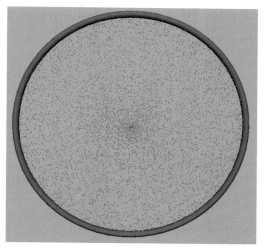

Figure 8.6: The "gate": a NURBS torus scaled

Figure 8.7: Energy particles are drawn into the center of the ring.

Although the particles are indeed falling toward the center of our "energy" ring, the effect right now lacks any real interest. Fortunately, our friendly `noise` function comes to the rescue.

4. Select the particles again and press the Down arrow key to select the particleShape node. Now add the following float attributes to the particleShape node (using **Modify → Add Attribute**): **lsMin** (with a default of 1), **lsMax** (with a default of 8), **clumpyness** (with a default of 1), and **speed** (with a default of 1). We will use these attributes to control how our noise expression works.
5. With the particle shape node still selected, set **Lifespan Mode** to lifespanPP Only. (This allows expressions to control particle lifespan.)
6. With the particle shape node still selected, choose **Window → Animation Editors → Expression Editor**. In the Expression Editor window, click the Creation radio button, type the following, and click the Create button.

```
lifespanPP = lsMin + (lsMax - lsMin) * noise(pos * clumpyness);
```

On playing back your animation, you should see something similar to Figure 8.8.

This expression creates holes in the "energy" particles based on the value of the **clumpyness** attribute and the particle's emitted position in space (the **pos** attribute). The value output from the `noise` function (–1 to 1, remember) is multiplied by **lsMax** minus **lsMin** (making the spread bigger), which is then added to the value of **lsMin**. With this setup, the noise function produces a value less than 0 during a large percentage of time, meaning that the particles die immediately. We can alter our formula in a couple of ways to eliminate the subzero return values. The simplest is to "normalize" the expression as follows:

```
lifespanPP = lsMin + (lsMax - lsMin) * (0.5 + 0.5 * noise(pos *
clumpyness));
```

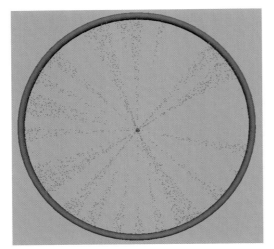
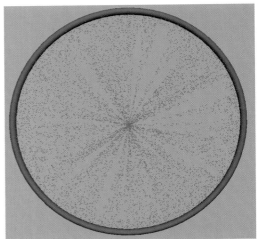

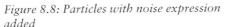

Figure 8.8: Particles with noise expression added

Figure 8.9: Particles with renormalized noise expression

The 0.5 + 0.5*noise portion of the expression rescales the noise function so that it returns values between 0 and 1 rather than values between –1 and 1, thus removing the sub-zero values. A more elegant solution is to use the smoothstep function to do the same thing:

```
lifespanPP = lsMin + (lsMax - lsMin) * smoothstep(-1, 1, noise(pos *
clumpyness));
```

This time we're using the smoothstep function, which smoothly normalizes the third term (the noise function's return value) using the first two values as input based on a cubic polynomial. Thus, smoothstep takes the return values of noise, which are between –1 and 1, and renormalizes them to the 0 to 1 range, and it does this in a smoothly varying fashion. If you edit your creation expression with the second expression, you should end up with something similar to Figure 8.9, which shows much more extensive coverage within the circle, along with smoothly varying lifespans down to 0 in areas that are not covered.

You are now free to vary the three attributes referenced in the expression. **lsMin** and **lsMax** determine the range of lifespans (how long the particles live), and **clumpyness** scales the noise space and thus determines how quickly lifespan goes from maximum to minimum as one travels around the ring (the pos, or position value). Changing **clumpyness** to a number less than 1 (such as 0.35) produces particularly interesting results. You can also animate any of these values to produce other results. Animating **lsMax** from 0 to 5 or so over 100 frames, for instance, creates a nice run-up animation for our energy ring. Setting **lsMin** to 0 instead of a nonzero value causes some particles to die immediately, opening distinct holes in the emission pattern. You can accentuate this by setting the smoothstep function's first parameter to 0 or greater.

One thing still remaining is to change the lifespan variation over time as well as space. We can do this by using the last attribute we created—**speed**—to modify our expression once again. (Notice that we've set the smoothstep lower bound to 0 in this revised expression.)

Edit your expression to read as follows:

```
lifespanPP = lsMin + (lsMax - lsMin) * smoothstep(0, 1, noise(pos *
clumpyness
    + time * speed));
```

You can make a variety of changes to produce more interesting results. For example, you can add some rotation to your gate (rotate the torus in Z) and make the particles the child of the torus. (Select the particles, Shift+select the torus, and press P on the keyboard.) Now watch as your particles animate in a complex vortex fashion while the gate spins.

If you prefer to keep your rendered "gate" still, simply duplicate the torus, and scale this duplicate torus out slightly (or the original in slightly). To create an even more interesting look, try changing the particle render type to multistreak rather than point, and change its color to some energetic color (orange, blue, or white). In the Hardware Render Buffer Attribute Editor window, turn on Multi-Pass Rendering in the Multi-Pass Render Options tab, increase the Render Passes setting to a high number (such as 25 or more), and set Motion Blur to a high value such as 20 or 30 to blur the individual particles together into a cloud of energy. You can also add a ramp to drive the **opacityPP** attribute of the particles, causing them to fade in and out of existence. After some tweaking, you might end up with something similar to Figure 8.10. (the scene file to create this image, noisyGate.ma, is on the CD) along with a rendered movie of the gate in action, noisyGate.mov.

With hardware-rendered particle types (such as point, streak, multistreak, and spheres), you must render the particles in a separate pass in the Hardware Render Buffer. This rendering engine uses the power of your machine's graphics processing unit (GPU) to render particles, which can really speed up particle rendering.

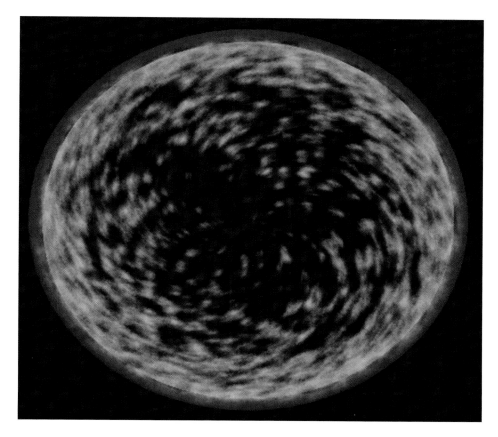

Figure 8.10: The final energy gate

Generating a Hermite Electric Arc

This example is inspired by some work we developed for a recent science fiction trilogy with confusing mythological references that needed some electrostatic discharges to arc over a hover ship's engines. One benefit of the `noise` function is that it can be used to make a curve look much like an electrical discharge arc (lightning, for example) when animated over time; so we can use the `noise` function to help us create this effect.

The basic idea for this effect is to update a curve arcing between two surfaces at each frame using the `hermite` MEL function. This function implements a curve using startpoints and endpoints as well as tangents to define the shape of the curve. All this information is extracted from the surfaces between which the curve arcs. Two disclike surfaces are set up, facing each other, to be the termination points of the curve. The start and end points of the hermite curve are controlled by two particle systems, each of which crawl along the surface of their respective hemispherical surfaces using the `noise` function to influence their motion in UV space.

Scene Setup

First we're going to create the shapes that emit the arcs and create a group of particles on each shape from which the electric arc will be emitted.

1. Open a new scene in Maya and create two hemispherical NURBS surfaces, as shown in Figure 8.11. (Alternatively, you can model any NURBS shape you want for this exercise.) It's best to create the surfaces with UV bounds of 0 to 1.
2. Select one of your objects, and then choose **Particles** → **Emit from Object** ❑. In the option window, choose **Edit** → **Reset Settings**, set **Emitter Type** to surface and **Emission Rate** to 10, and create the particles.
3. Select the particles (you may do so most easily in the Outliner), and name your new particle group startPtPars. This step is important, because your expressions will use this name to access the particle group.
4. Select the particles, and then Shift+select the surface geometry from which they emit. Choose **Particles** → **Goal** ❑. In the option window, set the goal weight to 1.0 (100%). This locks the particles on the surface of the sphere, so as they move around later on they won't come off the surface.
5. Select the particles and open the Attribute Editor. Under the Add Dynamic Attributes twirl-down section, click the General button. Using the Particle tab of the resulting window, you can add a number of useful attributes to the particle system. In our case, choose

Figure 8.11: Spherical shells that will act as the termini for the electric discharge curve

the **goalU**, **goalV**, **goalOffset**, **parentU**, and **parentV** attributes. Click OK. In the Attribute Editor, under the Per Particle (Array) Attributes section, you should now see these attributes available for editing, as shown in Figure 8.12.

6. Select the emitter (not the particles; the emitter will be a child of its surface) and, in the Attribute Editor, check the Need Parent U/V box under the Basic Emitter Attributes section. Adding this attribute allows the UV information from the hemisphere to control the placement of your particles.

7. Select the particle node, press the Down arrow key to select its shape node, and open the Expression Editor. (Choose **Window → Animation Editors → Expression Editor.**) Click the Creation radio button (which causes this expression to be run only on creation frames for each particle), and create the following expression.

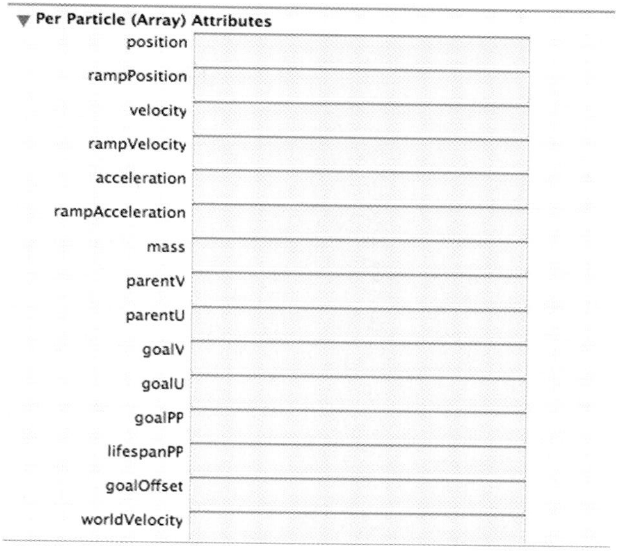

Figure 8.12: The Attribute Editor with custom attributes added

```
startPtParsShape.goalU = startPtParsShape.parentU;
startPtParsShape.goalV = startPtParsShape.parentV;
```

These two lines of code set the **goalU** and **goalV** values of the particles to the **parentU** and **parentV** values; in other words, the particles will "stick" to their birth positions along the parent surface's UV space as they are animated in the next steps.

8. Run your animation forward about 24 frames (or one second, which should give you about 10 particles), and then select the particle node. In the Attribute Editor, select the startPtParsShape tab, and then, under the Render Attributes twirl-down, set Particle Render Type to Spheres. Now check to see if you have 10 spheres on the surface of your object. If not, step forward (or rewind) until you have 10 on the surface. Later in this example, we'll create an expression that makes our spline curve "hop" between particles, which is why we want multiple particles on the surface.

You might need to rescale your sphere particles' radii, depending on how big your emitter surfaces are. To rescale the particles, select the particle node, open the Attribute Editor, select the startPtParsShape tab, and twirl down the Render Attributes section of the window. Under Render Attributes, click the Current Render Type button, which enables a Radius field below it. In the Radius field, adjust the spheres' radii to any desired size.

---

9. With the particle node selected, choose **Solvers → Initial State → Set for Selected.** This "freezes" the particle system and becomes your initial frame when you rewind the animation.

10. Finally, select the emitter and set the rate to 0, effectively turning off the emitter. Upon rewinding your animation, the 10 particles should still exist on the surface of the emitter.

*Figure 8.13: Two
hemispherical
surfaces with 10
particles on each
surface*

*Figure 8.13: Two
hemispherical
surfaces with 10
particles on each
surface*

Repeat steps 2 through 10 for the other surface, naming the particles endPtPars for this step. When finished, your scene should look similar to Figure 8.13.

11. Select both surfaces and the particle groups, and group them all together (press Ctrl+G). Name this group arcGrp. With the arcGrp group selected, choose **Modify** → **Add Attribute**, and create a float attribute called **speed** with a default value of 0.01.

12. Select everything in the scene, and choose **Modify** → **Freeze Transformations** to reset geometry and particles to their default state. This is not strictly necessary here, but in complex scenes it's often best to freeze transformations just to be on the safe side.

Basic Particle Motion

Now we have completed the setup work. It's time to move on to creating some expressions to control the particles' movement! First, we'll add runtime expressions to the particles to get them to move around over time.

Select the startPtPars set of particles, press the Down arrow key to select the startPtParsShape node, and open the Expression Editor. (Choose **Window** → **Animation Editors** → **Expression Editor**). Click the Runtime before Dynamics button and type the following expression.

```
float $speed = arcGrp.speed;

float $offsetV = $speed * noise(time * 0.3 + startPtParsShape.particleId *
100);

startPtParsShape.goalV += $offsetV;
```

The first line of this expression sets the variable *$speed* to the value in the custom attribute speed on the arcGrp node. The second line loads into the variable *$offsetV* a varying value achieved by multiplying *$speed* by the output of the noise function. The input to the noise function has two parts: the first simply scales the value of time (which relates to how quickly the noise function varies over time); the second reads in the value of each particle's ID and multiplies it by 100, effectively moving each particle into a different portion of "noise space" so that they don't all move in lockstep. Finally, the third line actually moves the particles by updating the goalV value based on the $offsetV variable. Thus, we get particle motion over the surface of the hemisphere. Repeat this process for the endPtPars particles, using the following expression, which is nearly identical to the last expression, save for the 200 unit offset per particle ID instead of 100 units.

```
float $speed = arcGrp.speed;

float $offsetV = $speed * noise(time * 0.3 + endPtParsShape.particleId *
200);

endPtParsShape.goalV += $offsetV;
```

Play back your animation, which should now have particles moving around the outside of your two hemispheres. To allow motion in both directions, you need to alter the runtime expressions of your particles to include the goalU direction as well.

Adding the Curve

Now that we have particles moving along the surface of our hemispheres, it's time to add the curve that will arc between them. First, however, we need to add a few more custom attributes to the arcGrp node so that we can properly control the curve via expressions.

1. Select the arcGrp node, and then add the following **int** attributes (default values in parentheses):

   > **startPtId** (0)
   > **endPtId** (0)
   > **numCrvCVs** (50)
   > **maxHeight** (30)
   > **crvDegree** (1)
   > **offAmp** (1)

When finished, the arcGrp Channel box should look like Figure 8.14. The **startPtId** and **endPtId** attributes provide a way for your curve to jump from particle to particle; the **numCrvCVs** attribute determines how many segments the curve has; the **maxHeight** value determines how much the curve arcs away from the surfaces; the **crvDegree** attribute controls the curve degree—degree 1 being a linear curve with hard corners, degrees 2 and 3 becoming progressively smoother; and **offAmp** controls how roughly the arc varies over its length—a value of 0 here creates a very smooth curve, while a large value (such as 5) can create some crazy-looking curves. In general, the default values of these attributes create a nice-looking effect.

2. In the side view, select the EP Curve tool and click a few times to create a simple 4 CV curve. We just need to slap something down quickly for the expression to modify (see Figure 8.15). Rename the curve arcCurve. This will be the starting point for our expression to control the curve's motion.

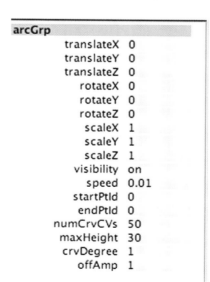

arcGrp	
translateX	0
translateY	0
translateZ	0
rotateX	0
rotateY	0
rotateZ	0
scaleX	1
scaleY	1
scaleZ	1
visibility	on
speed	0.01
startPtId	0
endPtId	0
numCrvCVs	50
maxHeight	30
crvDegree	1
offAmp	1

Figure 8.14: The Channel box for the modified arcGrp node

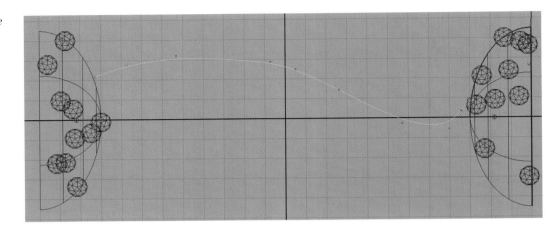

3. We need to add some extra nodes to our surfaces in order to extract the normal for each surface at each particle point for each frame. Type the following lines into the Script Editor, and then highlight and execute them (by pressing the Enter key on the numeric keypad).

```
createNode -n "st_baseNormal" "pointOnSurfaceInfo";
connectAttr -f r_base.worldSpace[0] st_baseNormal.inputSurface;
```

The first line creates a pointOnSurfaceInfo node (called st_baseNormal), which will be used to obtain information on the selected surface's normal value at each point.

The pointOnSurfaceInfo node provides basic information about a surface at a given UV position, including that point's 3D coordinates, normal, and tangents in U and V space. There also exists a pointOnCurveInfo node that provides similar information for a curve and a closestPointOnSurface node that returns the closest 3D point on a surface as well as its UV coordinates to a given point in space. These nodes come in quite handy for a number of FX scenarios.

The second line connects this pointOnSurfaceInfo node to the world space information of the selected base—in this case r_base. Be *sure* you name your surfaces r_base and l_base, or you'll need to adjust these lines, as well as the expression that follows.

A normal is the vector that points perpendicular to a surface at any given point. This is a useful value to know for any number of reasons. In our case, we want to align the start and end tangents of our curve to the normal so that the electric arc points away from the surface wherever it lies on that surface.

---

4. Let's do the same thing for the end base (l_base). Execute the following lines in the Script Editor.

```
createNode -n "end_baseNormal" "pointOnSurfaceInfo";
connectAttr -f l_base.worldSpace[0] end_baseNormal.inputSurface;
```

Now that everything is set up, we can turn to creating a fairly complex expression to control and update the curve over time. You can either type in the expression in Listing 8.1 or copy the file from the CD (`arcExp.txt`) and paste the text into the Expression Editor. (Note that if you're typing it in, line breaks occur only at semicolons.) Because this is a long expression, you can read the comments for information concerning how each segment of the expression works. The "big picture" is that the expression regenerates the original curve at each frame using the `hermite` function with all its parameters supplied by the control attributes we created on the arcGrp node. A single particle is selected in this expression (particle 0 for the startPtPars group, and particle 1 for the endPtPars group), and the curve follows along with this particle as it moves over the surface of the hemisphere. In the middle of the curve, the code iterates over each vertex using the `hermite` function to calculate the current CV's position. The position information is perturbed using the `dnoise` function, which moves the curve around in space, making it look more "electric."

`dnoise` is the vector (or 3D) equivalent of `noise`. It returns three noise values each time it is called. In this case, the three values are mapped to the X, Y, and Z coordinates of each point.

Listing 8.1: arcExp

```
////////////
//Use the desired particle identities from both surfaces to define the
//start and end points of the arc
int $startParId = arcGrp.startPtId;
int $endParId = arcGrp.endPtId;

//Now find the position of each of these particles
vector $startPt = `getParticleAttr -at position -array true
("startPtParsShape.pt[" + $startParId + "]")`;
vector $endPt = `getParticleAttr -at position -array true
("endPtParsShape.pt[" + $endParId + "]")`;

//////////////
//This next section determines the surface normals at each of the start and
//end particle positions, to be used later in the hermite function
float $maxHeight = arcGrp.maxHeight;
float $tmp[];

//The following lines grab the uv values of the identified particle and
//make them the parameters for the pointOnSurfaceInfo node we created for
//the start surface
$tmp = `particle -at goalU -id $startParId -q startPtParsShape`;
st_baseNormal.parameterU = $tmp[0];
$tmp = `particle -at goalV -id $startParId -q startPtParsShape`;
st_baseNormal.parameterV = $tmp[0];
```

```
//the $startTan vector variable now gets the normalized normal value from
//the surface point where the particle sits
vector $startTan = $maxHeight * <<st_baseNormal.normalizedNormalX,
st_baseNormal.normalizedNormalY, st_baseNormal.normalizedNormalZ>>;

//Now repeat for the end surface
$tmp = `particle -at goalU -id $endParId -q endPtParsShape`;
end_baseNormal.parameterU = $tmp[0];
$tmp = `particle -at goalV -id $endParId -q endPtParsShape`;
end_baseNormal.parameterV = $tmp[0];
vector $endTan = -$maxHeight * <<end_baseNormal.normalizedNormalX,
end_baseNormal.normalizedNormalY, end_baseNormal.normalizedNormalZ>>;

////////////////
//Now we're going to shape the curve between the two surface points
//First, position the points of the pre-created NURBS curve along a hermite
//curve shape spanning between the start and end particle positions:

//Retrieve the user-preferred degree of the curve...
int $crvDeg = arcGrp.crvDegree;

//... and define a curve command (as a string variable), including its
//first point (on the start surface), with "-r" specified to replace the
//original curve. When we later invoke this command it will replace the
//selected curve with the one created via this string
string $curveCmd = "curve -r -d " + $crvDeg + " -p " + $startPt.x + " " +
$startPt.y + " " + $startPt.z;

//Iterate over the points (starting at the second point, point 1), placing
//each one equidistantly along the arc
int $i, $numCVs = arcGrp.numCrvCVs;
float $distNormalized;
float $offsetAmp = arcGrp.offAmp;
vector $hermitePt;

//Before iterating, check to be sure we have enough CVs. If not, we could
//get a divide by 0 error below
if ($numCVs <= 1)
    print ("Error. You must have at least 2 points on your curve");

        //Iterate over the CVs
for($i=1; $i<($numCVs - 1); $i++)
{
    //Calculate the next point's base position along the arc
    $distNormalized = float($i) / float($numCVs - 1);
    $hermitePt = hermite($startPt, $endPt, $startTan, $endTan,
$distNormalized);
```

```
    //Offset each point along the arc using dnoise (the 3D, vector, noise
//function) The "+ time * 3" component determines where we sample in noise
//space to create the offset.
    $hermitePt += $offsetAmp * dnoise($hermitePt + time * 3);

    //Add the resultant point to the curve command string
    $curveCmd += " -p " + $hermitePt.x + " " + $hermitePt.y + " " +
$hermitePt.z;
    }

    //Add the end point position and complete the command by referencing our
    //"arcCurve" node
    $curveCmd += " -p " + $endPt.x + " " + $endPt.y + " " + $endPt.z;
    $curveCmd += " arcCurve";

    //Create the new curve (replacing the old one) by evaluating the string we
    //have built up previously
    eval($curveCmd);
```

Once you have successfully added this expression, try adjusting some of the custom attributes on the arcGrp node. For example, change the **crvDegree** attribute to 3, and notice how much smoother this curve looks than the degree 1 curve. (You will need to rewind or play the animation to see the changes take effect.) Play around with these settings and have some fun with your creation! You might also want to hide your particles now so that they are not visible on the control surfaces. Figure 8.16 shows the curve in motion.

You can take many other steps to make this curve effect even more fun. For example, you might want the curve to "hop" between particles on the surface, you might want to add multiple curves connected between the surface particles rather than just one, you might want to extrude a tube down the length of the curve, and you might want to add Paint Effects strokes on the curve.

To create a "hopping" expression for the start position of the arc, you can create the following expression.

```
    if (!(frame % 20))
        arcGrp.startPtId = floor(rand(10));
```

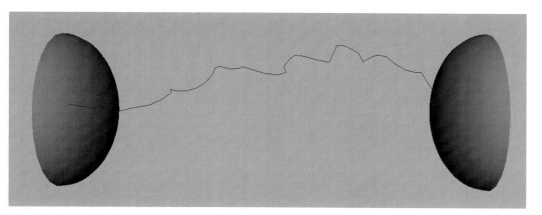

Figure 8.16: The completed curve in action

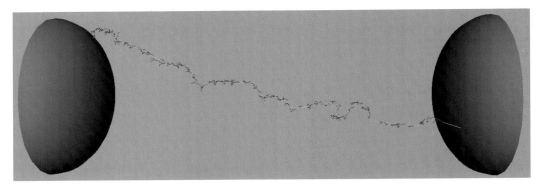

Figure 8.17: The arcCurve with the goldSparks Paint Effects brush attached

This expression simply updates the startPtId (which references which particle the curve should start from) with a random number each time the frame number is a multiple of 20 (via the `modulo` function). If you want the curve to hop to different endpoints, update the previous expression appropriately—here you might want the endpoints to update when the frame number equals a different number, such as 25 or 31.

To add Paint Effects to the curve is fairly straightforward as well. Follow these steps:

1. Choose **Paint Effects** → **Get Brush**. In the Visor pane, choose Electrical from the Paint Effects tab, and then click the goldSparks.mel brush. (You can try others as well if you like.)

2. Now select the arcCurve and choose **Paint Effects** → **Curve Utilities** → **Attach Brush to Curves**. This attaches the gold sparks paint brush to your curve; you should see little "lightning bolts" branching from your curve, as shown in Figure 8.17.

3. Although the default brush is adequate, you can tweak the brush a bit to get really nice results. With the stroke selected, open the Attribute Editor, select the goldSparks1 tab, and adjust whatever settings you like. We made some changes to the Brush Profile settings, altered the colors in the Shading and Tube Shading sections, added some Shader Glow in the Glow section, adjusted several of the Tubes settings (Creation, Growth, Turbulence, and so forth), added some small Gaps, and even added a bit of Flow Animation to the strokes. Finally, we keyframed the Flow Speed and Gap Size a bit over the animation to get more varied results as the stroke animated over the curve. When done, we ended up with a look like Figure 8.18. The full animation (`noiseyArc.mov`) and the scene file that created it (`noisyArc.ma`) are on the CD for your perusal.

Always Learning

This chapter has described a number of tools and techniques to produce complex, appealing animation using the `noise` function to build a whole effects system. Although noise is fairly simple to implement, it creates a look that is at once convincingly real in its "randomness," yet at the same time is continuous in a way that truly random numbers aren't, making the results of noise feel more real and natural than strictly random numbers would produce. Even though some of our expressions get a bit complex, just remember to start simply with your expressions and build up to more complex examples as you get more comfortable

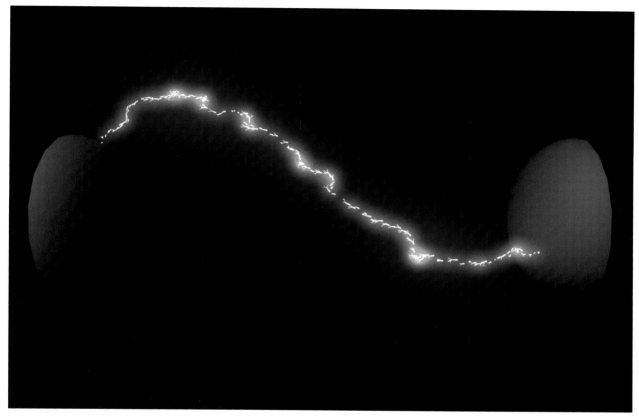

Figure 8.18: A rendered frame of the arc with a tweaked goldSparks Paint Effects brush on it

with the `noise` function and its uses. If you were not already familiar with some of the other nodes and commands, you now have some new areas of Maya to explore and discover. FX animation and development requires a firm understanding of CG concepts as well as basic scripting skills. It's then a matter of knowing how those concepts are implemented in a graphics package and how to work with them. Maya provides a fairly elegant scripting interface via MEL and a number of prebuilt nodes, such as the pointOnSurfaceInfo node, that supply useful information to the user. You might want to check out the node and MEL command help pages for more interesting stuff. Chances are, if you need some particular bit of information, you'll find a command or node that provides it.

We hope you now know more about the `noise` function and its uses and that you will add it to your Maya tools arsenal the next time you need to create some complex animation effects!

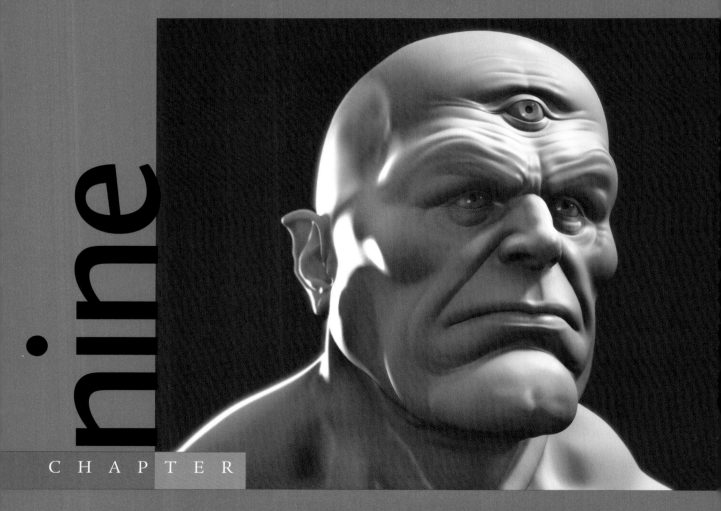

nine

Advanced Character Modeling Using Polygons and Subdivision Surfaces

Tom Capizzi and Krishnamurti M. Costa

Subdivision modeling *has become the standard for character modeling in most video and film environments. Maya has implemented a powerful and user-friendly way to use subdivision surfaces. The purpose of this chapter is to show you a proven method to create a complex shape—a character's face—using subdivision surfaces.*

The human face could be the most easily recognizable, familiar, and expressive 3D shape known to humankind. Anyone can easily spot the subtle nuances and details, but this shape is notoriously difficult for an artist to get just right. In this chapter, we'll create a human face from a conceptual sketch, an exercise that will give you the ability and tools to tackle any model that uses organic forms and shapes.

We'll employ the concepts and artwork of Krishnamurti Costa, a prominent and talented 3D artist. We'll document his techniques and processes in detail, explaining every step he uses to create his artwork.

Modeling Concepts

Certain modeling practices and guidelines are universal concepts that can be applied to any model. The way a model deforms, animates, and renders depends on how the model is built. The flow of the geometry requires planning, and the planning of the model begins before the first curve is drawn.

Modelers and studios use different processes to create polygonal models. Any given process will create different results. Many modeling tutorials suggest an approach in which

the modeler uses primitives to start a model and fills in the detail later. Some studios use 3D scans or hand-digitized 3D data to begin modeling.

The approach in this tutorial uses carefully placed rows of polygons to create an easy-to-edit polygonal cage. This technique is called poly-by-poly modeling. The polygonal cage is the basis for the subdivision model. If the geometry flows naturally along the surface of the model, texturing, lighting, rigging, and animation are much easier later in the production process.

Before modeling takes place, it is important to understand the model that you will be creating. How will it move? What kind of detail will be required? Where is the detail going to be? How will it be textured? What kind of lighting will be applied to it?

The production requirements for a model can be considerable and can change during the time the model is being created and used in production. It can be impossible to know exactly what will be required of the model before it is created, but a good modeler attempts to make educated assumptions about these requirements.

An experienced modeler knows that two things will probably happen when they are given a model to build for a project:

- If they are told that the model will not have to be too detailed, the model will almost certainly appear full screen at some time.
- If the model is detailed to support any amount of close-up scrutiny, the rendering deadlines will require that the model's level of detail be taken down to the absolute lowest levels possible to expedite production.

Luckily, subdivision modeling supports both scenarios. When you carefully plan your model and execute using levels of detail in the subdivision, the model can hold up to careful scrutiny, and the detail can be reduced quickly and easily to render out fast and easy.

Using Conceptual Art: Laying Out the Views in 2D

The character we'll work with in this chapter is stylized, but it has human features to provide a variety of modeling situations that can be explored for this tutorial.

Instead of creating a 3D model from scratch, we'll use artwork to illustrate how a model can be created in a professional environment. Seldom is an artist given a project to work on that they have complete creative control over. When an artist is shown how to model from a piece of artwork, they can easily use that technique in a professional situation in which they will be asked to create models from conceptual art.

The drawings in Figure 9.1 are excellent examples of the level of specifics needed in the artwork to create a detailed subdivision model.

A minimum of two views are necessary to create an accurate 3-dimensional model from 2-dimensional artwork. In these views, called orthographic views, the overall dimensions must line up between the drawings. The overall length, width, and placement of the details such as eyes, nose, and mouth must be aligned between the two drawings, as in Figure 9.2.

Modeling Standards

Modeling standards change from studio to studio. In some cases, for example, it's fine for a subdivision model to have a lot of triangles, and in other cases triangles are strictly forbidden.

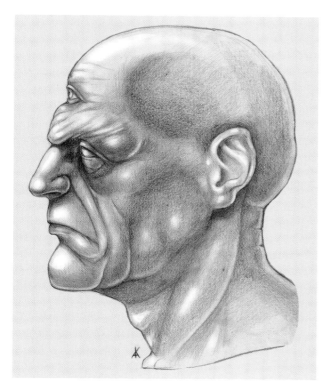

Figure 9.1: Detailed front and side views of a character

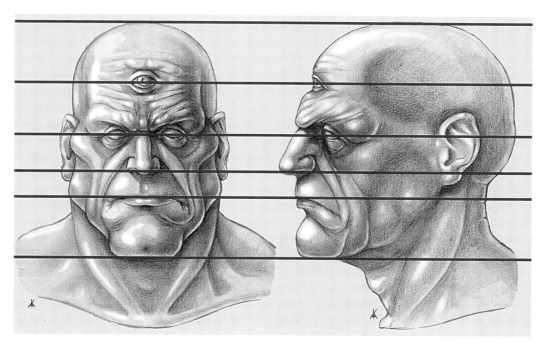

Figure 9.2: Two
views aligned

Generally, if it looks good in animation and lighting, you'll be allowed some freedom in the process used to create the model.

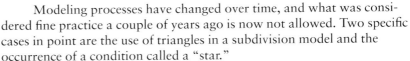

Modeling processes have changed over time, and what was considered fine practice a couple of years ago is now not allowed. Two specific cases in point are the use of triangles in a subdivision model and the occurrence of a condition called a "star."

Subdivision models work much better with four-sided polygons than with three-sided polygons. In our exercise, the model has no triangles whatsoever. With careful placement of edges, and by using the tools explained here effectively, it is possible to create high-quality models that have no triangles.

A star is a place where five edges come together in one corner. This condition can cause many problems in animation and lighting. They create irregular flashing and twisting when the object is used in production. The model in Figure 9.3 has been built to the standards specified here and was produced using just four-sided polygons. Stars, on the other hand, are harder to avoid because they're caused by the edge loops crossing. You can control stars and place them where there is little or no deformation. When it is impossible to avoid a five-cornered condition, always avoid putting the star in a place where there will be a great deal of movement.

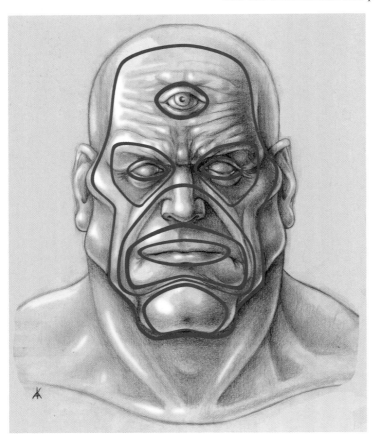

Figure 9.3: A star condition in a polygon layout

Animation Flow

The first concept to consider when planning the flow of geometry in a model is animation flow. The "flow" of the geometry must support the way the model will move. A model must have geometry that can be moved along the lines that the model will be required to move.

The areas that are required to move in this model are the eyes, mouth, and jaw. The flow of animation in these areas will surround these areas. By outlining the general vicinity surrounding the areas of movement, as shown in Figure 9.4, we can visualize how the geometry will need to flow along the model.

This geometry flow is simple to understand. Geometry must flow radially away from areas of movement (see Figure 9.5). The careful arrangement of radial polygon rows placed along the paths of motion make the model easy to rig and animate. Rows of polygons that surround the animation areas

Figure 9.4: Areas of animation

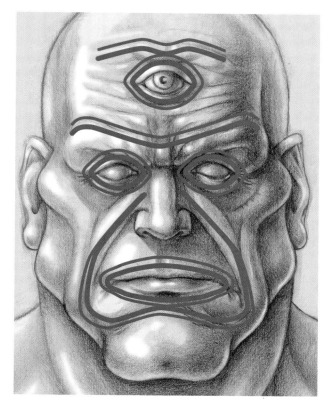

Figure 9.5: An animation flow diagram

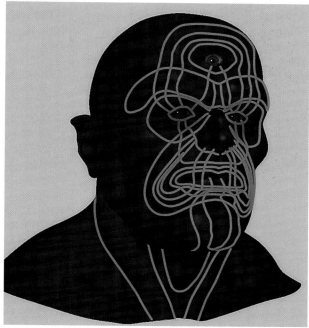

Figure 9.6: Muscle edge loops

create uniform movement in the model, define the anatomic forms better, and allow the model to render properly as well.

Edge Loops

A more complex idea that relates to construction is the concept of edge loops. Edge loops are related to animation flow, because they follow the muscle construction in the actual face, and the face naturally moves along the path of these muscles. But the edge loop concept takes the idea of animation flow and expands on it to cover the construction of muscle groups, bone areas, and areas of fat along the surface of the face.

Muscle edge loops are placed around areas of the face that will move: the eyelids, the lips, the brow, and the jawline. Model muscle areas carefully to avoid awkward intersections and triangles. These areas require the closest scrutiny when animating and present the most problems if not modeled correctly.

When defining the edge loops of the muscles, try to integrate the muscles by defining not only lines that are parallel to the areas of movement, but also lines perpendicular to the movement where muscles will connect. In Figure 9.6, notice how the lines flow around the lips, but lines flow through the lips as well. These lines allow the flow of the geometry of the lips to align with the flow of the geometry of the cheek and jaw muscles.

Fat edge loops, like those in Figure 9.7, define the areas of the face where movement takes place, but it is passive movement that is not driven by a direct force. This movement is caused by the muscles. You must model fat areas as carefully as muscle areas because they will move almost the same amount. Fat areas do not really have to interact with other fat areas. Fat areas exist as small islands of passive flesh that allow the muscles to move freely.

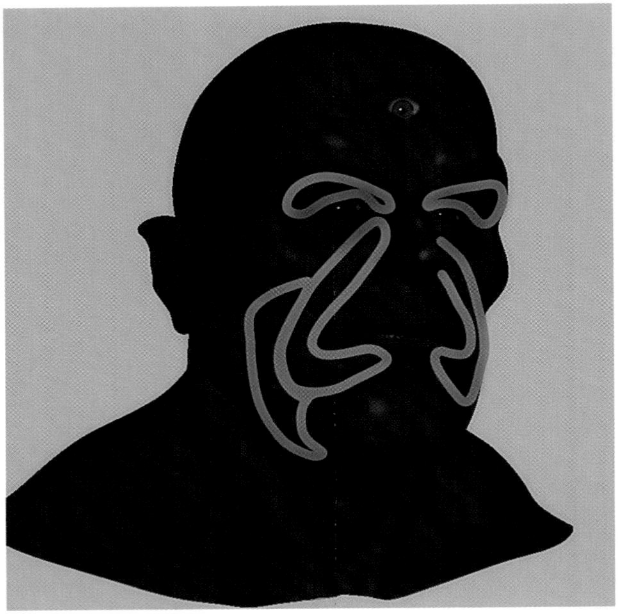

Bone edge loops are the hard areas of the face where the bone comes closest to the surface, as shown in Figure 9.8. These areas do not have much flexibility and will not have much movement within them. For this reason, it is convenient to use these as places where the model can have transition areas such as five-cornered intersections. Because these areas do not move much, some geometric flaws can go unnoticed if constructed carefully.

You use the entire edge-loop layout (see Figure 9.9) to plan the placement of the geometry during construction. Using careful planning and geometry placement, you can build a model that is easy to edit and animate. Even if the model will not be used for animation, a good edge-loop layout can help define the anatomic details of your model, just because bones, fat, and muscle loops are part of the same main volume.

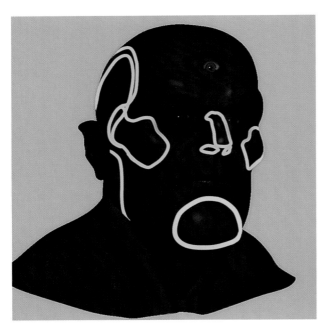

Figure 9.7: Fat edge loops

Figure 9.8: Bone edge loops

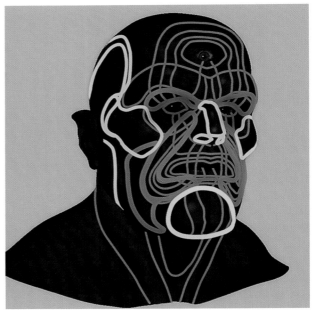

Figure 9.9: Edge-loop layout

Modeling the Face

Once you have a basic understanding of the flow of the geometry, you can begin the process of building a wire cage. The modeling process is much like any other kind of artistic endeavor. You work on the piece until the work is finished, and throughout the course of the work, many operations take place. You build something, tweak something, and erase something else. These steps build up over time until you have accomplished a number of small things that amount to a big piece of art you are proud of.

The problem with modeling in Maya is that the computer remembers everything you do. You can set history to a small number of steps to mitigate this overhead, but over time it is important to optimize the work flow by performing certain steps during the modeling process.

Save often. Save your file many times over the modeling process to unique and sequential names. These names are usually something like `workFile.0001.mb`, `work-File.0002.mb`, and so on

Delete history often. History slows you down to the point where simple tasks take a long time. Experienced modelers recognize quickly when the history starts to be too much and delete it.

Subdivide the model judiciously. Subdivision is a great way to create high-quality models quickly. The subdivision process itself, however, is computationally expensive. In this exercise, we build the model almost entirely using only polygons until the end, when subdivision modeling is necessary. During construction, view the subdivision model periodically to make sure the model is progressing correctly. In these cases, the model is subdivided to preview the progress, and then the subdivision operation is undone so the clean and light polygon modeling process can continue.

The process for modeling the face consists of placing the image planes in 3D, creating a wire cage that outlines the details of the face, and creating a polygonal cage from which to create the subdivision surfaces.

Laying Out the Image Planes in 3D

Load your images before manipulating the viewports. If there is any camera movement in the viewports before the image plane is imported, choose **View** → **Default Home** (at the top of each viewport) to reset the view.

Load drawings into the Maya viewports by choosing **View** → **Image Plane** → **Import Image** from the viewport menu. Locate the front and side images in the respective front and side viewports, as shown in Figure 9.10. This will create a perspective view in which the images can be seen positioned at 90 degrees to each other. The perspective view is where a lot of the wireframe modeling takes place. To see an example of the modeling windows set up with the image planes, open `subD_modeling01.mb` on the CD.

Now we are ready to begin laying out the model in 3D. To make the modeling process easier, build a rough wire cage using splines that will be the basis for the polygonal modeling process. The polygonal cage will be used to create the final smooth model that will be animated and rendered. The wire cage will be the skeleton for the model.

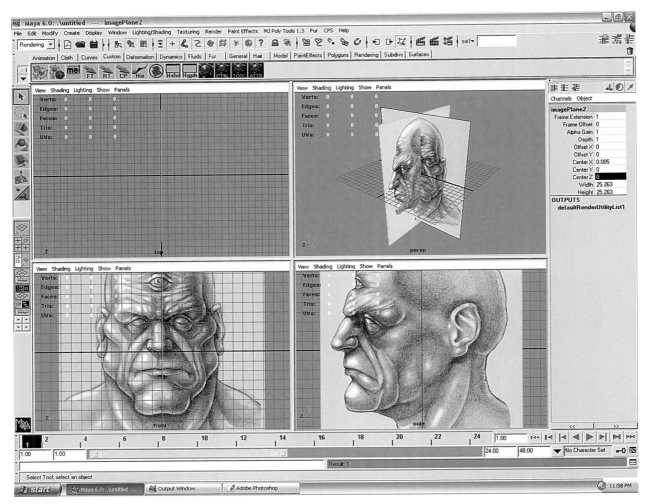

Figure 9.10:
Images loaded
into viewports

Creating a Wire Cage

The previous section explains in detail how to prepare for modeling a complex organic model. Now that we have done our homework and have a plan, it is time to set our plan in motion. The next steps will create a 3D digital armature for creating the polygonal head.

The wire cage needs to follow the animation flow lines and the edge loops. The wire cage represents your modeling strategy from which all the modeling will take place. For this reason, this modeling phase is one of the most important steps to get right. Once polygonal modeling has started, it is difficult to go back and change your strategy.

Build the wire cage using curves that are easy to control and still give an accurate representation of the form that you are trying to create. Choose **Create → EP Curve Tool □**, and then create degree 1 Edit Point NURBS curves with Uniform Knot spacing. These curves are the most similar to polylines (an entity type that is not supported by the Maya modeling software). Since we are building a polygonal cage from the wire cage, it is simpler to use degree 1 curves.

Start by drawing curves in the front view. Begin tracing the details of the drawings using fairly simple curves, as in Figure 9.11. Remember, the more points you use now, the more points you will need to edit later. Capture the outlines around the eyes, cheeks, chin, and the rest of the face as shown. Lay out the curves roughly around the areas of animation so the model can be built along these lines later.

Once the front view is finished, the curves in that view all rest in one place at zero in the Z axis. After you draw the front-view curves, you must edit the curves in the front view to match the side view. Begin, for example, with the curve in the lower eyelid, as shown in Figure 9.12. Translate the curve outward in Z to position the curve correctly. Edit the curve point by point to get the curvature correct along the Z axis.

Continue this process with the rest of the face. You need to edit the curves already drawn before adding details for the side view (see Figure 9.13). Curves such as the bottom of the chin and the brow might need additional information so that they flow

Figure 9.11: EP curves drawn on the face

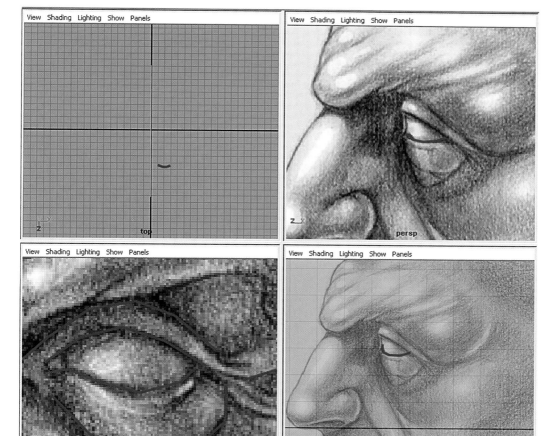

Figure 9.12: The lower eyelid curve edited

Figure 9.13: Front and side view of the wire cage

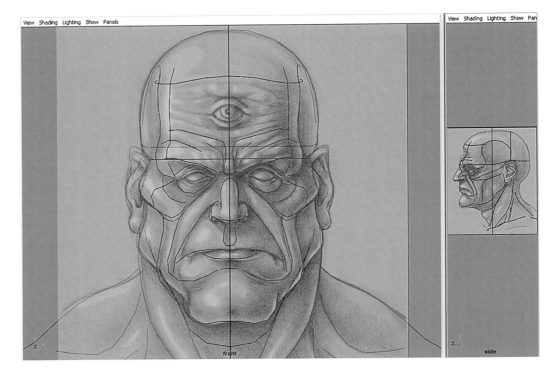

 correctly along the Z axis in the side view (see Figure 9.14). You can do this by adding curves in the side view that extend the front-view curves beyond their original extents and joining the curves later during the modeling process. To see the construction of the wire cage, open `subD_modeling03.mb` on the CD.

Work on the wire cage until it is a clean representation of your concept. This is a critical step in the modeling process. This wire cage will allow you to visualize your design in 3D before you begin creating polygons and subdivision surfaces using easy-to-edit degree 1 curves. You can edit this wire cage later, so do not waste unnecessary time finessing it. This is a strategy, not the final model. If your plan is basically shown in 3D, you can proceed to the next step.

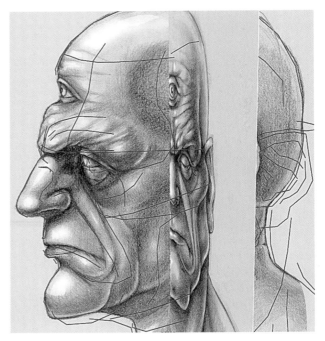

Figure 9.14: Perspective view of the wire cage

A Warning about Orthographic Projections

The process described here uses orthographic projections to create 3D models. This is a fast and accurate way to get 3D form from easily interpreted 2D drawings. This process has been used for years in traditional and digital artwork to make just about any conceivable 3D shape.

But there is a problem with this process. Orthographically created models tend to look boxy when completed. Take precautions so that this does not happen as the model comes together. The edges of the model, the places where the edges of the views come together, sometimes get an unnatural boxlike form; sculpt this out.

A good way to think of this is to picture the creation of a sphere using orthographic views. First, you lay out two really nice circles in the two orthographic views. You then cut out a piece of digital clay to be perfect circles from each of the two views. We're done, right? From the front the sphere looks fine, and from the side the sphere looks fine. But when the model is viewed from the perspective camera, the model has a really ugly outer edge going down the corner. It is up to you to round out the sphere from the basic shape created using the orthographic method.

The same thing can happen during the modeling process of a human face. It is your job to make sure that the corners of the model have beautiful 3D roundness. You can achieve this only by constantly rotating the model in the perspective view, looking at it from every imaginable angle, and trying to get the form as natural as possible.

Unfortunately, Maya has no "make cool" button. You must use your eyes and understand the finished form. There are some tools, however, that can help you along the way, and the section "Creating a Polygonal Cage" explains them.

Creating a Polygonal Cage

Most artists use their favorite tools to create their artwork. The same is true of modelers. You don't have to use all Maya polygonal modeling tools to create a great model. The trick is to get good at the tools you really need and know when to use them.

The next few sections show how specific tools are used at different stages of the modeling process. The tools that are used relate to the process that is taking place. As with all modeling projects, the model starts with simple forms and moves into more complex and refined shapes later.

The tools that are used at these phases of construction reflect the way that the construction goes from simple to complex. In the process of constructing the polygonal head, you'll use many tools, but you'll primarily do the following:

- Choose **Polygons** → **Create Polygon Tool** and **Polygons** → **Append to Polygon Tool** to create the entire main form of the head.
- Choose **Edit Polygons** → **Split Polygon Tool** to cut faces to add more details or change the edge-loop layout of the model.
- Choose **Edit Polygons** → **Extrude Edge** to extend the rows of polygons to cover large areas of the model quickly. Choose **Edit Polygons** → **Merge Vertices** to collapse vertices and close holes in the mesh.
- Choose **Edit Polygons** → **Sculpt Polygons Tool** and **Modify** → **Transformation Tools** → **Soft Modification Tool** to create subtle and controlled modifications to the geometry using a "faded deformation."
- Choose **Edit Polygons** → **Collapse** to reorganize the polygonal layout of the model surface by collapsing different edges into only one.
- Choose **Edit Polygons** → **Extrude Face** to create interesting areas of detail that maintain excellent geometric layout.

Creating and Appending Polygons

As I mentioned earlier in this chapter, the process we are using is called the poly-by-poly modeling method. This method works well because we are not making discrete patches of polygons from curves, merging them after the fact. The benefits to this process and the process of creating merged patches are as follows:

You need not predetermine the number of points per spline. When making patches, the number of polygons per patch is determined by making sure all curves have a specific number of vertices. Keeping track of this can be tricky and, at the very least, time-consuming. Since you are just making a polygon model that will be subdivided, this step is unnecessary using the poly-by-poly method.

You need not keep track of face normals. When you are making patches, the direction of the face normals depends on the way you create the patch. You need to keep track of the order in which you select your splines when making patches and the direction in which the splines were drawn. If you screw up the direction of the face normals and merge a model created using patches, your model will not subdivide. You will spend a lot of time reversing polygon normals until you get them all lined up.

You need not spend as much time merging faces. Some steps in this process require merging polygonal patches. For the most part, by building the model polygon by polygon, the merging occurs as the model develops.

Using this process, polygonal modeling begins with the creation of a single polygon. Using the edge loop layout, you can place polygons strategically and then duplicate them into rows by choosing **Polygons** → **Create Polygon Tool** (see Figure 9.15). To draw polygons, use the Snap To Curve function or press the C key while drawing the polygon. The points of the polygon snap to the wire cage that you constructed earlier.

The next step is to append the polygon into a string of polygons by choosing **Polygons** → **Append to Polygon Tool** (see Figure 9.16). The Append to Polygon tool works much like the Create Polygon tool, but you must first select the polygon that needs to be appended and then select the edges of the new polygon (the one you are building) that are beyond the original polygon (the one that was created using the Create Polygon tool) using the C key to snap the new edges to the wire cage curves that were drawn earlier. The Append to Polygon tool makes polygons that are already merged to the original polygon, and they do not require cleanup.

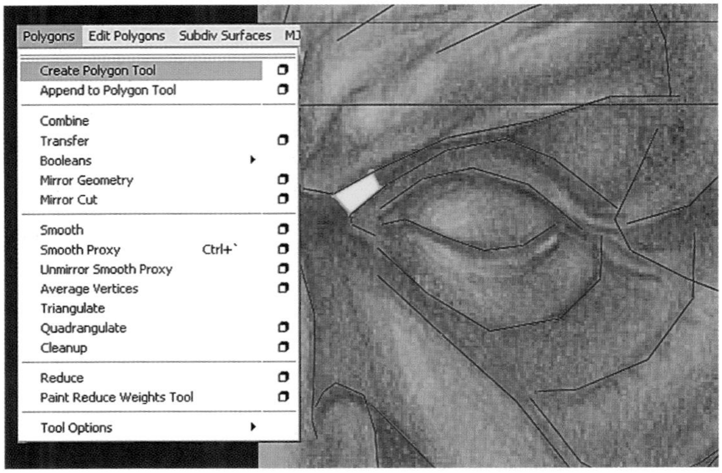

Proceed around the eye, and then press Enter to complete the process. For the next row of polygons, choose the Append to Polygon tool again, but use the lower edge of the polygon to create the next row of polygons. From the sequences of images in Figures 9.17 and 9.18, it is apparent how using the Append to Polygon tool can be a useful way to create a fast network of polygons.

Once there is an adequate number of rows to begin visualizing the shape of the eye

Figure 9.15: The Create Polygon tool

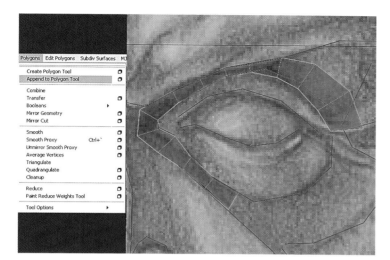

Figure 9.16: The Append to Polygon tool

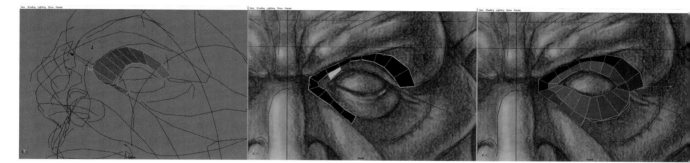

Figure 9.17: Append Polygon, inner rows

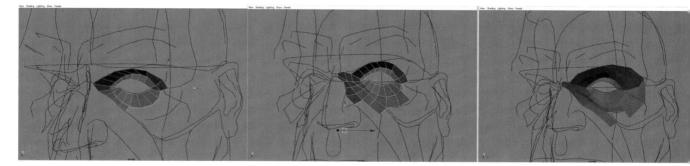

Figure 9.18: Append Polygon, outer rows

and cheek areas, you might need to duplicate the eye area across the X axis. When you do this, it is important to choose **Edit** → **Duplicate** → ▢; then set **Scale** to –1 in the X axis and set **Geometry Type** to Instance (see Figure 9.19). This will allow the model to update instantly as one side is changed. To see the initial polygonal modeling, and the mirroring across the X axis, open subD_modeling04.mb on the CD.

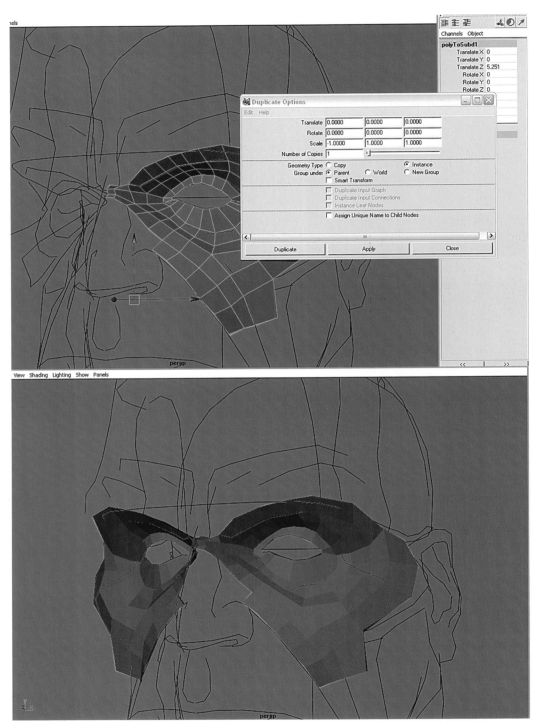

Figure 9.19: Duplicating an instance across the X axis

Continue to use this instanced geometry to view the model throughout the entire modeling process. Only when most of the modeling is done and you are about to convert the entire model to subdivision surfaces can you merge the instance with the rest of the model to make one piece of geometry.

The next area that requires attention is the mouth and chin (see Figure 9.20). This is done the same way as the eye area. Start the rows of polygons as single polygons, and then string them across using the Append To Polygon tool. Model the left side of the character's face; because that's the original, the right side is automatically updated. The mouth is laid in first, creating a template edge for the next row of polygons. The chin is completed, and then the upper lip area is laid in later.

The forehead (see Figure 9.21) and the surrounding areas of the face are tied in using the same process. When joining different areas of polygons, the Append To Polygon tool

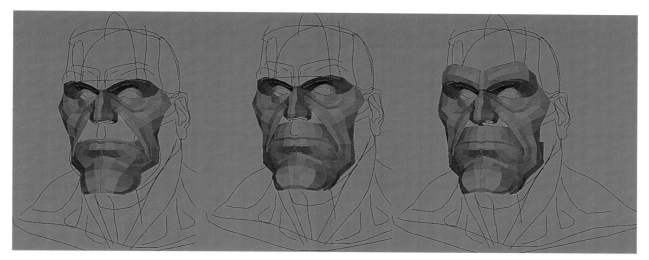

Figure 9.20: *The mouth and chin*

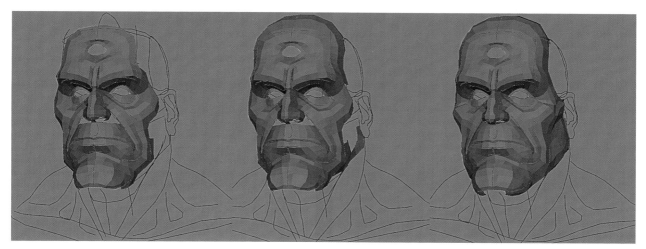

Figure 9.21: *The forehead*

will require using the Snap To Vertices option, or pressing the V key. Snapping to polygons across the span cleanly creates a bridge where the model forms one smooth mesh.

Splitting Polygons

The wireframe image shows the simplicity of the construction and how the polygonal layout adheres to the original edge loop layout. At this stage, many areas of detail have been added.

Since Maya first introduced the polygon modeling tools, the Split Polygon tool has been one of the most valuable in the modeler's tool box. This tool works extraordinarily well to maintain geometric integrity, while allowing us to significantly change the topology of the model.

> While using the Split Polygon tool, the UVs of the model accurately split and are not deleted. The polygons that are split are not detached, and there are no spurious duplicates of the polygons that sometimes occur when using other tools.

The Split Polygon tool is used through the modeling process to create areas of detail and to reroute some of the polygons in order to avoid triangles and five-sided intersections. When you use the Split Polygon tool in combination with choosing **Edit Polygons** → **Delete Edge,** you can keep a model's surface intact, but completely change the polygonal layout of the model to suit the needs of animation and production.

To create the areas of detail shown in Figure 9.22, we used the Split Polygon tool to make rows of polygons tighter in areas where natural seams occur along the face. To reduce the number of times the model requires different levels of subdivision, these details need to be as correct as possible. If you want to see the model with the details in place, open subD_modeling06.mb on the CD.

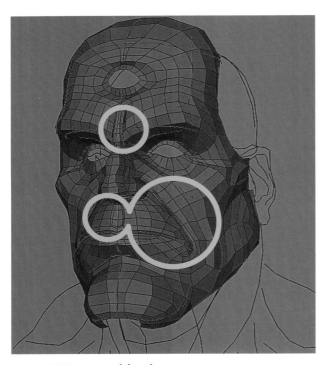

Figure 9.22: Areas of detail

Extruding Rows of Polygons

When the model gets to the point where there are just large areas to create with little detail, such as the top of the head and the neck, the Extrude Edge command is helpful. The next few figures show the detailed step-by-step process of creating extruded rows that will be clean and line up with the rest of the model.

By selecting contiguous edges manually or by selecting one edge and choosing **Edit Polygons** → **Selection** → **Select Contiguous Edges** (see Figure 9.23), select a row of edges where the model needs a new row of polygons.

The default extrusion behavior in Maya is to separate every polygon. To make sure the polygons stay together, choose **Polygons** → **Tool Options** → **Keep Faces Together** (see Figure 9.24). This forces the extruded polygons to keep the edges together during the extrusion process.

Choose **Edit Polygons** → **Extrude Edge** to create the row of polygons. This selection displays the Extrude Edge manipulator that you can use to translate, rotate, or scale the leading edge of the extruded polygons. When extruding the row of polygons, make

*Figure 9.23:
Select Contigu-
ous Edges*

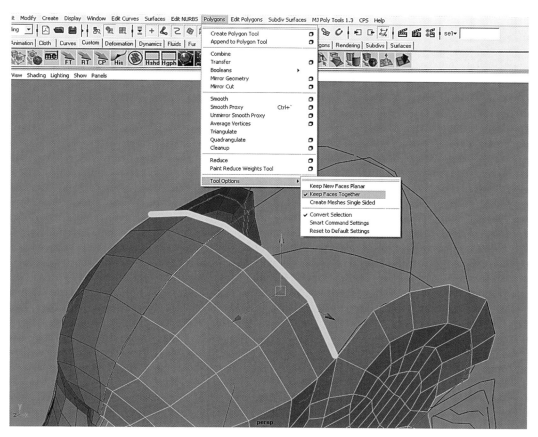

*Figure 9.24:
The Keep Faces
Together option*

sure that the row is built as close to the desired final location as possible. The manipulator, shown in Figure 9.25, makes this process as simple as it can be. Any editing that cannot be achieved without using the manipulator will need to be done by hand after the extrude operation is complete (see Figure 9.26).

When the extrude operation is complete, you'll need to weld the vertices at the edges of the polygon row you just created. The last vertex of the row will be disconnected from the remainder of the model and will need to be integrated.

Select the two vertices that need to be welded (see Figure 9.27), and then choose **Edit Polygons** → **Merge Vertices** ❑. Merge Vertices welds the selected vertices within a given tolerance (the Distance option in the dialog). To ensure the selected vertices are welded, the option for the weld distance is set fairly high. In this case, Distance was set to a level of 10.0.

After you set the options, click the Merge Vertex button to execute the merging process. The finished extruded row and subsequent merged vertex are shown in Figure 9.28.

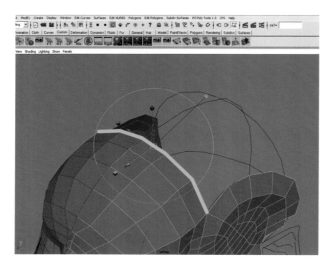

Figure 9.25: The Extrude Edge manipulator icon

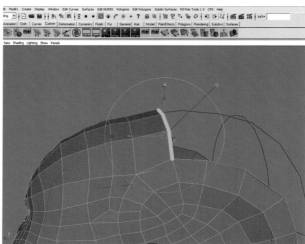

Figure 9.26: Extrude Edge complete

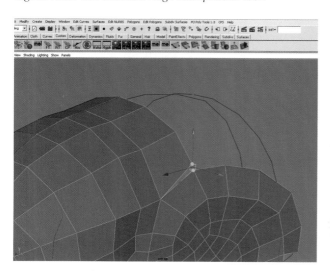

Figure 9.27: Selected vertices

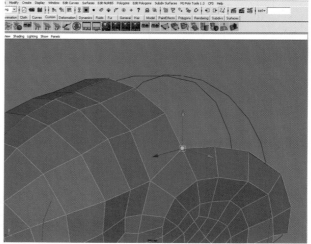

Figure 9.28: Merge Vertices complete

Modifying the Mesh

Several tools in Maya let you move geometry in a subtle way, as if the geometry were clay. In this model, we primarily used the Sculpt Polygons tool (choose **Edit Polygons → Sculpt Polygons Tool**) and the Soft Modification tool (choose **Modify → Transformation Tools → Soft Modification Tool**).

The Sculpt Polygons tool is great for gently pushing and pulling geometry in and out, but one of the most useful options in this Tool Box is the Smooth option (see Figure 9.29). It works by averaging the values of the affected vertices and blends irregular areas out into one smooth area.

Another tool that was introduced in Maya 6 is the Soft Modification tool (choose **Modify → Transformation Tools → Soft Modification Tool**), as shown in Figure 9.30. This tool uses proximity around the selected vertex to control the falloff of the transformation. The curve of influence from the selected vertex to the last affected vertex is clearly drawn out so the user

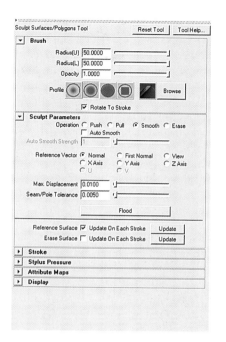

Figure 9.29: The Sculpt Polygons Smooth option

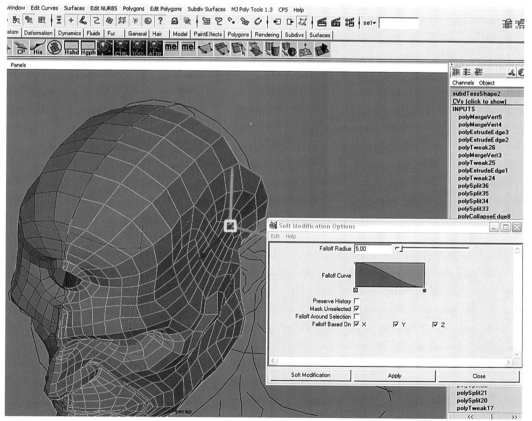

Figure 9.30: The Soft Modification tool options

can adjust the falloff and the amount of intensity the falloff has from the center to the outer edge.

These tools work exceedingly well when used in combination. The smoothing option in the Sculpt Polygons tool prepares the surface by distributing the geometry more evenly, and the Soft Modification tool moves the geometry in a soft, controlled way that the other tools cannot.

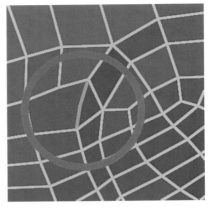

Figure 9.31: Select problem edges before choosing Edit Polygons → Collapse.

Collapsing Polygons

This technique allows us to modify the number of polygons without having to clean up edges and vertices by welding them. The process is simple, but should be thought out carefully before using the Collapse command.

Begin by identifying a problem area in the model. These are places where the model has polygons that are not four-sided or where the flow of the geometry does not coincide with the flow of animation or edge loops. You should reorganize your model's polygon layout to avoid problems later on in production.

Select the edges of the problem areas in the model, and then choose **Edit Polygons → Collapse** (see Figure 9.31).

The resulting geometry shows how the polygons in that area have been collapsed (see Figure 9.32). The polygons surrounding the area do not have problems with duplicate vertices or duplicate edges. The Collapse command takes care of the cleanup that is usually associated with this kind of work.

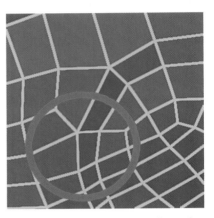

Figure 9.32: The resulting collapsed area

Extruding Polygons

For fast and easy construction of detailed areas, one of the most surprisingly useful tools is Extrude Face. In most organic models, some areas undulate in and out, making conventional modeling difficult. In this section, you'll see several examples of how this command can help when creating detailed areas around the head.

In Figure 9.33, the muscles of the neck are modeled in simple polygons using the Create Polygon tool and the Append to Polygon tool.

Select these polygons, and then choose **Edit Polygons → Extrude Face**. The default behavior for Extrude Face is to divide the faces into separate entities. The separating polygons are not usable and require a lot of cleanup if used by mistake. Be sure the default behavior of the polygon modeling toolset is selected by choosing **Polygons → Tool Options → Keep Faces Together** described in the earlier section "Extruding Rows of Polygons."

Once the Extrude command is applied, the faces appear highlighted with a manipulator present so they can be translated and scaled to fit into the appropriate detail. When you use Extrude Face, the polygons remain cleanly connected (see Figure 9.34). If you do not

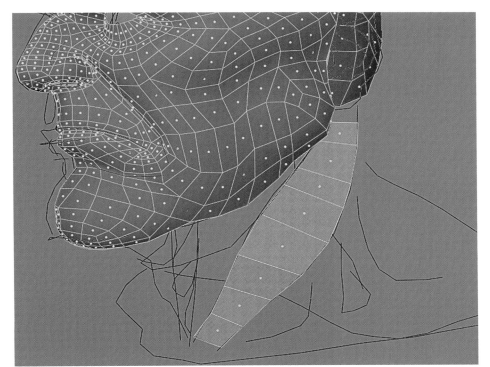

Figure 9.33:
Polygons of the
neck muscle

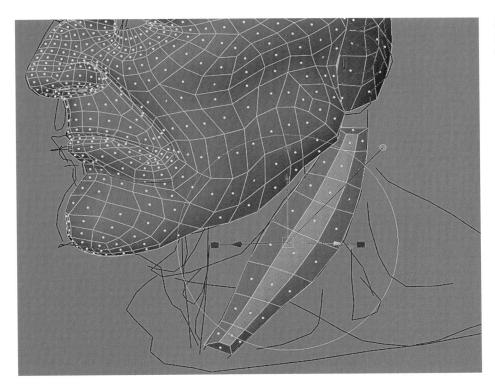

Figure 9.34:
Extruded faces of
neck muscle

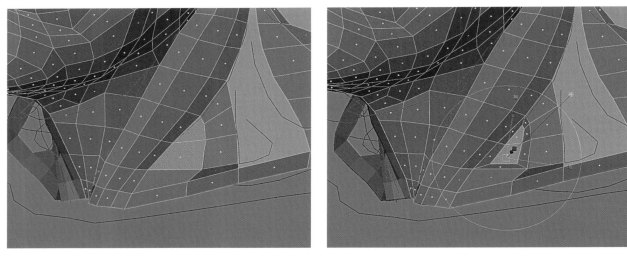

Figure 9.35: (left) Selected faces in neck area 1; (right) extruded faces in this region

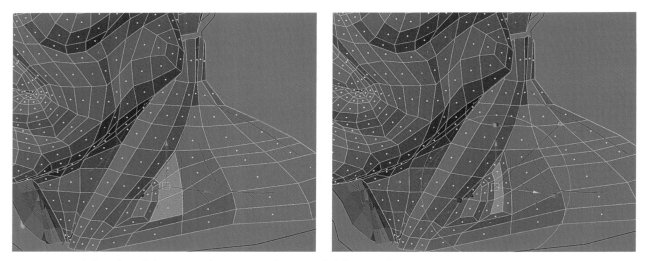

Figure 9.36: (left) Selected faces in neck area 2; (right) extruded faces in this region

correctly set your Keep Faces Together options and the faces separate, undo the operation and start over with the correct options.

This modeling technique is beneficial in many instances. Figures 9.35 and 9.36 are two more examples in which you can use the Extrude Face command in the neck area.

Now that we've described the basic tools, we can get into the specific techniques for building individual details of the model. The parts of the model that make all the difference when viewing the final work are the trickiest. Much of the process involved in the finishing touches of any model are more technique than technology.

Details of the Head

This section uses images that have been collected, showing a step-by-step approach to building each part of the model. The basis for the rest of the construction is in place using the processes that have already been covered, but the tools are used in different combinations.

When you create these areas, it is important to know how these elements are going to look when they are subdivided. To preview the subdivision surface of the model, choose **Modify → Convert → Polygons to Subdiv**. We use this command at this stage of modeling as a way to previsualize the subdivision surface; we won't commit to a subdivision model until the polygonal cage is completed. At the finishing stages of the model, you need to preview the subdivision often. Only by testing the subdivision can we see what the finished version of the model will look like.

The Back Area

You construct the back area by building a single polygon first. Choose **Polygons → Append to Polygon Tool** to create a polygon that goes from the base of the head to the edge of the lower back. Then choose **Edit Polygons → Split Polygon Tool** to split the polygon down the center (see Figure 9.37).

Select the edge that was created by the Split Polygon tool, and translate it to the center of the back (see Figure 9.38). This will serve as the base for the rest of the construction.

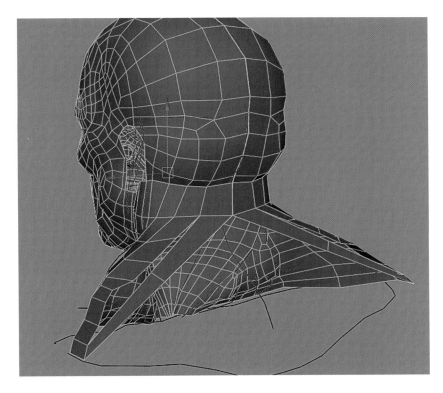

Figure 9.37: A single polygon split in half

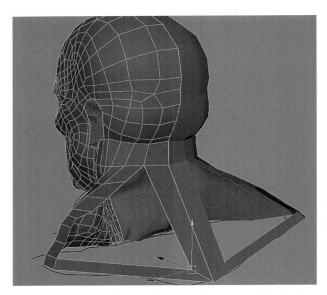

Figure 9.38: The edge translated to the center of the back

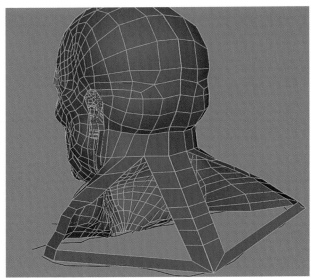

Figure 9.39: The center of the back split into sections

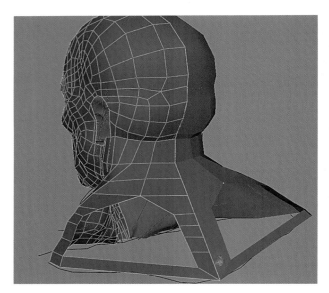

Figure 9.40: Joining the rows of back polygons

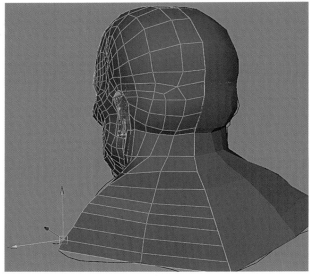

Figure 9.41: The back polygons joined in the center

Use the Split Polygon tool again to give the center polygon the same number of divisions as the edge row of polygons (see Figure 9.39). This sets up the mesh construction for the rest of the back.

Choose **Edit Polygons** → **Merge Vertices** to join the vertices along the vertical polygon rows (see Figure 9.40). This creates a simple mesh along the back that will become a more complex sculpted mesh.

Join all the remaining edges of the rows using the Merge Vertices command, and split the bottom polygon using the Split Polygon tool (see Figure 9.41). Now the surfaces are ready to become a more complex shape.

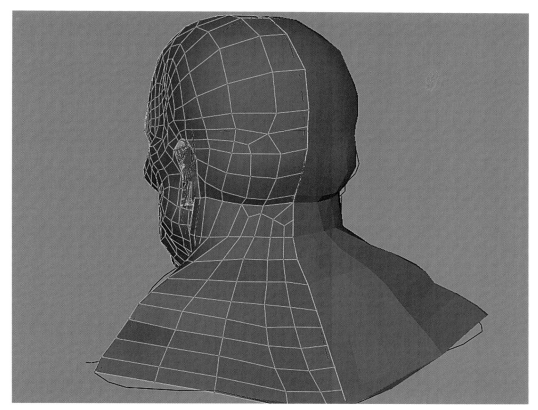

Figure 9.42: The back surface completed

Using the Split Polygon tool modifies the polygon mesh in the back and makes it into a surface (see Figure 9.42) that can be sculpted easily by selecting points and pushing and pulling them into an organic shape. The sculpting process can also be done by choosing **Edit Polygons** → **Sculpt Polygons Tool** or **Modify** → **Transformation Tools** → **Soft Modification Tool**.

The Ear Area

The ear is one of the trickiest parts of the human body to visualize in any medium, and perhaps the most difficult medium in which to capture this complex form is 3D. Using a digital medium or traditional sculpting methods have given artists problems. The only way to really get it right is to work from reference. For the initial construction phase of the ear, turn off the polygonal model's visibility and turn on the image planes. In the side view, use the image planes to trace the outer edge of the ear (see Figure 9.43) by choosing **Polygons** → **Create Polygon Tool** and **Polygons** → **Append to Polygon Tool**.

Block in the rest of the details of the ear by creating a single polygon inside the ear (see Figure 9.44), and then choose **Edit Polygons** → **Split Polygon Tool** to edit the shape. This creates a 2D template for the inside of the ear.

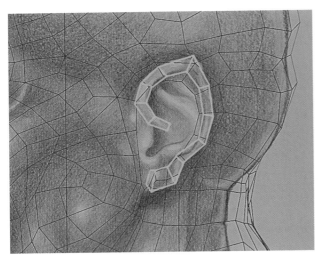

Figure 9.43: Tracing the outside of the ear

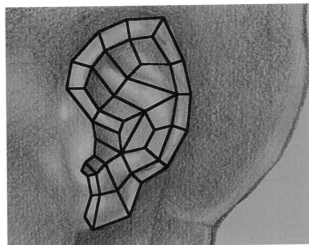

Figure 9.44: Tracing the inside of the ear

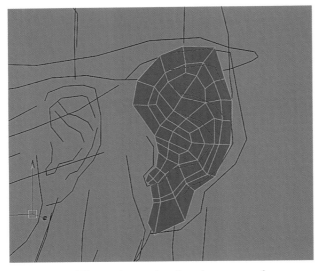

Figure 9.45: The ear is translated to the correct place.

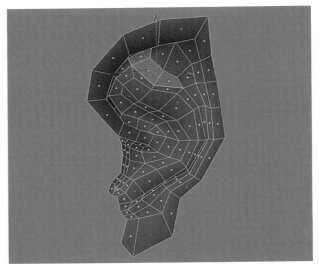

Figure 9.46: Adding detail to the ear

The mesh that was created using the image planes in the side view now have to be translated into the correct place in 3D (see Figure 9.45). Using the wire cage that was previously constructed, place the ear in the approximate location where it will eventually go in 3D.

Sculpt the ear model into the correct shape by pulling points. The details of the ear are still somewhat rough. Create additional details (see Figure 9.46) by choosing **Edit Polygons** → **Extrude Face**. Select the faces that constitute a detail of the ear.

To complete the extrude process (see Figure 9.47), scale down the inner polygons and then translate them in toward the inside of the head. This process creates a clean detail that requires no additional editing.

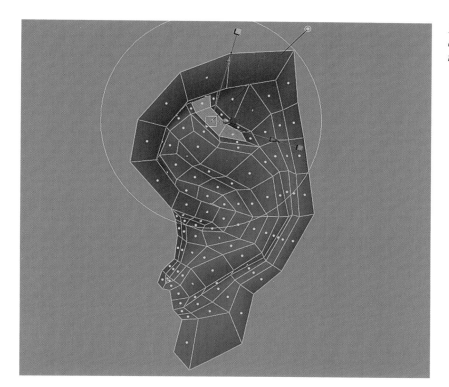

Figure 9.47: The extrude process to make detail

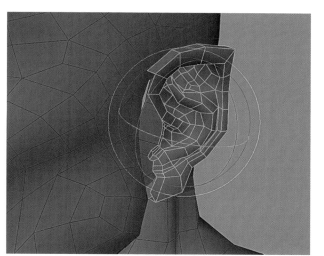
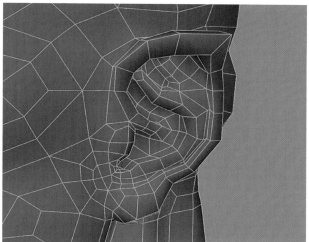

Figure 9.48: Combining polysets before (left) and after (right)

The ear is ready to be joined to the rest of the head. Make the polygonal model visible, and choose **Polygons** → **Combine** to combine the two meshes into one (see Figure 9.48). If you want to see the finished ear, open the subD_modeling14.mb model on the CD.

The Eye Area

The basic shape of the eye has already been laid out in previous steps. The rest of the eyelid now needs to be integrated into the face and adapted to an eyeball. Select the edges that surround the exterior of the eye so they can be extruded (see Figure 9.49).

Choose **Edit Polygons** → **Extrude Edge** to extend the edge of the eye toward the inside of the head (see Figure 9.50). Normally, in an animated model, an entire eye socket is associated with the eye area, but this eyelid detail will suffice for now.

You can add detail to the eye area by choosing **Edit Polygons** → **Split Polygon Tool** (see Figure 9.51). This creates a smoother transition between the areas of relatively light detail around the eye and the tighter rows of polygons in the eyelid area.

To finish the eyelid area, you must put an eyeball in place. This will not be the final eyeball, but you can use the placement and diameter of this object to create the final eyeball. Create a simple sphere (choose **Create** → **Polygon Primitives** ❏), and place it correctly to act as a guide to see if the final subdivision is working (see Figure 9.52).

Once the eyeball is in place, preview the subdivision model in order to see the progress in this area. Choose **Modify** → **Convert** → **Polygons to Subdiv** to visualize the subdivision version of this model (see Figure 9.53).

After previewing the model, undo the subdivision operation. Continue cleaning up the polygonal model and testing the subdivision by turning it on and undoing it repeatedly before committing to the final version.

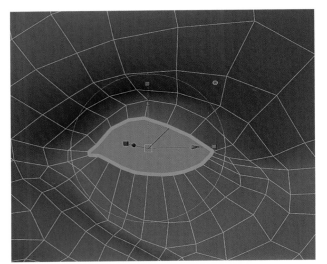

Figure 9.49: Selected edges around the eye

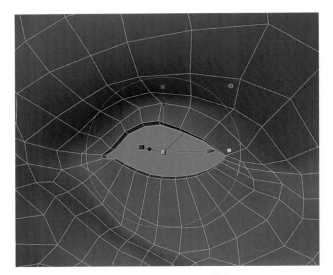

Figure 9.50: The extruded edge around the eye

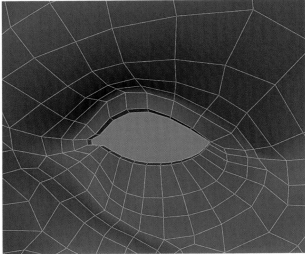

Figure 9.51: Additional detail around the eye

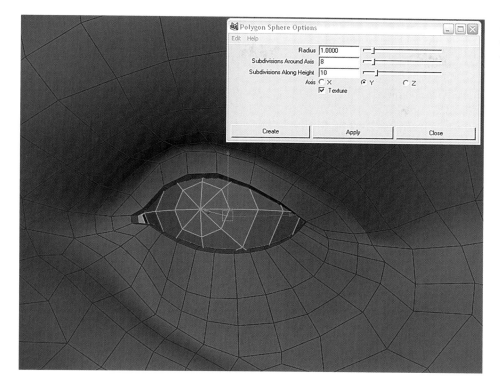

Figure 9.52:
Placing and scaling the sphere

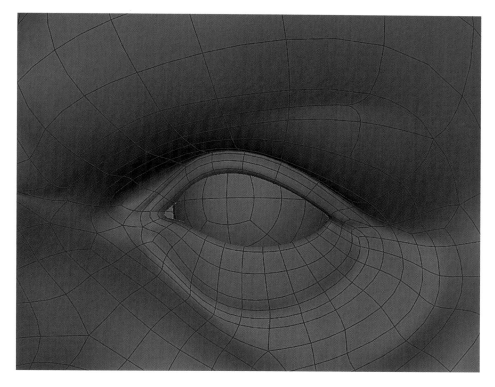

Figure 9.53: Subdividing the model for testing

Creating Subdivision Surfaces

Before you convert the polygonal cage to subdivision surfaces, it is important to delete all construction history. Subdivision modeling can sometimes get slow. Additional history that is unnecessary will make it much worse.

Once the polygon cage is completed to the point where you decide to apply the subdivision surfaces, you can finally merge the two sides of the face. With both sides selected, choose **Polygons** → **Combine** to combine the two halves into one continuous mesh (see Figure 9.54).

Select the adjacent rows of vertices along the center, making absolutely sure that no other vertices are selected except those that run up the exact center of the model (see Figure 9.55). If some stray vertices creep into the selection set, repeat this step until the selection set is correct.

Use the Merge Vertices command to seal the center line between the two halves of the model. If some errant vertices merge together during this operation, the operation accidentally closes one or more polygons in the model. It is important that this not happen during this step, so carefully check the results before proceeding to the next step. Any accidental problem at this stage will cause many more later.

In our example, we chose **Edit Polygons** → **Merge Vertices** ❏ and set Distance to 0.0020. By choosing only the vertices that you want to merge and using a relatively low threshold for merging, you can help ensure that these common mistakes do not happen. Of course, there is always the tried-and-true method of saving often as an insurance policy.

Figure 9.54: Combining the two halves of the head

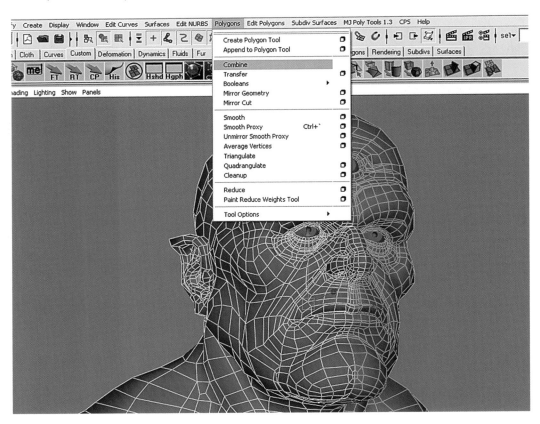

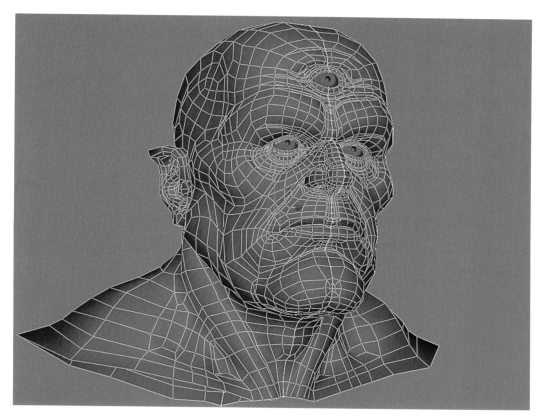

Figure 9.55:
Selecting the
center row of
vertices

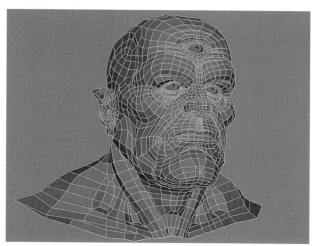

Figure 9.56: (left) The merged polygonal wireframe; (right) the merged model with edge loops

Once the two halves are combined, it is easy to see how the initial planning stages of the modeling procedure have paid off (see Figure 9.56). You can visualize the discussion about edge loops and areas of animation by looking at the wireframe. The original edge loops that were laid out before modeling started can be seen clearly.

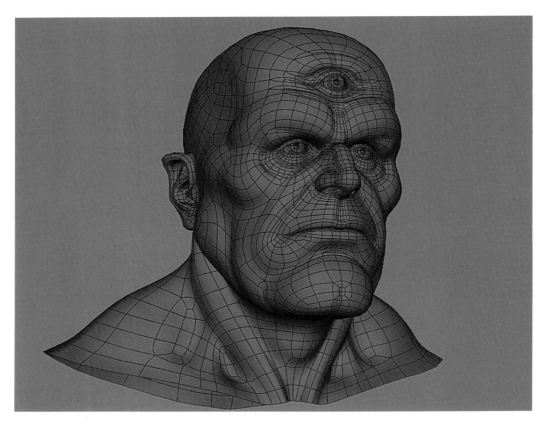

Figure 9.57: The converted model

We can now subdivide. We wait to do so until the last possible moment because the subdivided model is slow to work on and time-consuming to update. Choose **Modify** → **Convert** → **Polygons to Subdiv** to convert the model to subdivision surfaces (see Figure 9.57).

Here's another, more important reason that the subdivision step is not taken until the last minute: at this stage of the modeling process, asymmetric details are added to the model. Wrinkles and character lines are usually not exactly symmetrical. When these details are added, the model needs to be in a state where it is no longer creating perfectly symmetrical details across its two halves. You add these details using the subdivision modeling layers and modeling options.

Editing the Subdivision Model

Subdivision modeling is just like polygonal modeling, except that the model has levels that can be traversed and the menus are slightly different. Also, just like polygonal modeling, only a limited set of tools is necessary to create a great subdivision model. The rest of the modeling tools are great to use, and you should learn how to use them. But only a handful of the subdivision modeling tools in Maya were used to create this model.

Most of the subdivision modeling that was done on this model was surface editing using the options in the pop-up menus and choosing **Subdiv Surfaces** → **Partial Crease Edge/Vertex.**

Surface Editing

When modeling in Maya subdivisions, the marking menu (which appears when right-clicking the model) changes (see Figure 9.58). The new options let you edit the model at different levels using different entity types. With a knowledge of polygonal modeling, and an understanding of how subdivision levels work, you can begin to create models with subtle details very quickly.

If you want to add detail at the base level, or the subdivision zero level, choose the **Coarser** option on the marking menu. You can then select vertices, faces, or edges to edit. To work at a finer level or at subdivision level 1 or above, choose the **Finer** option.

The distinction between levels going from coarsest (level zero) to finest (the highest level of subdivision that a modeler would care to set) is how subdivision modeling differs a great deal from polygon modeling.

Notice in Figure 9.59 how the vertices do not display as simple points as they would in polygon modeling mode; they display as the numeral 0. Using a coarser setting allows us to

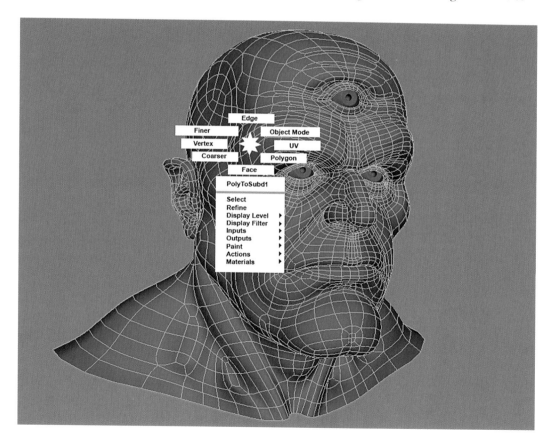

Figure 9.58: The subdivision marking menu

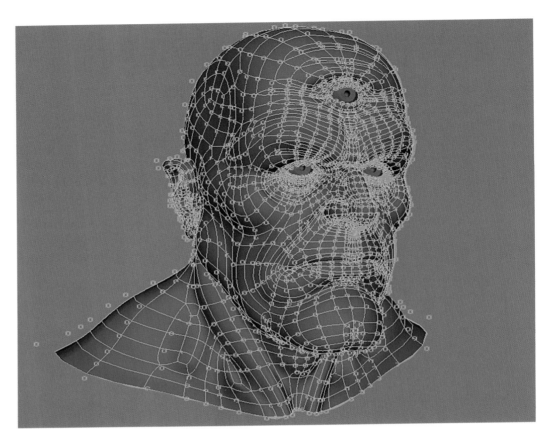

affect large areas quickly. Editing in this mode lets the modeler make progress quickly on large areas.

Similarly, the vertices at level 1 display as the numeral 1. Using a setting like this accommodates the creation of small details. The finer the selection, the tighter the details. Editing the surface using a level 1 or finer setting means that we are not making big changes to the model; we're creating small details (see Figure 9.60).

You can edit the edges along a surface in the same way you edit in polygonal modeling mode. The display between coarser and finer levels is an obvious increase in detail that is not designated by visible numerals (see Figure 9.61).

You can see the results of subdivision surface editing in Figure 9.62. The edited figure has many asymmetrical details and many small wrinkles that the unedited version does not. All these small details increase the realism and make lighting and texturing easier, without dramatically increasing the computational requirements of the model. Each subdivision detail is added to a localized region. The rest of the model that is not detailed is not affected by the additional small elements created using this technique. To see the 3D version of the unedited model, open `subD_modeling21.mb` on the CD. To see the 3D version of the edited model, open `subD_modeling22.mb` on the CD.

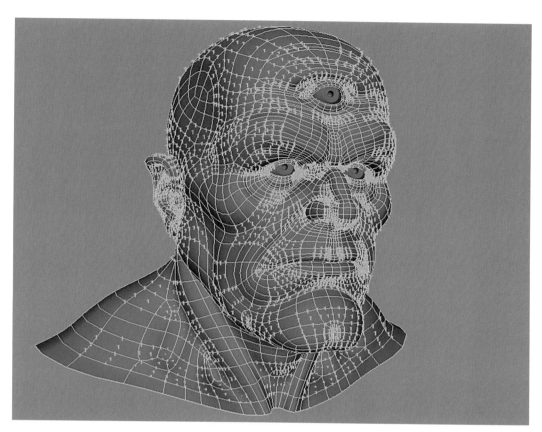

Figure 9.60: Vertices at level 1

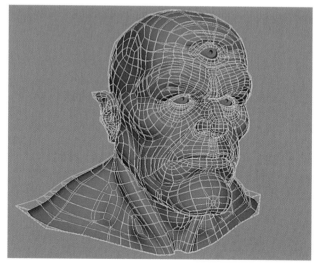

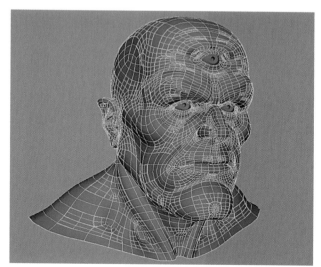

Figure 9.61: Edges at (left) level 0 and (right) level 1

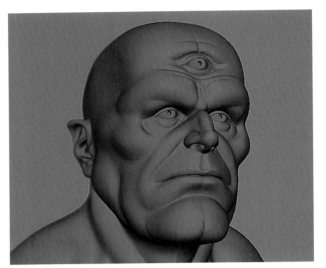 

Figure 9.62: (left) An unedited subdivision model and (right) an edited version

Using the Partial Crease Command

Choose **Subdiv Surfaces** → **Partial Crease Edge/Vertex** to create sharp, angular areas along selected edges and vertices within the smooth subdivision model. If the model needs details that would normally be created by adding geometry, this command adds the detail without adding geometry.

Usually it will not be necessary to go any finer than level 0 to use this command to create creases along the skin of the model. The edges along the lines that require detail are selected first. Figure 9.63 shows the edge of the eyelid highlighted, ready to use the Partial Crease Edge/Vertex command.

The line that was smoothed out now shows a crease where the selected edges were. This line will catch a dramatic highlight when rendered and will create a realistic appearance (see Figure 9.64).

Another area that requires a crease is the line that extends from the side of the nose to the corner of the mouth.

This character line usually animates quite a bit and is not an area where excessive detail should be added. The more complex the geometry in areas like this, the more likely it is that the blend shapes and facial animation rigs will have problems.

Using the Partial Crease Edge/Vertex command is a perfect choice for creating this detail. As in the example shown in Figure 9.64, the edges along the area are selected before the command is executed (see Figure 9.65).

When the command is executed, the line along the face is perfectly tightened. Using conventional polygon modeling methods would make this process difficult and complicated. The Partial Crease Edge/Vertex command simplifies the modeling in these areas a great deal (see Figure 9.66).

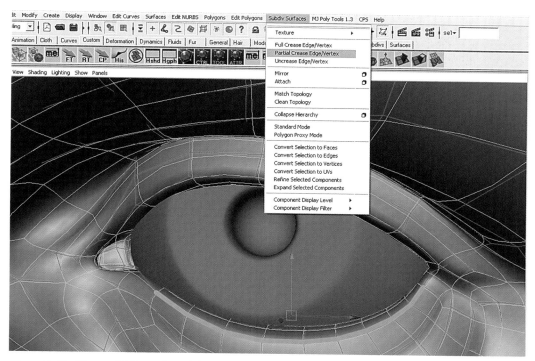

Figure 9.63: The eyelid line selected for the Partial Crease Edge/Vertex command

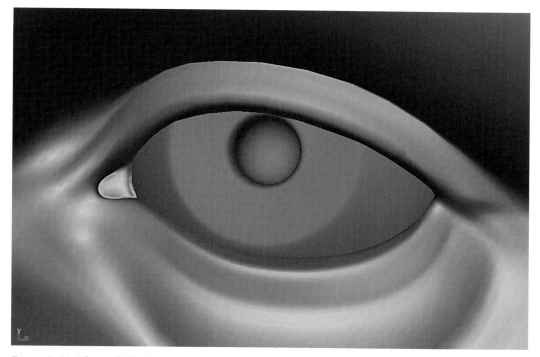

Figure 9.64: The eyelid highlight line

*Figure 9.65:
Selected edge
along the side
of the face*

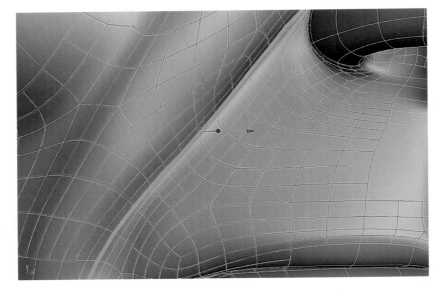

*Figure 9.66:
Finished crease
along the face*

   And our final model shows the results of our detailed work (see Figure 9.67). If you want to see the model in 3D, open `subD_modeling_final_details12.mb` in the CD.

Always Learning

We covered a lot of ground in this chapter—the process of creating a wireframe cage from an edge loop layout, the process of using the polygon-by-polygon modeling technique to create an organic model, and the process of using subdivision levels to create degrees of details. Subdivision modeling is quickly becoming the industry standard for creating beautiful organic models. These techniques are powerful and fast and are far superior to the techniques that preceded them.

Figure 9.67:
The final model

The problem is, digital art is like a moving train. To remain on track, we have to stay in front of it. These techniques are great, but something else may come along that will make these techniques obsolete.

In the end, you—the modeler, the artist—must be the one who makes the model great. You create the subtle form of the details of the face, the overall shape of the head and neck, and the little surface tweaks that bring the flesh to life. The tools in Maya are only the pencils and paintbrushes in your tool box; they cannot make the model great by themselves.

If you use the tools explained here, you will be able to develop more imaginative creations than those you developed using the tools that you have been using before. The flexibility and speed of polygon-to-subdivision modeling can help you make your creative visions truly come to life.

Figure 9.67:
The final model

Index

Note to the reader: Throughout this index **boldfaced** page numbers indicate primary discussions of a topic. *Italicized* page numbers indicate illustrations.

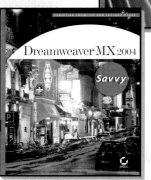

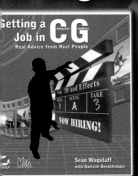

Photoshop® CS Titles
from Sybex

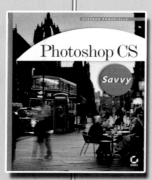

Photoshop CS Savvy™
by Stephen Romaniello
ISBN: 0-7821-4280-X • $44.99

In *Photoshop CS Savvy*, artist and teacher Stephen Romaniello reveals the secrets behind Photoshop's power—showing you how to combine theory with practical techniques to get results that are inspirational and satisfying. Whether you're a graphic artist, photographer, web designer, desktop publisher, or, if your goal is to become Photoshop savvy, this is the book that will get you there.

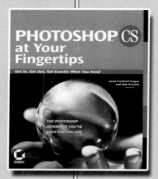

Photoshop CS At Your Fingertips:
Get In, Get Out, Get Exactly What You Need
by Jason Cranford Teague and Walt Dietrich
ISBN: 0-7821-4289-3 • $34.99

Photoshop CS at Your Fingertips: Get In, Get Out, Get Exactly What You Need is the first task-based reference to Photoshop that lets you search according to what you want to do. This book also includes at-a-glance shortcuts and time-saving tips as well as a visual reference to the Photoshop CS interface.

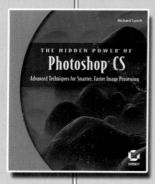

The Hidden Power™ of Photoshop CS:
Advanced Techniques for Smarter, Faster Image Processing
by Richard Lynch
ISBN: 0-7821-4255-9 • $39.99

The Hidden Power of Photoshop CS uncovers the little-known techniques that make Photoshop such a powerful program. It focuses on the methods that people using Photoshop professionally need to know — methods for retouching and correcting images, preparing images for output, and saving time and eliminating redundant tasks. With Richard Lynch's expert advice, Photoshop pros will work better and faster than they ever thought possible.

Photoshop Secrets of the Pros™:
20 Top Artists and Designers Face Off
by Mark Clarkson
ISBN: 0-7821-4191-9 • $44.99

Photoshop Secrets of the Pros throws you right into the thick of things, dropping you ringside for a series of digital duels and artistic collaborations as top artists challenge each other in Photoshop Tennis matches.

SYBEX®
www.sybex.com